SO,
WHAT'S
NORMAL?

So, What's Normal?

Life after Pedophilia, Abuse and Neglect

Rhonnie

Rhonnie & Company
Traverse City, Michigan

Published by Rhonnie and Company
P.O. Box 6219
Traverse City, MI 49697-6219

Publisher's Cataloguing-in-Publication Data
Rhonnie.
So what's normal: life after pedophilia, abuse and neglect / Rhonnie. Traverse City, MI : Rhonnie & Co., 2003.
    p. ; cm.
    ISBN: 0-9744305-0-1
    0-9744305-1-X (pbk.)

    1. Sexual abuse victims–Biography. 2. Victims of family violence–Biography. 3. Abused children–Biography. 4. Pedophilia–Psychological aspects. 5. Child sexual abuse–Psychological aspects. 6. Sexual abuse victims' writings, American. I. Title.

RC560.S44 R46 2003   2003095940
616.85/836–dc22 [B]   0311

Book coordination by Jenkins Group • www. bookpublishing.com
Cover design by Chris Rhoads
Cover illustration by Dierdra Julia Everard
Interior design by Barbara Hodge
Editing by Rebecca Chown

Printed in the United States of America
07 06 05 04 03 • 5 4 3 2 1

Dedication

This book is dedicated to Josephine, whom I fondly called "Jo", and all of the other silent Heroes in this world who may wonder if their kindness has gone unnoticed. "Jo's" love, strength, and compassion instilled in me the truth, that one person can become a bright light, a beacon of hope for those who would otherwise live a dark and grim existence. Instead of continuing the cycle and remaining part of the problem, One person can become a part of the solution. Words can never express how blessed I feel to know a person like you, Jo. My friend, my confidant, my inspiration, my "mother". I love you.

Contents

Acknowledgments

I would like to thank my husband, Delbert, for patiently sitting alone night after night this past year, never once complaining about the time I spent writing this book. It was a personal sacrifice on your part, but you hung in there until I finished.

I would also like to thank my children whom I love with all my heart: Andy, Danielle, and Elizabeth. Kids, you were my first true loves, and your lives have enriched my whole being. Not only did you give life new meaning for me, but you also helped me understand Gods higher purpose for mankind.

For just being part of my life and for blessing me with your presence in it, I would like to thank my surrogate kids, Jesse Ames, Stacy Stark, Jimmy Smith, Harley Wales, Mary Lightfoot, and Michael Weitzman. I would like to give an additional heartfelt thank you to Michael for sacrificing his personal time to assist on the book cover idea and to my daughter Danielle for her constant assistance in helping me with the more difficult areas of my book.

I would like to thank a very special young lady, Deirdra Julia Everard, for the beautiful art piece for my book cover.

I would like to thank the handful of other people I call my friends: Julie Riley, Nancy Sheffer, Pat Mills, Linda Burchette, Carol Komrska, Danielle Bukowski, Pam Kunnath, Sindi Wineman, LeeAnn Wares, and Susie Penney.

I would like to extend a special thank you to Chuck Bethea for hanging in there with me as I was writing this book. You are a man of conviction and passion, and I admire you greatly.

Denise Schmuckal, I also thank you for sharing a passion for helping innocent victims.

Greg Worthington, I owe a special thank you to you for adding your story. You have a personal as well as a professional interest in helping victims of pedophilia that is inspiring.

I would like to thank Mary O'Connor for daring to go after what you believe is the right approach for repairing the broken family as a whole, stricken by addiction and abuse.

Finally, last but not least, I would like to thank Rebecca Chown, my editor, for making this book all it could be and for embracing the importance of my message. I would also like to thank the Jenkins Group for their kindness and the wonderful team of experts they so proficiently provided to make this endeavor possible.

Introduction

⟡

One Woman's Remarkable Journey

By Charles W. Bethea, Ph.D.

So, *What's Normal?: Life After Pedophilia, Abuse and Neglect* is a blunt book. It recounts a tale of almost unimaginable savagery and ultimate triumph from the personal perspective of a remarkable woman, and her recollection of battles with dismay, horror, and betrayal from earliest childhood on.

I have been privileged to know Rhonnie, the author, in my capacity as her therapist as we have explored her childhood, marriages, and where she goes from here in the endless struggle to overcome the abuse she recalls both as a child and as a young woman. Rhonnie's story is one of a woman who has forged ahead without roadmaps, even when her trust was repeatedly betrayed. It is one of a woman who did not know where her efforts would take her or when there would be relief, but she trusted her emerging resolve that matters could only get better.

Along the way, the author struggled with such core questions as "Does life have meaning?" "Is there any hope?" and "Where is God?" Professionally, I've been able to observe Rhonnie move through many phases, from rage and dismay to acceptance, serenity, and a new sense of mission. Her faith has been central in her journey, and throughout her childhood and into her adulthood, Rhonnie has experienced a sense of God's presence that sustains her and that inspires children and adults who have been brutalized by others. She has taken courageous initiative whenever possible and has "let go and let God" when not. The old adage "Without God, we can't; without us, He won't" was never truer than it is in Rhonnie's case.

Today, Rhonnie maintains an abiding compassion for individuals who have been abused, while abhorring the evil of incest and other forms of sexual degradation. Although figures vary and there is vast underreporting, indications are that 25 percent of women and 10 percent of men are sexually abused before adulthood. These millions in turn live lives of dysfunction and impairment and are at significant risk to repeat the same abuses in successive generations. One of the many triumphs of Rhonnie's story is that she refuses to be a part of perpetuating this cycle that so many abused individuals are caught up in.

As significant as Rhonnie's own healing, however, is her mission to extend hope and help to others. Conveying her message of recovery that is the essence of this book is but the beginning of her efforts. She is committed to aiding with speaking engagements, training, and funding rehabilitative therapy through her nonprofit foundation Leaps and Bounds, with the ultimate goal of significantly reducing the sexual, physical, and emotional abuse of children, families, and neighbors.

Though this book is a story of rare courage and faith, above all it replaces rage and despair with hope and triumph. While intensely personal, this book is also universal with its revelations and repeated messages of hope. *So, What's Normal?: Life After Pedophilia, Abuse and Neglect* is a journey of horror and pain yet eventual triumph, and I am impressed that it is but the beginning of Rhonnie's efforts to aid others.

Foreword

✹

The Mystery of Pedophilia

By Gregory J. Worthington, PsyD, LLP

My father-in-law is a pedophile. Unfortunately, I found this out the hard way when my wife and I received a call from her then seventeen-year-old sister who disclosed to us that her father had been "inappropriate" with her. Upon further questioning, she related that he had done things of a sexual nature to her "once or twice." Despite the initial shock, my wife wisely asked her to come and stay with us for a few days and she accepted. When she arrived, we tried to define and understand what had happened. During this discussion, some half-truths were discovered and we all agreed to be honest and open with each other. As soon as we had agreed to this new rule, the entire story came out. Her father had been sexually abusing her regularly since age nine or ten. I could write an entire book trying to describe the depth of our shock, dismay, revulsion, and anguish and still not capture the essence of the experience. My sister-in-law never went back to the home of her abuser. My wife and I adopted her and now she is our daughter.

How could I have a pedophile for a father-in-law and not know it? There is no clear-cut way to detect pedophiles or to determine who is likely to become one. Volumes have been written on this subject and researchers have explored many questions in trying to understand the issues that contribute to the formation of a pedophile. Major difficulties in creating a "profile" of a pedophile include disagreements over how to define deviant sexual behaviors and problems in finding and accessing truthful subjects who accurately represent the general population of pedophiles (Murray, 2000). Despite these difficulties, some general characteristics of pedophiles are known. Men are more likely to be pedophiles than women. Pedophiles can range in age from late teens through middle age. It seems that pedophiles more frequently choose girls as their victims, almost twice as often as they chose boys. Pedophiles can be members of their victim's families, or they can be strangers. They can molest children anywhere, but the home of the victim is frequently the setting for the abuse (Murray, 2000). Many pedophiles claim to have been sexually molested themselves as children (Freund, Watson, & Dickey, 1990).

The actions of the pedophile can take many forms. Some pedophiles only look at children or child pornography, some expose themselves, some fondle the child or have the child fondle them, some engage the child in oral sex acts, and some demand penetration (American Psychiatric Association, DSM-IV, 1994). While some pedophiles use force or threats, many rely on persuasion and friendship to gradually groom the child for later sex acts.

Pedophiles have described themselves as being introverted, shy, sensitive, and depressed, and many reported being sexually aroused by children of both genders (Ames & Hovston, 1990). It is clear that pedophiles can play many roles, including father, mother, stepfather, stepmother, uncle, aunt, grandfather, grandmother, family friend, babysitter, brother, sister, cousin, teacher, religious leader, or stranger. In other words, a pedophile could be anyone.

No one knows for sure why some adults are sexually aroused by children. One explanation is that some adults simply have deviant sexual arousal systems (Araji & Finkelhor, 1985; Finkelhor, Williams, & Burns, 1989). This would be supported by findings that many pedophiles demonstrate enduring and exclusive sexual interest in children (Araji & Finkelhor, 1985). Another theory is that pedophiles lack healthy sexual and emotional gratification from adult relationships and choose children as an outlet instead (Freund, Langevin, & Cibiri, 1972). In support of this theory, one study demonstrated that pedophiles tend to lack social skills and some fear adult heterosexual relationships and therefore choose children as sexual partners because children tend to be less socially demanding and are more vulnerable and available (Oberholser &Beck, 1986). Disinhibition is another theory that attempts to explain pedophilia. This theory states that, through a variety of mechanisms such as poor impulse control, alcohol or drug use, or the presence of psychosis or other forms of mental illness, the normal inhibitions against having sex with children are overcome or are not present (Finkelhor, 1984; Finkelhor et al., 1990). Since many pedophiles claim that they were sexually abused as children, some theorize that a learning model is involved in explaining the behavior of pedophiles since they are repeating what was taught to them about sexual behavior (Ames & Hovston, 1990; Finkelhor, 1984).

Exploring profiles and causal factors of pedophilia can increase our understanding of pedophiles, but these factors should never be allowed to excuse the acts. Adults do not have sex with children by accident. These acts are purposeful, intentional, conscious behaviors based on choice. These acts leave indelible marks on the lives of victims and persons who care about victims. These acts are also, unfortunately, not uncommon. One out of three girls and one out of seven boys experience sexual abuse before they are age eighteen (Bass & Davis, 1994; Russell, 1984; Herman, 1992).

My father-in-law played many roles in his life. He blended in many different circles and held jobs at all levels. At times he was charming, funny, loving, and articulate. At other times he was unreasonable, angry, jealous, and mean. We always knew he had a temper and that he was dysfunctional at times, but we never suspected that he was a pedophile.

After we adopted our new daughter, we had a great deal of re-defining to do. One issue we faced early on was what role the pedophile would play in our lives. Some treatment programs claim that complete rehabilitation is possible and therefore families should be reunited while others claim there is no effective treatment for pedophiles. While there are many options, most treatment programs fall into two camps: either victim advocacy or family system approaches (Maddock & Larson, 1995).

Victim advocacy approaches emphasize the rights and protection of the child victim and offer treatments to the victim to assist in recovery from the trauma associated with the sexual abuse and related effects. The perpetrator is typically viewed as having an underlying pathology that expresses itself in deviant sexual behavior (Maddock & Larson, 1995).

The family systems approach assumes a circular causality and interdependence of family members where sexual problems are viewed as a form of family dysfunction representing an imbalance in the system that requires treatment. Family systems approaches typically require treatment for all family members to facilitate structural change within the family. What's more, many family systems approaches do not believe that removal of the perpetrator is always necessary or desirable, as it can upset family stability and can cause more trauma to the family by placing undue emotional and financial hardship on the mother and other family members (Maddock & Larson, 1995).

Our new daughter entered our lives when I was in my first year of doctoral training in clinical psychology. Through my experience of her, I have come to appreciate the depth and breadth of the wounds that were inflicted upon her as well as the wounds that were inflicted upon each member of our family. Through my clinical work, I have treated many other survivors of sexual abuse, including refugee survivors from Bosnia. The negative effects of sexual abuse are profound and lasting and greatly impact the survivor's interpersonal relationships, sense of safety, and sense of self.

Thanks to both my personal and professional experience, I have come to believe that the pedophile's greatest allies are secrets and lies. When considering whether rehabilitation of pedophiles is possible, one must remember how high the stakes are. Any attempt to reunify a family torn apart by the actions of a pedophile must be predicated on the notion of trust. In my opinion, the risk of placing trust in a person who uses secrets and lies to engage in sexual acts with a child is too great. In our new family, we chose not to trust a person whose entire life was based on secrets and lies. We chose to place our trust in our new daughter. We chose to be advocates for her. We chose to have no place in our lives for a pedophile.

With the sexual abuse of children so prevalent, it is hard to not be discouraged. Parents need to be vigilant and cautious so that pedophiles have limited access to children. When abuse is discovered or disclosed, proper supports and treatments must be sought and every effort must be made to establish and maintain a sense of safety in the life of the victim. From the foundation of safety, recovery can begin. With proper support, love, care, treatment, faith, and perseverance, our daughter was able to not only survive her ordeals but to heal from her wounds, and now she is thriving.

In the book you are about to read, Rhonnie shares the story of her own childhood sexual abuse. Through her words, we can begin to understand her pain, suffering, and heartache. Through her courageous example, we can see how she has broken cycles of abuse and what she has done to create and maintain a sense of safety and new meaning in her life. Her example adds fuel to the hope that all victims of childhood sexual abuse can recover and go on to live healthy, fulfilling lives abounding with healthy, meaningful, and enriching relationships.

References

American Psychiatric Association. (1994). *Diagnostic and statistical manual of mental disorders* (4th ed.). Washington, DC: Author.

Ames, M.A., & Hovston, D.A. (1990). Legal, social, and biological definitions of pedophilia. *Archives of Sexual Behavior*, 19, 333-342.

Araji, S., & Finkelhor, D. (1985). Explanations of pedophilia: Review of empirical research. *Bulletin of the American Academy of Psychiatry and Law*, 13, 71-83.

Bass, E., & Davis, L. (1994). *The courage to heal*. Third edition. New York: Harper Perennial.

Finkelhor, D. (1984). *Child sexual abuse: New theory and research*. New York: Macmillan.

Finkelhor, D., Williams, L.M., & Burns, N. (1989). *Sexual abuse in day care*. Newbury Park, CA: Sage.

Freund, K., Langevin, R., & Cibiri, S. (1972). The female child as a surrogate object. *Archives of Sexual Behavior*, 2, 119-133.

Freund, K., Watson, R., & Dickey, R. (1990). Does sexual abuse in childhood cause pedophilia? An exploratory study. *Archives of Sexual Behavior*, 19, 557-569.

Herman, J. (1992). *Trauma and recovery: The aftermath of violence from domestic abuse to political terror*. New York: Basic Books.

Maddock, J.W., & Larson, N.R. (1995). *Incestuous families: An ecological approach to understanding and treatment*. New York: Norton

Murray, J.B. (2000). Psychological profile of pedophiles and child molesters. *Journal of Psychology*, 134 (2), 211-225.

Oberholser, J.C., & Beck, J. (1986). Multimethod assessment of rapists, child molesters, and three control groups on behavioral and psychological measures. *Journal of Consulting and Clinical Psychology*, 54, 682-687.

Russell, D.E.H. (1984). *Sexual exploitation: Rape, child sexual abuse, and sexual harassment*. Beverly Hills, CA: Sage.

Prologue

Why I'm Telling My Story

Christmas of 2001, it seemed, was the culmination of my life's work of overcoming the sexual, physical, and emotional abuse I endured as a child and young adult. My husband, Delbert, my three grown children, and our "adopted" family, a menagerie of young men and women, met at our house for a midnight adult Christmas Eve rendezvous. We talked and laughed and opened presents for what seemed an eternity. It was one of those glimmering moments in time that was sheer joy, and, for that night at least, we all were children again.

The next morning, we celebrated Christmas all over again with the three grandchildren by Delbert's daughter Marie and her husband, Collin. We opened more presents, and Delbert cooked everybody a wonderful family breakfast.

Everything seemed so perfect. After huge struggles and seemingly insurmountable differences, my husband and I, who both had more than one previous marriage under our belts, had successfully combined our families to create one big happy family. The new year promised happiness, togetherness, and a sorely needed new beginning, but it didn't last long. Happiness, as it always had been, was fleeting.

Just days into the new year, I answered the phone at work. It was my husband, and very calmly he said, "Jon's dead." Jon was our nephew, the son of Delbert's brother Robert.

"What? How?" I questioned, my mind beginning to race.

"A drug overdose," Delbert said in an eerily even tone.

"What!" I gasped.

"It was heroin, a heroin overdose. Robert just called to tell me," Delbert answered.

Our nephew, barely twenty years old, had been found dead at the home of Delbert's ex-wife in Arizona and allegedly had been given the fatal dose of heroin by this woman's son, who was also his cousin and a heroin addict for the past nine years.

As horrified as I was, I wasn't necessarily surprised. Jon's mother, the same ex-wife's sister, had done drugs with all three of her sons from the time they were in their early teens, and the boy's father was also a poor parent. Diagnosed with bipolarism, which is the new terminology for manic depression, a disease that affects your moods by alternating periods of depressed moods and periods of manic or excited moods, Robert was a manipulative man who had always been neglectful of his children. He and Laurie had been separated for ten years by the time Jon died, and he seemed never to have had any money or time for his own children, though he'd lavished both time and money on other peoples' kids. His children had simply gone without, and his philosophy was verbalized in this manner: "My kids are going to be gone someday soon, and at least I will still have these others in my life."

As serious as bipolarism is, Robert seemed to use his illness to his advantage. He became suicidal when he was broke, and made his mother worry about him incessantly, and this is where Delbert came in. At such times, Delbert would offer him a job or money so as not to worry their mother so much, and it was funny how Robert's depression always evaporated as soon as somebody laid cash in his hand.

Jon's death not only took its toll emotionally, but it also placed a huge financial burden on Delbert and me. Neither of the boy's parents could afford to bring him home to Michigan or to pay for his funeral, so we ended up bearing the burden of trying to collect money from Delbert's enormous family to pay the necessary expenses.

This didn't go over well. Very few family members pitched in, and perfect strangers seemed happier to donate than the family. The general attitude was that Jon's death was an accident waiting to happen, an inevitable end for this young man, and we consequently bore most of the burden of getting his body back to Michigan and arranging his funeral ourselves. Sadly, Jon was a victim of circumstances and apathy not only in his life but also in his death.

A few days after Jon's passing, Delbert's daughter Stormy turned up at our front door with the daughter she'd just gained temporary custody of and had had for only two weeks. Also in tow were a new puppy who wasn't housebroken, an adult Labrador retriever, and two cats. Stormy, who was just turning thirty, had left her allegedly abusive husband in Kansas City, Kansas, and had no place to go. I was genuinely hesitant about her coming to our home, since she had a volatile past with her dad and me, but I couldn't turn them out into the cold.

Delbert was happy to see his daughter and even more elated at the chance to see his granddaughter again. This thirteen-year-old child was the product of Stormy's first marriage when she was only sixteen years old, and the father, who was twenty-three at the time, had had custody nearly all her life.

The same day Stormy and company arrived, another surprise showed up on our doorstep. It was Laurie, the mother of our dead nephew. Though we, too, had a strained past, thanks to her being Delbert's ex-wife's sister, and her lack of parenting skills, I let her stay in our home until her son was laid to rest. I could not turn her away, as I couldn't imagine losing a child and then not having a single soul who cared or anybody to lean on.

In the midst of all this, my daughter Liz, who was nineteen, lost her job. This visibly shook her, as she had studied cosmetology for two years and had a job at one of the premier salons in town. Soon after, the home she and her sister, Danielle, age twenty-one, lived in was put on the market, and they had to move. Like the others, they had nowhere to go but here.

Also at home was my twenty-five-year-old son, Andy, who had been living with us since September, wanting deeply to clean up his life and kick his drug problem. I was his refuge when he had no options left, but this meant eight people were unexpectedly crammed into our one-bedroom, one-office, newly remodeled home. Everyone was on top of each other, and Delbert and I simply had no privacy. I wasn't able to say "No" to these people in need who had no other place to go, but they were all broke. It was also winter, the slow season for both Delbert and me, and making ends meet became more and more difficult. Simply feeding that many people every night was soon an enormous strain.

While all this was going on, the court case came up for Robert and Laurie's son Aaron, whom we had turned into the police three months earlier for molestation of another granddaughter. Aaron had been briefly staying with us, and the incident had happened right in our house. He and our seven-year-old granddaughter had been wrestling and playing around, and our granddaughter had confronted him on the spot. She stood her ground when he tried to say he'd touched her accidentally, and she showed me what he'd done. I didn't want to react unreasonably and alarm her, so I told Aaron to apologize to her. He did, and the incident was all but forgotten in her mind. This was the goal I'd wanted to achieve, and I was proud of her. What a gutsy little girl.

But when I glanced over at Danielle, who was sitting nearby through this whole fiasco, I saw she had a horrified look on her face. She got up and took me outside and told me she'd cleaned my computer files the day before and had found child pornography downloaded onto my computer by Aaron. Keeping my promise to the kids to watch the movie they'd brought over to the house proved very difficult after that. With Aaron still in our home, I'd sat there and agonized, watching every move he made. I couldn't tell you to this day what movie was playing, but the children were none the wiser to my anguish. When the movie ended, we took them home, and upon our return Delbert promptly removed Aaron from our house. The next day, he reported the incident to our counselor, who promptly called the police.

As bad as this sounds, it was only on the day of Jon's funeral that I was able to truly grieve for him. Up until now, I had been too busy with my job, with managing my chaotic household, and with making funeral arrangements and trying to collect the necessary funds to grieve. Looking at this young man lying in his coffin and then at his two brothers, I realized that none of them had ever stood a chance. I could see they probably wouldn't make it as adults, either, as they had no one to turn to in their lives.

A few days after the funeral, without any warning, Stormy's first husband showed up at the local state police post and demanded that Stormy bring him his daughter. Stormy had broken the terms of her temporary custody by leaving the state of Kansas with the child, and since he had his legal papers in order, there was nothing any of us could do. Our young granddaughter was devastated. She wanted to stay in Michigan, but we had only an hour to get her belongings together and take her to the police station. The poor child was bawling her eyes out, begging the police not to make her go with her dad, and Delbert was traumatized watching her suffer such anguish. This unfortunate situation just added more fuel to the flare-up of drama currently in our lives.

In the meantime, Laurie was following Delbert around like a lost puppy. She wanted a man's attention, and she didn't care whose man it was. Between Laurie and Stormy, I felt like my home was infiltrated by spies: Laurie to report back to her sister 'Sherrill' and Stormy to report back to her own maniac mother who, after twenty-eight years, still wasn't over Delbert. Though she was to stay with us only until the funeral, pleas like "I don't have anyplace to go," "I'll sleep in the furnace room," or "Just give me until the fifth of the month till my check gets here" made it difficult to ask her to leave.

We could find no relief in any quarter, and this three-week period became a turning point for Delbert and me. Our house was no longer our home, and we were simply overwhelmed. With so many dependent people living with us, our lives were in a constant state of confusion and chaos. Something had to give, and unfortunately it was us. Delbert started slipping into depression and, being the stoic man he is, couldn't face the fact that he was having an emotional breakdown. Like his brother Robert and daughter Stormy, he is bipolar, but he quit taking his medication and gave it to Stormy after she told him she didn't have any money. He said she needed it more than he did. I told her the seriousness of taking of Delbert's medication, and she said she would stop, but Stormy had proved numerous times in the past that she cared for no one but herself, and, true to form, she failed to quit asking for his medication.

The pressure at home was enormous, and finally, the situation blew up. It was admittedly ugly, but I finally told Laurie to leave. Other than that positive outcome, the result was disastrous. All that had happened in just a few short weeks was too much for Delbert to handle, and he informed me that he, too, was leaving. I just stood there in disbelief and watched my world and all that I had worked for with Delbert and our families crumble before my very eyes. I can explain my feelings only by saying that I felt like I was drowning. My life literally passed in front of my eyes, and I was totally devastated. Delbert, the only man I had ever loved and trusted, was leaving. Sadness overwhelmed me, and my world as I knew it was gone. I had never experienced such pain in my life; it was as though a cloud of darkness had engulfed me and I no longer could see any light. I had always been the rock that everyone else leaned on, and now I was left alone with no one to lean on. This was the one time in my life I felt like I wouldn't be able to recover and begin again, and I was shattered, as I'd thought Delbert and I were stronger than this.

Even though I knew intellectually that you could never run away from yourself, I decided that was what I needed to do. I wanted to sell the house and move. This home that had been so uniquely "us" was now choking me, and everything was a reminder of who we once but no longer were. I simply couldn't keep up appearances any longer. I was so transparent; everybody knew my inner state by looking at me. My plan, though it would not necessarily make me happy, would at least get me out.

As I was preparing to leave this community that had been my home for so long and to make a fresh start elsewhere, I learned that Delbert's brother Robert had just been arrested for first-and third-degree sexual molestation of a ten-year old girl who was now fourteen. As far as I was concerned, this explained why he had always found it so important to spend his money on children other than his own. He had been grooming this young girl for evil purposes, and I was disgusted when I heard the news.

Then, to my surprise, Delbert came home. Though he'd been gone only five days, it seemed like five years. He'd decided that divorcing me wasn't the avenue he wanted to take, and as elated as I was at his return, I couldn't help but despair that somebody my age with reasonable intelligence kept finding herself in so many predicaments. I had been to counseling off and on throughout my life when I felt it was needed, and I had worked hard to function normally. I had raised my kids as well or better than most, given my circumstances. In addition, Delbert and I had been going to counseling together for a year and a half after another incident in which he had felt like giving up and had briefly walked out.

Quite simply, how could my life be so dysfunctional when I had worked so hard to *not* be dysfunctional, and where did all this drama come from? Just like clockwork, as I asked myself the same questions I'd asked so many times over the years, one more stressful event occurred. Delbert's mother, whom he adores, passed out in her home, hit her head, and was rushed to the emergency room. She was in the hospital nearly two weeks with pneumonia, a high fever, dangerously high sugar levels, and E.coli bacteria in her blood. To my relief, this time Delbert didn't run. Instead, he put his trust in me, and together we got through the current crisis.

Essentially, we both realized that while we were dysfunctional and our families were dysfunctional, we genuinely loved each other. We concluded that all we could do was continue to go to counseling and grow together. We both believed that life together was better than life apart, and our flicker of hope was the insight we were gaining from counseling.

The bottom line was that we both had to face the fact that most of our lifetime disappointments were really our own doing, created by our own bad choices. This was a particular surprise for Delbert, who all along thought he was fine the way he was and that it was those around him causing his grief.

That he came to such a realization makes Delbert a giant in my eyes. He's fifty-seven years old now, and this isn't easy, but he's not only going to counseling for himself and our marriage, but he's also doing it for his family so he can continue to love them without enabling them to continue in the dangerous behaviors they've become accustomed to. The story doesn't end here, but thanks in great part to the ongoing saga caused by our decisions and the decisions of our children and other relatives, I have written this book with several specific goals in mind.

In writing this book, I have bared my soul to all the world, the good, the bad, and the ugly, and I want my readers to understand just how essential it is to do this. You don't have to write a book to come to terms with yourself, but you do have to be honest. Self-denial is, by definition, a psychological defense mechanism in which confrontation with a personal problem or with reality is avoided by denying the existence of the problem or reality. I know that facing yourself is the hardest thing in the world to do, but once you admit your problems, you've taken the biggest step toward making your life better.

I also want to communicate to my readers what life is like for the child who grows up in an abusive home totally devoid of love, compassion, direction, and guidance. Such children don't really know what it feels like to be "normal"; they can only have a glimpse from the outside looking in. The abuse they endure becomes permanently woven into their personalities and consequently shapes their futures. Some manage to change their lives and move in a positive direction, but others simply give in and give up.

It is my belief that it is our responsibility as adults to protect children from abusive parents and/or pedophiles. We must get directly involved when we see children in danger and take the necessary steps to report such crimes. It doesn't matter if the perpetrator is somebody we love, is a distant relative, or is a complete stranger. Our focus must be on the safety of our children. By the same token, children also need protection from parents who stay with an abuser and turn a blind eye to the abuse of their own children or, worse yet, participate with the abuser. As unbelievable as this sounds, I am living proof that it happens.

I would like to say emphatically that it is possible to overcome horrible childhood abuse and to go on to live a fulfilling life replete with love and joy. This isn't to say that the road never darkens again, but peace and happiness are possible. Unfortunately, a life of abuse isn't easy to overcome. It takes sheer determination to break away from behavior that has been passed down, accepted, or ignored through generations, and I can clearly see the patterns of abuse being repeated in my own family as well as my husband's. In addition, taking this stand against abuse pretty much guarantees that you will be scrutinized and scourged by those family members who aren't able or willing to do the same, but to break away from a cycle of family abuse, there can be no fence riders. You must make the decision to change and stick with it. You either take your stand, or ultimately, you are sucked back into the pits of hell and cause your own children the grief and agony you've lived through.

What choice is there, really? I firmly believe that those who decide to have children need to become selfless. However, what happens far too often is that parents become selfish. This is a recipe for disaster. When you are a parent, your focus must remain on your children, or they are the ones who will suffer. Generally accepted and ignored family molestations passed down from one generation to the next has to stop with *you*. If you don't think you can break the pattern for yourself, then don't have children or you will cause needless suffering to even more innocent victims. While I made mistakes and poor decisions along the way, I never gave up my relentless pursuit of peace, and I never stopped trying to learn better ways to make wiser decisions. Most important, I always made sure the needs of my children came first.

It is a sobering thought that as bad as the statistics on sexual abuse are, these numbers are undoubtedly grossly underestimated. According to Jim Hopper, Ph.D., "Most abused and neglected children never come to the attention of government authorities. This is particularly true for neglected and sexually abused children, who may have no physical signs of harm. In the case of sexual abuse, secrecy and intense feelings of shame may prevent children and adults who are aware of the abuse from seeking help."

The bottom line is that official government statistics do *not* indicate actual rates of child abuse. For my part, I simply know too many people who have endured sexual, mental, and physical abuse, and without exception, none of the cases I'm familiar with has been reported. This frightens me, as it only confirms what I've always felt: more child molesters/pedophiles are on the loose than have been caught. Make no mistake: they are lurking about, and chances are you know one and are clueless to who it is.

The childhood sexual abuse I endured was generational: it was perpetrated by my father, his father, by some of his brothers, by some of their kids, and so on. It also existed on my mother's side of the family. Today, it is alleged at least one of my siblings is a pedophile with a fixation for young boys. I don't know how far back it goes in my family, as my father's relatives refuse to talk about it. It is their "dirty little family secret," but pretending it never happened guarantees that the abuse will continue. I have seen this time and time again in my family and in my husband's, as well as in others. If ignored and swept under the rug, sexual abuse grows like a cancer.

My final goal in this book is to put real feeling and emotion to the word "abuse." It is hard for the many millions who haven't endured such a life to look at a person who is seemingly healthy and whole and to understand that "abuse" does not refer merely to an incident or event. There is a tortured soul inside those who have been abused, and I want all my readers to understand this so when they hear the word "abuse," it will no longer be just another word to them.

Unfortunately, those of us who grew up with savage abuse never were allowed to enjoy our childhoods. Even as adults, we see large spaces of blank nothingness or of pain when we look back. However, the good news is that we all can have a chance to see what a wonder childhood can be by creating it for our own children. This is where I have found my satisfaction, joy, and peace in life, and other victims of abuse can, too. I consider children my second chance, a magnificent gift from God. I have seen enough abuse in this world, and I hope my story will touch those who are struggling to break the cycle in their own lives and they will find hope. Better yet, maybe my story will touch the hearts of those mothers and fathers who are abusing their children and they will stop.

At age forty-seven, I believe that while life can be stranger than fiction, we all can survive if we are ferociously tenacious, though not without trials and not without heartbreak. So, here is my story.

Chapter One

The Nightmare Begins

I was born May 18, 1955. It was a spring morning, and I was the third of six children. I guess you could say this was the moment all my problems began. My mother loves to say that I was the homeliest baby she had ever laid eyes on. In fact, as she tells it, I was so ugly she didn't even want to hold me, but by the time two days had passed, I had somehow become her most beautiful baby. Though I have never found anything redeeming about this humiliating story, as a little girl, I had no idea it was merely a prelude to the grueling torture and abuse that was to come.

As hard as I've tried, I don't remember ever feeling any closeness with my mother or father. I see pictures of us, when my brother, sister, and I were little, before all six of us were born, and it appeared that our parents adored us. We were dressed nicely, our hair was combed, and we were a cute-looking, "all-American" family. How could anyone have known we were anything but? Truly, if photographs could talk, what stories they would tell.

To me, my childhood is like a puzzle with pieces missing. There are large holes, and no matter how hard I try to remember, I can't. I guess that is one good thing about being a child–children have a defense mechanism that allows them to block trauma from their memories. Given the nature of the memories I have, I'm somewhat thankful I can't remember more. What I do know is that I honestly can't recall when things started getting bad. It may be that they always were bad. What I can tell you is that my mother loved my father so much that she sacrificed her children for him. Somehow, she became twisted, and what was abnormal became normal to her.

My mother, a small woman about 4'10" who always looked somewhat childlike, came from a poor family from the deep South. Grandpa was the fix-it guy in the neighborhood, and from what I understand, Gramma was a hard-working woman who picked cotton. When her kids were old enough, they helped. Gramma also cooked for some of the wealthier people in the area and was given the leftover food to take home to her family. My mother was still a little girl when the family moved to a small town in northern lower Michigan where my grandpa started working on the ships that traveled Lake Michigan.

Gramma had a stroke while my mother was young, and I don't think my mother ever forgave her for that. She was raised mostly by her sisters, one whom she hates to this day, one whom she is indifferent about, and one whom she likes and relates to. Mom always felt she was treated callously by her siblings and had an unfair start in life, but I don't know much about her family, as she was ashamed of her poor Southern roots. She consequently has gone to great lengths to distance herself from her family and has even changed her name from "Betty Jo" to "Betz." She also refuses to speak with the Southern drawl the rest of her family still possesses.

It is important to note that my mother has always considered herself to be a victim. She has a "poor me" attitude, and I have often heard her say that by the time she was born, there was just no love left for her mother to give her. That is certainly the pot calling the kettle black, and Mom still fails to understand that Gramma was incapable of this through no fault of her own.

My gramma on my father's side moved her family to northern lower Michigan after her husband's death. Growing up, we knew very little about our father's father. All we knew was that he was dead and never spoken of. We all guessed there was some sort of family secret about him, but our grandpa remained a mystery to us until we were older. Gramma was brought up a very strict Catholic and in fact had three sisters who were nuns, all three of whom were tragically killed in a car accident. Gramma also taught at the local Catholic school for many years. She raised nine children by herself, but my father, who changed his name from Norbert to Robert but goes by Jack, was her favorite. He used this fact to manipulate her and was always a very handsome man. He was also cunning and conniving, with a high IQ, which certainly aided him in his predatory ways in life.

I have only a few vivid memories before the age of four. I know I wasn't any older than that, as I remember the apartment we lived in. It was right above the snack bar my parents owned and operated. The snack bar was a little mom-and-pop eatery with a jukebox and pool table in our small, rural community in northern Michigan and it was right across the street from the small Catholic school. I don't remember being happy or sad at this time in my life, but one of the most vivid memories of my childhood takes place in that apartment.

One day, there was a light shining brightly in the bedroom where I slept, and I was drawn to that light. I remember it as being blinding, so bright it should have stung my eyes when I looked at it, but it didn't. I walked into the light and felt a warmth wash over me. When I looked at the ceiling, there was Jesus smiling at me. His face was as big as the ceiling itself and was bright and luminous without being translucent, and I clearly remember that I wasn't afraid at all.

I do not pretend to know why Jesus presented himself to me that day, but I have a feeling he wanted me to have this moment as a glimmer of hope in the darkest hours of my life, and, indeed, from that point on, I knew I would never be alone in this world, even if in a physical sense I was.

Throughout the part of my life that we lived above the snack bar, I remember that my brother Bob and my sister Jackie and I, all children under the age of seven, were routinely left unattended while playing outside, just a few feet from a main road in town. One particular day when Jackie and I were approximately five and four years old, respectively, we were playing outside with a few of the neighborhood kids, and we all decided to go across the street to the small playground at the school. A janitor cleaned the school on the weekends, and this day his teenage son Frank was there in his place. Frank approached us kids and asked, "Who wants a bag of sunflower seeds?" Jackie, always the bravest, said, "I do!" He then asked Jackie to go with him. Jackie wanted to see the inside of the school, and the school doors were wide open. We all stayed outside and waited for her.

Jackie said the cool tile floor felt really good on her bare feet as she and Frank walked down the hallway. She said that Frank took her into the bathroom with him and got down on his knees and pulled her pants down, exposing her bottom and vagina. He then took down his own pants just far enough to bare his penis, which he took in his hand and rubbed on Jackie's vagina. She said he did that for a while. When he finished, he pulled her pants back up, gave her a bag of sunflower seeds, and sent her back out to play.

When we got home, Dad asked Jackie where she'd gotten the sunflower seeds, and she told him Frank had given them to her. Dad must have known something was up and asked her further questions. When she told him what had happened, instead of confronting Frank or calling the police, he laughed. Any father in his right mind would have gone over to that school and at the very least beat the hell out of that man for touching his daughter, but not my dad. His reaction was exactly the opposite.

Mom's reaction wasn't that of a normal mother even way back then, either. She was standing right there when Jackie told Dad, and she reacted with the same apathy he displayed. No doubt my parent's lack of reaction made many other children accessible to Frank, for he continued to work at that school and grew up to become a grade school teacher. Imagine Jackie's anguish a few years later when the substitute teacher for her class was Frank. At the time the incident took place, Jackie wasn't traumatized. All she knew was that Frank was going to give her a bag of sunflower seeds. We were so deprived of food even then that getting such a treat was of the utmost importance. It wasn't until Frank was her substitute teacher that Jackie realized he made her feel squeamish, and that was after she had begun enduring sexual abuse at our father's hands. It was in retrospect that she realized what Frank had done to her was wrong and that our parents thought it was funny.

On another occasion when we were playing outside, once again unattended by Mom, we again crossed the road to play at the playground across the street. On our way back home, as we were running across the street, Jackie was hit by a car. Other than a few scrapes and bruises, she was okay, but the kindly old couple driving the car was simply mortified that they'd hit a little girl. They wanted to give Jackie some money, but they were quickly let off the hook by Mom and Dad and went on their way. I have thought of that incident many times over the years and shudder at what could have happened, but even then Mom and Dad seemed not to understand or care that their small children needed supervision.

The bulk of my memories begin when we lived in the house about a mile or so outside of town. My family moved to this house when I was turning five years old. In this house, my family was isolated, as there were no neighbors close by. Most of the kids' bedrooms were upstairs, while the little boys slept downstairs, and we all shared rooms. Our house was very old and seemingly without insulation. Upstairs, the rooms were hot in summer and icy cold in winter. They got so cold that sheets of ice formed down the inside of our windows and we could see our breath when we exhaled. We slept on mattresses that sagged in the middle and had springs sticking out of them. They seemed to be as aged as the house, and the only way to stay warm was to sleep doubled up and close to each other. We were poor, but we were poor by choice, I later called it.

Dad was a successful businessman and made plenty of money, but he would not spend any of it on us. Eventually, we learned that he hated us for ever being born. He also hated our mother for getting pregnant and trapping him into marriage in the first place, and you can probably imagine that his firstborn son Bob, was especially despised and picked on by Dad.

When Jackie came along, she became the apple of Dad's eye. She was the one he always liked best and could seemingly do no wrong. Then there was me. I guess, like Bob, I got in Dad's way, not to mention that I was another mouth to feed. Collectively, Bob, Jackie, and I were known as the "big kids." I can't even imagine why Mom and Dad had Rod, Tay, and Roger, known as the "little kids." Their whole lives, they were nothing but afterthoughts to Mom and Dad and just seemed to get in their way.

Home was strange in many ways. We weren't allowed to play with any other children, and we ate odd food for dinner such as rice with ketchup and celery in it. Hamburger gravy was another meal we frequently ate, and let's not forget the frequent helpings of bean soup. I can't remember all our meals, but to us they were gross. We literally ate slop. We also routinely ate surplus food, including Spam, and our peanut butter was surplus peanut butter with a funny canned taste. The big pails it came in ended up becoming our lunch boxes for school. That was terribly embarrassing; we might as well have announced to the world how poor we were. I grew up thinking the only vegetables on earth were canned peas, beans, and pork and beans, which were also surplus. We didn't know what a salad was, and God forbid our parents ever took us to a restaurant. They never even took us to the one they owned and lived above. There was no such thing as a balanced diet in our home, but it wasn't because our parents couldn't afford food. They just fed us filler foods to quiet the ache in our bellies. As I mentioned, Dad had money and plenty of it. He had dump trucks, cement trucks, septic trucks, a cement plant, an outboard motor boat, an airplane, and later a semi truck. He and Mom ate steaks at times, but we kids never did. We ate our slop and watched while Dad cut up steak and fed it to Mom bite by bite. Once in a great while, we were lucky enough to have meat such as chicken.

Even Jackie, Dad's favorite, got in trouble once on account of food. One night we had chicken for dinner, and when Jackie reached for a second small piece, Dad took his fork with the pointy tines down and hit her in the hand with it, causing her to bleed. He then looked at her in a disgusted manner and called her a glut. You see, when we had chicken, Mom would get the whole breast herself, and Dad would eat the drumsticks. What was left over was split up between us six kids. On this particular day, there was some chicken left, and Jackie didn't know she couldn't have more than one piece. She was just hungry for real food, as we all were back then.

There were many food disparities in our house. My father had rye bread and real butter to go with his oatmeal in the morning, but not us. We never had toast with our oatmeal or real butter. We ate oleo, which tasted a lot like grease. We hated oatmeal, but it was cheap, and as Dad often said, "It's good for you!" Besides, oatmeal was part of the surplus food, so we were stuck with it almost every morning of our lives. I think if we could have had toast and butter, it would have helped the oatmeal go down a little easier. We used to beg Dad for a bite of his toast, and once in a while, he'd give us one. It was very special to taste his privileged food, and none of us ever forgot the rare occasions this happened.

After dinner at night, if we were lucky enough to have dessert, it was my job to go into the basement and get a jar of peaches or pears that Mom had previously canned. Dad knew I was deathly afraid of the dark and spiders, so, of course, this was the perfect job for me. We had an old Michigan basement, with dirt floors and only one light that was usually burned out, midway down the stairs. The light switch was on a string you had to pull to turn on the light, which meant I had to feel around for the string. I could feel the spider webs grazing my skin as I searched for the string, and I would continue to feel them across my face as I made my descent into the dark basement. After I got the peaches or pears, I would run back up the stairs as fast as my legs would carry me.

The whole process probably took a total of forty-five seconds, but it was so torturous it seemed to last a lifetime. I just knew some of those webs had spiders on them, and I would shudder and brush myself off quickly. Fortunately, it wasn't every night we got to have dessert, which was my saving grace. As a matter of fact, I don't think we ever had dessert unless Dad was present and suggested it.

In our family, the older kids looked after the younger kids, and now I cannot ever remember not being a caregiver. We were given tremendous responsibilities as young children, and we began chores at a very young age. This was the beginning of what I remember as our life of hell, and it was also the beginning of our group spankings. Bob, Jackie, and I, three children under the age of eight, even did dishes standing on chairs. Not only were we too little to reach the sink, but also Jackie and I were still small enough to take baths in the same sink we washed the dishes in.

Each dish had to be spotless, and the rule was that we each got one "wap" per dirty dish. A "wap" was one swat with the belt on our bottoms. I'm sure there were times when every dish passed the inspection, but I don't remember any. We all hated dish time, but we had to take turns washing, rinsing, and drying and putting away. The one who did the washing was the one who was spanked the hardest, as this individual was held the most responsible for the dirty dishes.

It went this way: every night when we finished the dishes, Dad scrutinized every cup, every dish, and every single piece of silverware, as well as each of the pots and pans. He always took his time doing so and indeed overemphasized his examination to intensify our fear. He looked hard for anything we missed, minute as it may have been, and added up the "waps" as we stood there frozen, watching him go through his lengthy examination process.

We stood and watched silently as he put every dish that did not pass his tedious inspection in a pile. As the pile grew, so did our panic and fear, but we had to stand there and await our fate. The process seemed to last a lifetime, and increasing our fear and agony this way was undoubtedly the best part for Dad of this sadistic torture. My stomach would knot up as I waited, and anticipating my punishment would be more than I could bear. When he was done, he would line the three of us up so we could get the number of "waps" he had counted up. Pulling his big black leather belt from his belt loops and snapping the leather together as he walked toward us gave him one final opportunity to terrify us and draw out our fear.

Knowing what lay ahead each night certainly made for dismal dinners. We were so young it would have been easier for Mom and Dad to do the dishes themselves, but Dad told us he was teaching us the right way to do dishes. Mom went along with this, as she had Dad on a pedestal and was convinced he could do no wrong. She apparently didn't realize or care that this was too much responsibility for such small children in the first place, and she likewise either didn't notice or care that Dad enjoyed punishing us. She also either didn't notice or care that her small children were being severely traumatized by Dad's sadistic nature, but in retrospect this shouldn't have been a particular surprise.

You see, very early in life, even as toddlers, we all became familiar with Mom and Dad's punishments. "Clobbers," or open-handed smacks upside our heads, were popular with Dad and Mom alike. Dad would add a special twist to this punishment by taking his open hand and cupping it around our heads and then pulling it back and cupping it back around our heads as if measuring the distance. He would do this four or five times before letting his hand fly and actually hitting us. He did this so he could keep us off guard, so we wouldn't be able to tell which time he pulled his hand back was going to be the real "clobber." We would just stand there cringing in fear, bracing ourselves and tensing up, while we waited. He liked to see us fly across the room and fall down. When that happened, he felt we'd had a good "clobber."

"Hair yanking," or shaking our heads violently by a fistful of hair, was one of Mom's choice punishments. She would come up and grab a handful of hair and shake our heads as hard as she could. I got instant headaches from this, and it was the sort of punishment that kept working even when it was over. Mom was a small woman, and this punishment seemed to suit her small stature, as she couldn't hit us very hard.

Another of Mom's favorite punishments was tying us back to back whenever we squabbled with one another. We then had to try to fight each other that way. I don't know what the purpose of this punishment was. It never solved anything and was instead a tremendous irritation. We struggled and struggled, and eventually one or both of us would give up. I always seemed to be tied back to back with Rod, who would fight his heart out, which meant I got hurt on top of everything else.

"Clunks" were another form of punishment. This meant getting hit in the head with Mom's or Dad's knuckles. It sounded like knocking on a piece of wood and left our heads with huge knots that were tender to the touch. All these punishments were instituted in our household to control us kids, and I know now that, like all good pedophiles, Dad was deliberately keeping his victims isolated and under his complete control. Mom didn't have such designs; she simply went along with whatever Dad did, though she did genuinely find having six kids around bothersome and unpleasant.

Gramma, Dad's mom, tried to help out all she could, especially with Bob. She often took him to stay with her. She never said anything about how Dad treated him, or any of us for that matter, but I know she knew how awful Dad was. Jackie and I also took turns staying with Gramma, and she taught me how to play the piano. I didn't like having to practice the scales over and over again for what seemed like a million times a day, but it was far better than being at home. Gramma lived across the street from a big graveyard, and her house was nestled in a pine grove. When the wind blew, the trees made an eerie sound that frightened me. Even though the nights were scary, I was still grateful to be there and have a break from home. It was more than a mile walk to the bus stop to go to school, but that was kind of fun, except for the boy who lived down the road from Gramma who picked on me relentlessly and washed my face in the snow in the winter.

Even though Gramma never hugged us, I loved her. Although she was a staunch woman who was not physically affectionate, she provided the only real care I had felt up to this point in my life. Her being unaffectionate did not seem unusual, as my parents were unaffectionate. The difference was, that Gramma was not mean to any of us, and when we did something wrong, she corrected us but didn't punish us in any way.

One of the best things about going to Gramma's was that we got to eat real food. We had corn flakes in the morning; dinners always included meat, potato, and vegetables-and we actually got dessert with dinner, which was always butterscotch pudding. That was my favorite, and because she always made it for me, I knew my gramma loved me. She also made me peanut butter and honey sandwiches for my sack lunch and wrapped my sandwiches in saran wrap, not wax paper. I was always embarrassed about having my sandwiches wrapped in wax paper because the kids at school said only poor people used wax paper. Even better, Gramma's lunches always tasted good. The honey crystallized the bread and made it taste like a candy bar, and she always included an apple, too. It was worth going to Gramma's house just to eat her food, and I felt like I was rich when I was there. I guess that was one of the few privileges of being one of the "big kids."

Mom and Dad had treats for themselves all the time, but normally they hid them from us. Hidden or not, we were not allowed to touch any of their food. Sometimes they would walk up to the little store on the corner about three-quarters of a mile away in the evening to get themselves a treat after dinner. They would, of course, leave us kids home alone while they did so. They never brought anything home for us, and they always ate their treats before they returned.

At the time, I didn't realize our lives were so abnormal. What I did know was that people made fun of us because we looked poor. Though we older kids had been dressed well when we were tiny, as we got older, our clothes got worse. Mom used to make shifts for Jackie and me. These shifts were made from two pieces of cloth sewn together with arm holes, head holes, and zippers in the back. They were like shapeless sacks. I had a yellow, a red, and a black shift to wear for the whole year. Each of us kids also had one pair of shoes, purchased at the beginning of the school year, and it didn't matter if our feet grew out of the toes of that pair of shoes before the next fall. We would not get another pair.

Socks were also a rare commodity. What socks we did have were old and didn't match, so we always wore various mismatched pairs. Thank God they were at least all white. It didn't seem to be a concern to Mom to make sure those few school outfits were clean for the whole week, and we often had to wear dirty clothes. The townspeople felt so sorry for us that sometimes we got off the bus to find boxes full of clothes on our porch. As if that weren't embarrassing enough, if we wore something that had belonged to somebody at our school, they would point it out and say something that made us feel less than human, a feeling we were certainly used to by then.

Through the summer months, we always went barefoot. There really wasn't a choice. We either had to go barefoot or wear our old worn-out school shoes with holes in the soles. I'll tell you, we had some tough feet back then. The property our house sat on was right next to the gravel pit my father owned. Between our yard, which was mostly clay, and the gravel pit and sand hill we used to play on was a large stretch of gravel. Getting across that gravel was always a painful process, as the rocks stabbed into our feet as we walked over them, and Jackie and I soon discovered an ingenious invention to help us get across those stones. Somewhere along the line, we discovered that if we walked in the wet clay and let it dry on our feet, it dried almost like shoes, which made it easier to get across the stretch of stones. It felt good when the cool, wet clay squished up between our toes, and we were proud of ourselves: we'd solved our own problem and made our own shoes! We even tried to make platform shoes by dipping our feet in the clay over and over again so it would last longer. It was a silly activity, and my sister and I laugh about it to this day. This is one of the few fond memories I have of growing up, but it's bittersweet. After all, the reason we had to make those shoes in the first place was that we weren't considered to be worth the money for a simple pair of shoes.

Of all the siblings in my family, I was closest to my sister Jackie. We were only thirteen months apart, and it seemed only right to chum up with her, as we were so close in age. Even though she was controlling and mean at times, I cannot hold anything that happened when we were children against her or my other siblings, as we were all just trying to survive. Jackie could be my best friend or my worst enemy. I suppose that was the best it could be back then, but I do know I never really trusted her completely. Although she wasn't always trustworthy, it was better to have somebody close to you in our family than nobody at all. Maybe this was when I learned that sometimes it's best to keep your enemies close to you so you can keep an eye on them. We argued some, but I got along with her most of the time. Without her, I would have been quite alone.

As we grew older, life took on a reliable pattern for us. In the summertime, we were routinely locked out of the house from morning until lunch and then locked out again until evening. Mom would put wet hankies on our heads so they wouldn't burn and say, "You kids go on outside and play." We knew what that meant we weren't coming in until lunch. After lunch she would again say, "You kids go on out and play." I don't know what Mom and Dad were doing in the house. I really don't remember them interacting much at all. All I know is that they didn't want six kids getting in their hair all day long. Some of those summer days seemed to last forever, but we knew better than to try and go in the house for anything except an occasional trip to the bathroom.

We were basically on our own, and we did the best we could. That wasn't always easy, as our youngest brother Roger was only two years old and Tay was three and they had to be watched closely. Although it should have been fun to play outside, it seemed to be just another chore. The whole day, we were left alone to tend to ourselves. There were no toys to play with, save a few army trucks for the boys, and the little kids needed constant attention. There was rarely time to just have fun. The main road ran in front of our house, and the little kids always wandered out there. Even though Bob, Jackie, and I were older, we were too young to have this much responsibility, but the only time Mom and Dad got involved was when something went wrong.

Every once in a while during the summer months, Mom played tennis with Dad's sister. We would all pile into our old station wagon and go pick up Aunt Jane and her two boys. Our car was all rusted out, but Mom and Dad didn't seem to think it was a big deal to have twelve-inch holes in the floorboards. As Mom drove down the road, oblivious to the danger at hand, we all sat in the back and watched the pavement pass under the car, afraid to move for fear we would fall through onto the highway and be killed. A piece of plywood would have covered those dangerous holes, but our welfare and safety simply weren't a priority.

Mom also occasionally took us to one of the local beaches with her friend Marsha and her two kids. We lived very near Lake Michigan, and there were also numerous inland lakes close by, but the beach Mom always chose was a scummy one, not the beach most people in our area went to. I hated this beach and didn't like going there, as a lot of migrant workers swam there in the evenings. It wasn't that I didn't like people of a different race; it was that the Mexican men scared me. These grown men sat on the beach in their bathing suits with baggy leg holes and tried to get Jackie's and my attention. If we looked at them, they spread their legs apart and leaned back with their penises hanging out of their suits. They also followed us around. If we went into the water for a swim, they went into the water, too. I never wanted to unwrap my towel from around my waist because they stared so much. This surely detracted from any pleasure we took in being away from home, but once again Mom paid no attention to any of us. She just sat there talking with Marsha, oblivious to the danger at hand. We would have told her what was going on if we'd thought it would do any good, but we figured she probably wouldn't believe us or care.

Mom's brother came to stay with us for a short period one summer to work with my dad when I was six or seven. He was a weird man. His hair was black, curly, and greasy, and he had a look that sent shivers up my spine. He was simply creepy. He played the guitar for us and would make up little jingles, and he slept in an upstairs bedroom near us that we called the "old room." One morning, Jackie told me to sneak into his bedroom and steal a fifty-cent piece out of the pocket of his pants, and she told me right where his pants were, on the floor at the foot of his bed. I really didn't want to do it, but Jackie always overpowered me and convinced me to do things for her that she didn't want to do herself, and she convinced me it was my turn to steal a fifty-cent piece, as she had done it before. Reluctantly, I agreed to take my turn, and I sneaked into his room on my hands and knees very quietly. Sure enough, his pants were lying right on the floor where Jackie had said they would be. I was so quiet I was barely breathing, but suddenly I heard him say softly, "Rhonnie ... Rhonnie."

I was caught! My heart was pounding as I looked up and there he was, lying in bed all covered up except for a makeshift hole in the blanket through which he had stuck his penis. I was so scared I got up and ran out of that room and into ours and told my sister what had happened. Although I was sure this was the reason she had asked me to go in our uncle's room, she denied this had happened to her. I should have known better than to listen to her; she had set me up to do something she didn't want to do herself. To me, it seemed the money was all she cared about, not what a pervert our uncle was.

Shortly after this incident, this same uncle was giving Jackie piggyback rides, and pretty soon it was my turn. I was now afraid of him and tried to steer clear of him as much as possible, but Jackie coaxed me to take a piggyback ride from him. He looked at me and said, "Come on; it will be fun!"

I remember standing on the porch and him standing below me as he was telling me to get on. All that time I knew I didn't want to be anyplace near him, but I got on anyway. He held onto me under my back legs in the normal way, but then he reached his hand up between my legs and put his fingers in a tickling motion on my privates and sang a disgusting little jingle he made up, "Tickle tickle tickle ... tickle!"

I was scared as he ran with me around the backside of the house. After he put me down he tried to coax my sister into another ride, but she refused. Then he looked at me and tried to get me to take another ride, but I got away as far as I could. Soon after, Jackie asked me if he had done the same thing to me as he had just done to her. I told her yes and then wondered why she wanted me to get the same treatment from my uncle that he'd given her. The only thing I could think of was that she wanted me to endure this so we would have something to talk about. As always, we both knew we couldn't tell our parents, as we figured they wouldn't do anything about it anyway or, worse yet, wouldn't believe us.

When he wasn't with us, this uncle still lived at home with my gramma and grandpa. Some time after these incidents, after he had moved back in with them, our family took a day trip to visit our grandparents. This uncle business was still in the forefront of my mind, and made the trip ominous, and when we arrived, one of our cousins warned us that there were peepholes in the wall in our grandparents' bathroom. Sure enough, she took us in there, and we saw them. Not one or two, but ten or twelve peepholes all together, stuffed with toilet paper so that whoever it was who had been peeking through them could no longer see anything. I don't know whose peepholes they were, but I can say with certainty that Grandpa never gave me the creeps in any way. I have only good thoughts and feelings about him, and I don't remember him ever being inappropriate at all.

On the other hand, I knew my uncle was capable of such behavior. Since he wasn't there that day, we had a reprieve, but we all sneaked up to his room and found tons of pornographic books lying everywhere. He was a real pervert, and thank God he never had children, even when he married.

Winters weren't any better than summers in terms of Mom and Dad taking care of us, and regardless of the weather, we were routinely locked out of the house on winter weekends, too. This was okay with us, even though we were always cold. We would double up our clothes and socks, put bread bags in our boots, and, if we didn't have any mittens, put socks on our hands. There were a lot of hills nearby, and we lived at the base of a hill, so we always went sledding. That was fun, and the kids from town and some from the neighborhood all came to these hills, too. Since we weren't allowed to have anyone spend the night or play at our house, getting a chance to interact with other kids made toughing out the bitter cold worth it.

One time while tobogganing, we all decided to go down the big hill behind our regular sliding hill. We were just kids, and we'd forgotten that at the bottom of this extremely steep hill was a barbed-wire fence. After we made our climb up that hill, we all piled on the toboggan and began our descent. We were going really fast when I realized we were going to run right into the fence. I was in front, and, not knowing what to do, I stuck my leg out of the side of the toboggan to try to stop it. I stopped it all right, and we all wiped out before we hit the fence, but my leg was injured. My kneecap was turned to the side, and I couldn't walk on it. The pain was intense, but the other kids helped me, and somehow I finally got home with my poor swollen leg.

True to form, Mom and Dad failed to take me to the doctor. They seemed quite unconcerned about my injury and likewise didn't seem to care about the pain I was in. They didn't even give me an aspirin, though my leg and knee were so swollen my skin was turning blue. How could they not care when my kneecap was turned to the side? The only thing Dad said was that I was stupid for sticking my leg out of the toboggan in the first place.

I was very concerned about being able to go to school like this, but Dad said I would have to hop on one leg, which I did. I spent at least three weeks hopping on one foot until I could finally put my foot on the ground. I'm sure that wrapping it tightly would have helped, as would crutches. I was embarrassed to be hopping around like that, and in retrospect I wonder about the teachers. Didn't they care? They could clearly see the pain I was in, but they did nothing, nor did they approach my parents about my leg. Though it eventually healed sufficiently for me to walk on, I am reminded of this injury every time it gets cold and every time it rains, when it begins to badly ache. I also sometimes forget that I can't stand and rest on that leg, as my knee still regularly gives out on me.

I don't have very good memories of school. There were only about seventeen kids in my class until the sixth grade, when we added a few kids from the Catholic school. Being considered poor was hard on us, and since our last name had the word "poor" in it, though it was spelled differently, the other children called our family "Poorpoor." They pretty much had free reign, as no one stopped them. In fact, one teacher picked on us right along with the other children. She was an old, bitter woman, and I'm sure in her warped way she thought this would help build character. The kids were just doing what the other kids were doing, but an adult in a position of authority should have known better. We were noticeably the outcasts of the school, though a few of the farm kids seemed poor also and were teased as relentlessly as we were. My brothers, sisters, and I already had chips on our shoulders as a result of our home life, and the constant teasing at school was just one more thing we had to deal with. This is probably why I don't remember too much of school other than the people in my grade and incidents such as being teased.

For my siblings and me, there simply was no escape. School was bad, and home was hell. Our teachers should have been able to guess what we endured at home by looking at us, but kids just didn't talk about those things back then. As a child, you just pretended those unspeakable things didn't exist. Even though there were slight similarities between school and home, school was our reprieve. Though the kids were often cruel, it was still better than the constant state of fear we lived in at home.

By the time I was old enough to go to school, home life had truly become hell on earth. Stepping off the bus at the end of the day was almost like walking into another dimension. It wasn't just the constant chores we were forced to do. The atmosphere was thick and tense always, and then there was the process of walking on eggshells that began immediately if both Mom and Dad were home. Although we never witnessed them arguing, we knew by their tone that they were often mad at one another, and we paid the price. Our weekends were filled with chores, and we spent countless hours working in the house or in the yard. There were always plenty of chores to do. As we got older, besides doing the dishes, we became responsible for cooking and cleaning, and doing the laundry became Jackie's and my responsibility as well. This was an all-day job that more often than not became an all-weekend job.

We did the laundry out on our back porch with an old ringer washer. The cord of the washer was frayed, and there was bare wire exposed on some parts of it. My sister and I worried constantly about being electrocuted, since the porch would get completely wet and the water collected in small pools in the low spots, but we somehow managed to keep the cord out of the water. We had to wash and hang clothes out on the line to dry and iron and fold them as well. This was back in the days before permanent press was invented, when almost everything had to be ironed. We used to divide up the ironing, but the job was never ending. Our chores took so long we rarely had any time for ourselves.

Although we had no furniture to speak of, Mom and Dad insisted that the house be spotless, and we were beaten if it wasn't cleaned to their specifications. We already knew that Dad was really big on spankings and that he enjoyed group punishments, and before long, if one child did something wrong, we all were punished. Dad would line all six of us up and spank us one at a time and, just like with the dishes, he seemed to enjoy dragging our punishment out and amplifying our fear by taking his belt in both hands and snapping the leather together as we got in line. There was enjoyment on his face as he watched the terror wash over us, and he would then abruptly grab the left arm of whoever was first in line and just start wailing on that child, who would run in circles and scream and writhe in pain during the beating. He never hit us just a couple of times in these instances; he wailed on each of us at least ten or fifteen times. The rest of us were forced to stand there in dread, crying, awaiting our own painful fate as we watched.

When it was Bob's turn, Dad would yell, "Dance Bob, dance!" He seemed to enjoy tormenting and beating Bob the most. The fear in those of us waiting became even greater the longer we watched, for Dad seemed to build momentum as he went along. It was as though spanking us energized him, and he seemed to become more aggressive with each passing swing of his belt. He would spank each of us from our backs to our legs until we were black and blue from his belt. He started out slowly and built momentum, and his breathing became heavier the longer he worked us over. He never stopped until he was satisfied, regardless of what we had done or how much we were crying, and the louder we screamed, the harder he hit us. He had an insatiable sadistic nature and actually seemed to enjoy our tears and pain, and in retrospect I can safely say it was as though he were having an orgasm in the process of hitting us. He may well have, as he seemed quite satisfied when he finished.

Mom was usually right there, justifying Dad's choice of punishment. She seemed to go along with the idea of group spankings and indeed seemed quite pleased with this punishment. It was as if she thought Dad were defending her somehow by punishing those who had done her wrong. We were, after all, nothing but monsters who deserved such severe punishment, and she never missed a chance to tell us that. To her, it probably seemed Dad was proving how much he loved her by punishing us.

All of us children lived in fear every single day of our lives, as Dad and Mom's moods dictated our fate for the day. We couldn't step out of line the least little bit or we suffered grave consequences. Bad moods with Mom or Dad meant bad days for us; good moods meant better days for us. Better, but still not good or anywhere near normal.

One day we must have all been fighting with one another and were beaten. To further make their point, Mom and Dad waited until we were sound asleep that night and then they came upstairs. This was a big deal, as they only made it up once or twice a year. I don't recall ever being tucked in by them or receiving a goodnight hug or kiss, prayer or story, or even a drink of water. Once upstairs this particular night, they started yelling at each other. Mom yelled, "Jack, quit hitting me!" Then Dad yelled, "You hit me first." Then he yelled, "Jackie, Rhonnie, tell Mom to quit hitting me!" Then Mom yelled, "Bob, tell Dad to quit hitting me!" This went on for quite a while. They were teaching us with this new creative punishment just what it felt like to have to put up with kids fighting with each other. Then they yelled, "This is what all of you sound like!" and stormed downstairs.

On another occasion when we were too noisy during their "quiet time," which was any time they were together, they came upstairs in the middle of the night, Dad loudly blowing his trombone while he and Mom marched all around the bedrooms, waking us up. When they were done, they screamed, "How do you kids like having your quiet time interrupted with all this noise?" and then once again they left. We were simply terrified to be awakened like this, and it was hard to calm down and go back to sleep. I remember lying there shivering and scared, and I also remember that this was a feeling I knew well.

Somewhere along the line, though I can't remember when or why, I became Bob's female counterpart and almost as much an object of Dad's hate and sadistic behavior as Bob. I remember feeling a lot sorrier for Bob than myself, though, as Dad really enjoyed being cruel to him and couldn't get enough of it. Dad was simply contemptible with Bob and found endless ways to punish and degrade him. Bob was held back in the third grade, and after this Dad's favorite name for him was "Stupid." Bob's teacher even told Dad that Bob was stupid. Of course, this was the same teacher who enjoyed picking on our family with all the other children.

Years after his struggles in school, Bob went to the eye doctor, and guess what? He wasn't stupid at all; he just needed glasses. For most parents, vision would have been an obvious thing to check, but not ours. Dad and Mom just didn't want to spend any money on doctors for their children. We were not only burdens to them, but also we were second-class citizens.

One day, Dad must have been feeling especially cruel and made Bob carry water buckets to the gravel pit, a good block's distance away. He made Bob put a full bucket of water in each hand and then walked behind him, yelling, "Move Bob, move!" All the while, he kicked Bob at the base of his back with the inside of his foot. Tears just streamed down poor Bob's face as he tried to go faster with the heavy load without spilling it or falling down. I stood there watching Dad torture Bob, knowing he had to endure this, with my heart aching. This torturous event was purely for Dad's amusement. He wasn't carrying any water and in fact had running water at the gravel pit.

Another time, Bob was upstairs in his room, and the rest of us kids were all downstairs with Mom and Dad. We kept hearing this voice saying, "Help! Help!" We finally went upstairs and found Bob hanging upside down in his closet with a belt strapped around his ankles. We didn't know what he was doing, but Dad just stood there and laughed hysterically and didn't let Bob down for quite a while. He had to humiliate him first, but finally he undid the belt around Bob's ankles, and poor Bob fell to the floor. He was so embarrassed. He said he'd strapped his ankles like that because he'd wanted to do sit-ups and didn't want to fall to the ground and hurt himself.

I don't know if that's what he was doing or not, but I felt so sorry for Bob. Bob was just a young boy; he may very well have thought of this invention to do the sit-ups. Even though we all laughed along with Dad, our laughs were nervous ones to keep Dad happy. Dad got a lot of mileage out of this incident and brought it up every chance he could, and though I felt guilty for laughing at Bob and was ashamed of myself, there was nothing I could do. I did what I had to do to survive. We all did.

My version of being Bob's counterpart meant becoming Dad's slave, and sure enough, Dad saw to it that I had a lot of extra duties. I remember one time in particular when I was seven or eight years old and he made me scour the bathtub. Scouring the tub was nothing new to me, but this time was different because he stayed in the bathroom and stood over me, watching every move I made. I was nervous, because I knew why he was there: he was just waiting for me to do something wrong. I didn't want to give him a reason to hit me, so I worked very carefully, but I was scared and nauseated as I scrubbed the tub. Sure enough, all of a sudden I felt a thunderous crack against my head as he clobbered me and yelled at me, telling me how stupid I was.

I began to cry and begged him, "What? What?" He just kept yelling at me and clobbering me. I scrubbed as hard and fast as I could with tears streaming down my face, and then came another blow to my head. By this time, my little hands and body were shaking, and my vision was blurred with tears. I could no longer see what I was doing, and in a desperate attempt to get him to quit beating me, I used more cleanser. He just kept clobbering and berating me, telling me how stupid I was.

I had absolutely no idea what I was doing wrong, and nothing I did seemed to appease him. I scrubbed even harder, hoping that would make him stop, but he was beating my head so hard I could no longer fight to keep it up, and it began to make contact with the cast iron bathtub. Each time he hit me, my head connected with the tub. I just tried to keep scrubbing harder and harder, hoping he would see what a good job I was doing, but I couldn't seem to do the right thing, and I thought he was never going to stop.

My mom finally came in and said, "Jack," and at last he stopped. She must have thought he was never going to stop either, for she never interrupted his punishments. His breathing was heavy, and he was tense. Then in a tone thick with disgust he said, "You're so stupid; you're supposed to use cold water to rinse the tub, not hot water. Hot water costs money." With that he walked away, giving me a look that told me exactly how much he despised me. It was the look that told me I would never please him, no matter what I did.

When you are little and feel that you will never have the approval of your dad or mom, it hurts more than any physical abuse, and I was literally dumbfounded. I was never told about the hot water before that day. Had he told me, I surely would have done it right, but had he told me, he wouldn't have been able to use this as an excuse to beat me. I knew that day I would I never be able to please him, no matter what I did, and I began to feel there was something wrong with me. I didn't yet realize there was something wrong with him.

I had been afraid of Dad before this incident, but after this I was petrified of him. I began to tremble at his mere presence, and I started getting diarrhea often. This was also when my migraines began. I tried hard to be loved by my parents, and I tried to do everything they told me to do, exactly the way they told me to do it, but nothing ever seemed to be right or good enough. I think it was at this point that I realized Mom and Dad just weren't going to love me, no matter what I did. This beating in the bathroom was the first punishment I'd received alone, without any of the other kids, and it was also the first time I'd realized I was at Dad and Mom's complete mercy. That day, I learned that I lived by the mercy of their hands, and I realized I could die by those hands. This memory of complete helplessness in a horrifying situation is still emotionally charged for me today, and I can hardly write about it as my vision is again blurred with tears.

Among other chores, by the time I was around seven years old, I also had the duty of making the oatmeal every morning. That seemed to be the breakfast of choice in our home, as it was inexpensive. The only time we deviated from having oatmeal was if we had spoiled milk and Mom made pancakes. It didn't matter if it was a school morning or not; it was my job to get up earlier than the rest of the family and make the oatmeal. It wasn't just making the oatmeal that was bad. What was even worse was that it had to be made Dad's way, which meant I had to stand right next to the stove and stir constantly. I was barely taller than the stove and had to reach up to stir, which meant my arm would get so tired it ached and the skin on it would nearly blister from the heat, but Dad insisted it be made this way, as this was the only way to get it creamy and without lumps.

I not only hated this chore, but I also hated the fact that Jackie never had to do it. One time I guess I complained enough, and finally Dad told Jackie she had to make the oatmeal the next morning. She burned it and wasn't punished, which really surprised me. Shortly after that, I decided that if burning the oatmeal worked for Jackie, it might just work for me. The difference between Jackie and me burning the oatmeal was that I got a really bad beating for it, and I never even thought about burning the oatmeal again.

Though Mom wasn't as bright, Dad was simply cunning. He was like one of those villains in comic books. He was completely maniacal and capable of dastardly deeds and he used his intelligence to control and connive many people, including his children. There was no question as to whether his tactics would work. He knew they would. Punishments sealed his authority with us, and manipulation by fear was his controlling factor. As close as Jackie and I were, he pitted her against me and then began pitting us all against one another.

For instance, Jackie could do no wrong, and I did everything wrong. This ensured that we vied for his attention, and made his control over us even stronger. Winning favor with Dad was of the utmost importance for our survival, as it meant there was a lot less torture for you. As I said before, I don't hate Jackie or anybody else in our family for anything they did as children for their survival. When I was little, I probably did hate them sometimes, but I understand now why we did what we did. We were all living in our own personal hells.

One time my younger brothers and sister and I stole a can of root beer from Mom and Dad's forbidden stash and went upstairs and hid in a bedroom closet to drink it. It tasted so good, each gulp was followed by an "Ahhh." This was a huge treat, even if it was a stolen one, but Jackie, by now the household enforcer of us all, told Dad about it. As we sat hidden quietly in the upstairs closet and drank this pop, we heard Dad coming upstairs. He walked into the bedroom where we were hiding and said, "I smell pop." We got really quiet and scared, and our last gulps of pop turned in our stomachs and made us feel sick. He didn't sound even slightly mad and said as he sniffed the air, "It sort of smells like root beer." We knew then that we were caught. We were too little to know you couldn't smell pop, so we reluctantly emerged from the closet with the nearly empty can.

Somehow we were fooled by his calm demeanor. We were still frightened, but we thought that maybe he would yell at us or put us in a corner. Oh, God, we were so wrong. Instead, he walked us out from the little bedroom into the spacious hallway and pulled his belt out of his belt loops, and this time there was no tormenting us by snapping the leather together. He grabbed the kid closest to him and just started beating him. I wasn't first in line; it was Rod who was closest to Dad, and by counting I could gauge the kind of beating I was going to get. Dad hit Rod over thirty times, and this beating was different than all the others. He held nothing back and indeed beat Rod so hard that I was completely overwhelmed with fear. I burst into tears, and knew my fate would be much worse, as Dad always built momentum and got meaner and madder with each kid.

Dad had an unquenchable anger that day, and I thought we were all going to die. I wanted to run away, anything to avoid my impending beating, but endure it I did, along with the other kids. All four of us were beaten until we were bloody. My father simply went ballistic, and I believe it must have been God himself who kept him from beating us to death. To say my sister felt bad about telling on us is an understatement. She never knew he would fly off the handle like that and beat us so severely. She said she had to run out into the field and cover her ears with her hands and make loud noises so she couldn't hear us. To this day, she still feels horrible for telling. This was without a doubt the worst beating I ever endured as a child, and it was over a four-cent can of Spartan brand pop.

Dad also pitted us all against Bob and incited us to hate and humiliate him as he did. This worked best with Jackie, who picked on Bob right along with Dad. Because Dad and Jackie were so close to each other, Jackie never did find a balance in her feelings toward Bob. She just always hated him because Dad did and to this day she feels the same way, only now she feels guilty about her feelings of contempt for him. Jackie also picked on me when it pleased Dad, and it often did. The younger kids figured it all out and did the same. All this manipulation was geared to allow easier access to us by a pedophile. Controlling us ensured access to each of us without any of us ever daring to tell each other or anyone else. Sure enough, we never did talk about any of this until we were older.

Jackie had a lot of privileges when we were small that I just couldn't understand. It was almost like a Cinderella story, with me as Cinderella and Dad as the wicked stepmother, only there was no fairy godmother to save me. We all had certain duties to perform, and I was just the one who had more than the others. One time I remember my sister sitting on Dad's lap as I was scrubbing the kitchen floor on my hands and knees. Both of them were watching me and making fun of me. It was quite commonplace for this type of thing to occur around the house. Boy, I remember being so jealous. I used to think that if only Dad loved me like he loved my sister, I would be so happy.

Somewhere around this time, Dad started driving a truck. At first when he used to come home from the road, we would run outside like his return was something special, but we finally quit getting excited when he came home. Even getting to collect the pop bottles from his truck didn't seem worth the trade-off of having him back. I would get a pit in my stomach and a feeling of impending doom when he pulled into the driveway. Being home with Mom was bad enough, but when the two of them were together, it was horrible.

I don't know how he managed it, since Mom was already jealous of the attention he paid Jackie, but somehow he talked her into letting him take Jackie with him on some of his trips. I was once again jealous that I didn't have the special relationship with Dad that Jackie did. Not that I wanted to go out on the road with him, but he seemed to love her so much and didn't seem to love me at all. She always got little favors from Dad, and she and Dad shared secrets, too. Dad never shared any secrets with me, and I really wanted to have that kind of closeness with him.

When he was home, Dad stayed right on top of us. He not only had complete control over all of us at this point, but he'd also succeeded in making Mom virtually insignificant. He did this by elevating his own status to that of supreme power in the household. He often overrode Mom's authority and brushed off things she said by telling us, "You know how your mother gets." I know now that he had very little affection for Mom and in fact increasingly enjoyed agitating her.

Dad also successfully raised Jackie's status in our household to the point that she had more authority in our house than Mom did. This was too much control for any young person to have, and soon it didn't matter to us whether Mom cared about us or not. We only cared if Dad loved us and, by extension, Jackie. Mom was absent most of the time now anyway, working at night and sleeping during the day, but she became more and more resentful of us, and treated us as unpleasant obstacles who drew Dad's attention away from her. I don't remember her being kind to any of us at this point, and, par for the course, she made herself out to be the victim, with us kids as the bad guys rather than Dad. She told all her friends stories about how awful we were, and in turn we were treated as ungrateful bratty kids that poor Betty had to put up with.

Though she didn't seem to care for any of us, she didn't hate anyone as much as she hated Jackie. Indeed, Jackie became her nemesis and her competition, no longer her daughter, and we all ended up having to tolerate her jealous, enraged behavior toward Jackie, not to mention her newly rejuvenated victim role. She became more bitter, more hateful, and more unbearable to be around and in fact seemed driven by her deep-seated rage and jealousy. Without a doubt, Mom managed to become the biggest troublemaker in the family, and that's saying a lot, as Rod was always a master troublemaker. Always wanting to be the damsel in distress waiting to be rescued by her hero, Mom began manufacturing problems and making any existing problems bigger than they really were just to see whether Dad would jump to her defense. Of course he did, since he enjoyed punishing us, and we got in trouble. This seemed to please her.

Watching a grown woman behave like this was disturbing, to say the least. Even a child could see what she was doing. She was especially pleased when Dad got angry with Jackie, and she seemed to try the hardest to get her into trouble. Jackie was, after all, her main competition for Dad's affection. For her part, Jackie was not about to step down to a lower level of status in our home after tasting the benefits of being Dad's favorite.

I still didn't know why Jackie was Dad's favorite, though I was about to find out, nor did I realize how unnatural my mother was until I had my first child and felt the overwhelming love a parent is supposed to feel for a child. Mom felt it was such a conquest if Dad showed affection to her. That was the big prize she sought, and she'd do or say anything to get it, including sacrifice her own children. She was so detached from reality that she never did see past what she wanted. Thus, we would all continue to suffer at the hands of both our parents.

Chapter 2

A Little Girl's Nightmare Worsens

Things had gotten really sticky around our house. Not only was Mom horribly jealous of Jackie, but I was jealous of her too. I also wanted the closeness she had with Dad, as well as the special privileges she enjoyed. Now, late at night, Dad would call her downstairs to share his special food. He called her downstairs often for pickled bologna and crackers, and I was nearly green with envy. I just knew I would never get to have such privileges. Dad just didn't love me like that, and I wanted him to more than anything.

I told my sister how I felt, and she seemed sympathetic, so one night when Dad called her downstairs, she told me to go instead of her. I was a little nervous about that, as I knew he would be expecting Jackie, but, after a fair amount of coaxing, I made my way down that long, steep stairway and into the living room. Sure enough, there were the pickled bologna and crackers waiting for my sister. Dad looked up, expecting to see Jackie, and said, "What are you doing here?" Then he got up from the couch and spanked my bottom and told me to get upstairs and in bed. I was crushed and in tears, not from the spanking, but because he had rejected me once again.

I don't know what I would have done without Jackie in my life. She was truly my comfort, and I knew she felt bad about how Dad had responded when I went downstairs. I just couldn't figure out why I wasn't allowed to enjoy the treats in life that were given to her, but when I was seven years old, this all changed. I had waited a long time for this to happen, and one night after I went to bed, I heard Dad calling my name.

I couldn't believe my ears! Could this really be happening? Was it really my turn to be treated as special? Was it really my turn to go downstairs at night while Mom was at work? Was it really my turn to be "privileged" just like Jackie? Was it really my chance to prove to Dad that I, too, was worthy of his love? I flew downstairs, hoping to share pickled bologna and crackers with him, or maybe even the ice cream Jackie sometimes told me about. This was heart-pounding excitement, and I was so thrilled I was beside myself.

When I got to the bottom of the steps, the lights were all off, and I didn't see Dad sitting in the living room. This was a huge disappointment, and my heart was broken just at the sight of the darkness and his absence. Where was he, and where was the special food? Then I heard his voice. He was in his bedroom, and he asked me to come in there with him. I knew immediately that something was wrong, and that sick feeling started in my stomach, but I was obedient and did just that. The lights were off, and it was dark in the bedroom, and I felt almost nauseous as I reluctantly walked in. I was already frightened, and not even being able to see Dad made it worse. To this day, I cannot fully erase this memory from my mind.

Dad was lying in bed, and he asked me to rub his legs for him and said they were really sore. I felt even more let down when I heard this, as it seemed I was having to do yet another slave chore for him. He said he had a vibrating device to put on my hand that would help when I rubbed his legs. He showed me how to put it on my hand and told me they really needed rubbing. I was even more afraid now, and I didn't want to put that thing on my hand. All I could think about was going back to bed and going to sleep. I didn't want to be in that bedroom with him with the lights off, but I was trapped. I was even concerned about the sound of Dad's voice. It was calm and smooth, a tone I had never before heard him use, and in retrospect, I know he was trying to make what he was doing seem okay to me. I didn't yet know what was going to happen, but I knew it was bad.

Now I had the vibrating device on my hand, and I started to feel even more sick, but Dad lay face down on the bed and told me to start rubbing the backs of his legs, on his calves. It seemed like I rubbed his calves forever, and my hand got numb and tingly from the vibration. I wanted to stop, but after a long time, Dad instructed me to move up to the tops of his legs for again what seemed to be forever. I was tired and wanted to go upstairs to bed, but I knew better than to tell him or he would become angry. I was trapped with no way out, and the longer I was in his room, the more I knew I was there for something sinister.

He finally turned over, and I thought I was done so I turned off the vibrator, but he told me I wasn't done yet and made me rub the front part of his legs. I didn't like that at all, and when he started breathing in the same way he did when he spanked us, I got really scared. I knew something was wrong, but I didn't know what to do. I had a desperate feeling inside my chest, and I was in complete turmoil. He then took my hand with the vibrator on it and moved it up to his boxer shorts area and with his hand over mine moved my hand toward his penis. Then he guided my hand back and forth until he figured I knew what he wanted, and then he removed his hand so I could do this all by myself. I knew I couldn't stop or he would be angry, and I wasn't willing to take the risk of a beating.

I rubbed him back and forth sideways over the opening of his boxer shorts until his erect penis popped out. My dad's breathing was harder now, like after he finished spanking us. He then put his hand on the back of my head and pushed me down toward his penis. I could smell him now, and this was a smell I will never forget as long as I live. Then he did something unspeakable and made me put his penis in my mouth. He started choking me with it, and the taste of him make me sick. I wanted to throw up, and I started to cry, but that didn't seem to affect him. I just wanted him to stop, and I was somewhat dazed while this was happening. It was sort of like a blackout, but not a complete blackout. He jammed his penis way back in my throat really hard, causing me to gag, and then it seemed like he peed in my mouth.

After that, it was over. He picked my head up while I was coughing and told me not to tell Mom, as he didn't want her to be mad at me for this. He then said, "You know how your mother gets" and told me not to tell anybody, as that would make him mad at me. To me, that was the worse thing in the world that could happen. That would mean I would be punished, and I was deathly afraid of him. By the way he said it, I knew exactly what he meant. He then added, "We can never tell."

I was too young to understand what was going on. All I knew was that Dad had done something very wrong, and I was ashamed. His unconscionable act took what little was left of my spirit and innocence that night, and I was left feeling more than just awful. I felt totally devastated, and I didn't even want to tell Jackie what had happened. Normally, I told her everything, but about this I couldn't bring myself to say one word. I now had firsthand knowledge of what she had to do to earn pickled bologna and crackers. I now knew why she and Dad shared secrets with each other and what those secrets were. I had waited so long to have what I thought was a special relationship with Dad, and this was it.

When I left Dad's room, I felt betrayed by him, but most of all, I felt scared this would happen again. Jackie went downstairs often to see Dad. I didn't want that to happen to me. I wanted this never to have happened, and I would have far preferred to remain his slave than to go through this again.

To my surprise, Jackie never said anything to me about it. She never questioned me at all, and this was very unusual behavior for her. She always wanted to know what was going on, and she didn't like not knowing everything and everyone's business. I knew she'd heard Dad call my name, but she was probably grateful for the reprieve it gave her. There would have been nothing she could have done anyway, but my life changed in many ways after this happened. For one thing, I now hated going to bed at night for fear Dad would call me downstairs again, which he did. I don't know how many times he called me, but I know it was a lot. Now, not only did I spend my days fearful of punishments, but I also spent my nights fearful of something more evil. This was when my recurring nightmares began. I would lie in bed afraid, not just because of Dad, but because of the horrifying dreams that plagued me nightly. In my recurring nightmare, a burglar would come into my bedroom at night and start choking me. I couldn't move, I couldn't scream, and I couldn't breathe. The burglar always had a knife, and he wore a mask over his eyes. He would choke me until I was close to death, his hands tight on my throat. I never died in that dream; instead, I woke up gagging and gasping for air at the last moment before death. These dreams were simply terrifying, and I truly believed that if I fell asleep, one of these nights I would surely die.

To me, nights now wielded a double-edged sword: if I stayed awake, I might hear Dad call me downstairs, but if I went to sleep, I would have this frightening nightmare. One was as bad as the other, and soon I devised a plan: I would lie awake so I wouldn't have the dream, but I would pretend I was sleeping. It was a good plan, but it didn't work. I tried ignoring Dad when he called me, but he just kept calling. When I didn't come downstairs, he came up and got me, and I quickly realized this was just something I had to endure, as I knew Jackie had to. The "code" was Dad telling me his legs were sore. I knew what that meant; I guess that was the big secret I got to share with him.

One night he lay down on top of me and tried to push his penis into my private parts. It really hurt, and I cried and begged him to stop. He finally quit after he'd peed on my privates. I was way too young to know it wasn't pee. He told me this was how babies were made, and someday I would do that like the big girls and have a baby.

After that night, going downstairs when Dad called me is a blur. I don't remember the specifics, and I don't remember ever having intercourse with my father, but I'm sure the sexual abuse didn't stop at oral sex. Nor do I remember at what age he finally stopped sexually abusing me. What I believe is that my lack of memory is part of a God-given defense we have as children to prevent even more trauma. As I mentioned earlier, children have the ability to block out memories that are too painful for them to live with and that occur in situations they have no control over.

Though I now hated my life even more than I had before, mostly I hated my father and what he represented to me. I hated his voice. I hated his walk. I hated him touching me anyplace, and I hated his smell. I hated how every conversation he had with Jackie or me had some kind of sexual overtone. I didn't even like talking to him anymore. I just wanted him to leave me alone and to leave our house, but that wasn't going to happen for some time yet.

For one thing, I soon realized Dad was obsessed with Jackie's and my blonde hair. When we were very young, Jackie's hair was a golden blonde while mine was almost white. My hair stayed light for quite a long time, but Jackie's started darkening when she was eleven or twelve. Dad wasn't going to have that, so one night while Jackie was baby-sitting for one of Mom's friends, Dad sneaked over with hair bleach for her. He didn't want Mom to know he was behind it, but he definitely preferred his number one daughter to remain blonde. He told her not to tell, and Jackie never did.

That wasn't the only sneaky thing he did. Jackie and I used to hear him talking on the phone at night after we went to bed using the same sexual overtones he used with us. We would lie upstairs in bed and hear his every word. Clever as he was, just in case some of us were still awake, he would leave out the dirty words and say things like "How is your hmmm?" or "When I see you, maybe we can hmmm." He was such a disgusting man, a real pervert. He often told dirty jokes to us kids and didn't think there was anything wrong with it. He also sang dirty songs to us. Mom thought it was cute, but this kind of thing isn't cute. Just being around him made me squeamish, because I knew the real motives behind the songs and the jokes.

One day some time after he'd begun sexually abusing me, Mom stopped me in the kitchen and pressed my shoulders against the refrigerator and got down on her knees to be eye level with me. She looked me square in the eyes and asked me, "What does your daddy do to you?"

She didn't have a threatening tone to her voice, but I was afraid to answer. Dad had told me that if I ever told Mom, she would get mad at me. I didn't want that to happen, so I said, "Nothing."

She was persistent and asked again, "What does your daddy do to you?" I refused to answer, but she kept on asking me in a steady, calm voice. I knew that if I told her, she would get mad and so would Dad, but I finally caved in. She was gentle with me, which was unlike her, and I was fooled into thinking she cared, so I said, "My daddy puts his wee into my mouth and pees in it."

All of a sudden she began shaking my shoulders violently and screaming at me, "What does he do to your sister? What does he do to your sister?" She was enraged, and I was scared. I remember looking into her eyes and seeing that they'd changed to a lighter color than normal. The kind tone in her voice had disappeared, and she had turned back into the cruel, mean mother I'd always known. She had tricked me into telling her my secret by making me think she cared about me, and I remember thinking that I didn't really know what he did to my sister; I knew only what he did to me. I also remember realizing that her concern was not for me and my safety—she was angrier at the thought of Dad doing something to Jackie. I remember thinking that I shouldn't have told her and that everything Dad had said would happen was coming true.

I was bawling my eyes out, and suddenly I knew for certain that Mom truly didn't care about me. I can't find the words to describe how I felt at that moment. All I can say is that I had the grim realization of how insignificant I was to her and Dad. She finally quit shaking me and let go of my shoulders, and she acted so disgusted with me that I was greatly surprised when nothing really changed around the house. It was almost as though this event had not taken place. Mom was a little more aloof with me, but Dad certainly continued to have free rein with us. My nightmare still continued, the real one as well as the dream.

As time went on, the only thing that changed was that Dad became more aggressive with his punishments and slave chores toward me. I don't know why this was so, but since Mom always followed suit with Dad, my punishments from her became more humiliating and degrading. I know only one thing for certain:

she must have known something was going on, or she never would have asked me about it. All the outward signs of abuse were readily apparent, and it must have been obvious even to her in order for her to approach me.

One of my new punishments was called "Eating on the floor with the dog" and it meant just that. This was Mom's brainchild, and she started this punishment after I told her about Dad. Assuming she confronted him at all, she was probably just trying to show him that she believed his lies over her daughter's words. This punishment had a condemning and belittling effect, and that was the whole purpose. Since I was no better than a dog, there was no place setting at the table for me. My dinner plate was placed on the kitchen floor in the corner by the back door, and I wasn't given any silverware. I had to sit there cross-legged and all alone with Bowser, our collie mix, while the rest of the family ate at the table within feet of me.

In addition, this was a family participation punishment, so while Bowser and I sat on the floor, the family ate and laughed and simply ignored me like I didn't exist. I would look up at them, and they would all carry on as a family, minus one. Dad would tell jokes and make the other kids laugh, and Mom would chime in, too. They acted extra funny and conversed more than usual with the other kids during this punishment, and that was part of the punishment—I was supposed to realize that I didn't belong with them. I wasn't allowed to talk to any of them, as dogs can't talk, and the rest of the family wasn't allowed to acknowledge my presence at all. If they did, they would be punished and maybe even suffer the same fate as me. To me, this complete isolation from my brothers and sisters was the most frightening part of the punishment. We kids were in this family together, and to take them away from me was devastating. We were all we had.

Of course, Mom and Dad made rude comments about me at the table, but I don't remember the specifics. I remember only that they made me feel awful and unworthy to be one of their kids. In fact, Mom and Dad made me feel that I was completely undesirable for anyone to have. I was the brunt end of their jokes for the night, and everybody laughed at me. Even on an average day, I seemed to be the brunt end of a lot of Mom and Dad's negative remarks. As I sat on the floor, I would get a pit inside my stomach, and of course I'd have no appetite at all.

Since Dad and Mom never bought dog food for Bowser, he was always happy to have me on the floor with him. He knew I would share my dinner with him, and his tail never quit wagging. I think if somebody had forced me to eat at those times, the food would have come right back up. At least Bowser was ensured a meal for that night, and that was a good thing for him. All he ever got were scraps otherwise, and with six hungry kids, you can probably guess there were hardly ever any scraps left. I guess that what I got from life at that time was just scraps, too, but I simply didn't realize life could be any different. As bad as this punishment was, I probably would have felt more humiliated if not for the fact that I loved Bowser. That old dog loved all us kids, and he was so happy that I was down on the floor with him.

As far as I remember, Bob was the only other kid who ever had to share in this punishment. Dad hated him, so of course Bob had to endure this as well, but Mom and Dad really didn't have to go to all that trouble to make us feel inferior and insignificant. I had felt that way long before Mom created this punishment, and I know Bob did, too.

My other new punishment was being a "Joe Smith." Joe Smith was a boy who lived in town with his elderly mom. She never really interacted with Joe that any of us saw. All his siblings were older and married, and Joe used to walk around town a lot and smoke cigarettes. My parents told us that was because his mom didn't love him and just ignored him. That was mean for my parents to say, as his mom did love him and his dad had died, but making me a "Joe Smith" meant pretending I didn't exist. Mom and Dad would go days and sometimes actual weeks on end ignoring me, and pretending I had never been born. That meant no bowl of oatmeal in the morning, no lunch, and no place setting at the dinner table. I was allowed to come and go as I pleased, and I would sneak food to eat, or Jackie would sneak some for me. I was even allowed to sleep in my own bed at night. I'm sure they knew I was sneaking food, but that wasn't really the point. The purpose of this punishment was to treat me as if I were invisible. Thus, even when I tried to talk to Mom and Dad, they acted as if nothing were there. They couldn't hear any of my words, and the other kids had to play along with this.

I would walk downtown, almost a mile away, and call home from the payphone. When Mom answered, I would say, "Mom, Mom, Mom, it's Rhonnie," and she would say, "Hello, hello, hello, Jack, there's nobody there" and promptly hang up.

During this punishment, the other kids were not allowed to talk to me, or they were punished. As long as Mom and Dad were around, they ignored me to save their own skins. When Mom and Dad weren't around, Jackie or Bob would take a chance and talk to me, but even then they had to watch it for fear they would get told on by one of the other kids. Rod was everybody's enemy and would have told on them. He thoroughly enjoyed getting people in trouble and was good at it.

It was torture to have to sneak around like a thief and steal a moment with one of the other kids, and that made the punishment a success I did truly feel as if I didn't belong and that I was unloved just like Joe Smith. Being shunned like that was the loneliest time in my life. I didn't have anybody I could go to for help or moral support; I just had to endure those feelings alone. I used to hide under the bridge near our home and listen to the cars drive over the top. The rhythm of the car tires going over the bumps on the bridge was comforting to me. Under the bridge, I was isolated from the whole world, and nobody could see me or find me. I was alone there, and I could cry in peace with no danger of my dad saying, "If you don't stop crying, I'll give you something to cry about!" We were never allowed to cry as kids, so even though I was quite alone under there, I also found some solace there. I would stare at the water and cry and ask God to take me out of this world and up to heaven. I felt so alone and isolated that I truly wanted to die, a feeling that took me many years to get over, but somehow I knew that God could hear my heart crying and that he would help me.

No one who saw me downtown ever asked why I was there alone, and sometimes when I was downtown, I saw Joe Smith walking around. He always gave me cigarettes to smoke, and I took them under the bridge with me. When at long last my punishment was over, I was supposed to realize how precious our family was and to be grateful for being loved, and I had to apologize to my parents for not appreciating the good things I had. That was always the hardest part, knowing I had to apologize to them and accept the plain truth that even though I hated life at home, it was surely better than being a "Joe Smith." My family, though abnormal, was my family, and they were all I had. I wanted to belong. Plus, I didn't want to lose my sister. That was sad, but at that time, it was all too true.

As time went on, dehumanizing me seemed to become almost a sport for Mom and Dad. Though none of the kids in our house were treated well, by the same token, none were treated as badly as Bob and me. Rod used to be spanked for wetting the bed, which happened every night, but those spankings were different from what Bob and I routinely endured. Even Jackie was punished once in a while by Dad, but she also got away with a whole lot. I, however, did not.

I remember taking swimming lessons with all the family one summer when I was eight or nine when they were offered at a local beach for free. Everybody else passed, but when I tried to swim, I sank straight to the bottom. It seemed the harder I tried, the worse it got. Likewise, the harder I tried, the more Dad made fun of me. He told the story of what I looked like trying to swim over and over again, and he built it up with every retelling, all the while laughing so that everybody else in the family laughed with him. This was humiliating to me, but when I retook the next round of lessons, I flunked again. I couldn't even dog paddle, and this meant Dad got to add even more to the already over-told story. After I flunked the third time, I gave up, but by now Dad had too much fodder to quit telling the story.

Looking back, I realize that I couldn't dog paddle because I was too flustered. Being humiliated on top of that sealed my fate; it was simply too much pressure. I was afraid that if I tried, I would fail, so that's exactly what happened. Interestingly enough, I learned to swim later in life when I wasn't under any pressure, but I still hate swimming to this day.

Dad also loved to torment Bob and me in other ways that involved our siblings' participation. If he thought Bob or I were acting up, he would say, "Oh, look, Bob needs attention; everybody look at Bob." Everybody would accordingly stare at Bob, and Dad would humiliate him until he was done with this punishment. As always, we did whatever Dad told us to do so that we wouldn't be next in line. Needless to say, he did the same thing to me. To this day, because of this punishment, I hate having people stare at me. I always think they are making fun of me, and though I know this isn't true, I have to constantly fight with myself to overcome this feeling.

Dad also used to sing a song to us called "Three Babies in the Woods." He would sit us down at bedtime and tell us he was going to sing it, and we would all plead with him not to. The more we pleaded, the more he enjoyed the idea of singing it. These are the words to that song:

Three babies in the woods, three babies in the woods, have you ever heard the story of three babies in the woods? They were stolen away, one bright sunny day, and left in the woods the people would say. They cried and they cried, they sighed and they sighed, and finally at last they laid down and died.

This song was simply awful, but I think his point was that we were all supposed to realize how unimportant we were, just like those three babies. This was just one more of Dad's sadistic methods of entertaining himself at our expense. Of course, he got a lot of extra mileage out of our pleas to him to stop. Such begging had only the opposite effect, but we were too young to know that.

For me personally, Mom and Dad's abuse also took the form of raw neglect, and a telling situation occurred when I stepped on a rusty nail that went through my shoe and into my foot. I was eight or nine at the time, and a day or so later, my foot became infected. My mom's friend Marsha was often at our house in the daytime, probably to baby-sit us since Mom was now working during the day, and she became very concerned about my foot after a red line developed that went up my leg from the nail hole.

Dad told me I had blood poisoning and that if the blood got to my heart, I would die instantly. Telling me this worried me sick. Why didn't they take me to the doctor? Was my life not worth saving? The red line was moving quite fast up my leg, and I watched it all the time, and hoped it would slow down and not get to my heart. I couldn't sleep at night, and I thought about this red line creeping up my leg. I didn't like to sleep anyway, and now I was afraid that if I fell asleep, I would never wake up.

Marsha was so concerned that she brought a friend to the house to see my foot. Judy was a Boy Scout leader, and she took one look at my foot and then soaked it, lanced it open, and sucked the poison out. When she was done, she put a salve on it and a fresh, sterile bandage. Even though it hurt when she lanced my foot, I knew in my heart she cared for me and my well-being. That in and of itself made me feel better and as though maybe I was safe from the sure death my father had talked about. She returned several times to do this, and not only did she save my life, but she also saved me from having my foot amputated. She always spoke to me in a soft tone, and I will never forget this kindness from a woman who didn't even know me. To this day, I don't know why it took a stranger to take care of me. By comparison, other than soaking my foot at the beginning of this injury, my mom did not tend to it at all, nor was she in the least concerned.

Virtually the same thing happened when I developed an ear infection in my right ear. I'd gone swimming with my cousin's fiancé, and we both got an infection. She went to the doctor and got treated right away, but I suffered needlessly for nine weeks, the whole length of the summer. Marsha put peroxide in my ear a few times, my only treatment, but eardrops would have cured the painful and disorienting infection within a few days.

Even birthdays and Christmases failed to produce much joy. Birthdays weren't celebrated much, though there are pictures of me when I was really young with a birthday cake and some friends. Christmas was a little more important, but the biggest part was decorating the tree. However, Dad made even this joyful task painful. We were allowed to hang only one icicle decoration at a time, not two or three, and we had to hang them straight, or we got clobbered. Dad stood over us the whole time we were decorating to make sure we did this right. Christmas mornings were exciting, as there were just enough presents under the tree to let us know Santa had come, and I got my first doll from an aunt when I was eight or nine. This was a doll that told you her name when you pulled a string.

We were just so deprived of love, compassion, and decent food that all six of us thoroughly appreciated it when anyone did anything nice for us. One time we were all waiting in the car while Mom was in the store. We were watching the Butternut man unload his supplies, and he dropped a bag of donuts that he didn't see. When he came out and still didn't see them lying on the ground, we said, "Mister, you dropped some donuts." He picked them up and looked at us and then brought that bag of donuts over and gave them to us. We were beside ourselves at this kind gesture and extremely grateful. We must have looked so pitiful to him. We told him thank you, and he went on his way. After that, whenever the Butternut truck drove by our house, we all ran out to the road and yelled, "Thank you, thank you, thank you!" We seldom had treats, so that was a big deal to us.

As we grew older, Dad's stinginess grew, too. He was so cheap that he refused to install a proper furnace for our old house and instead simply reinvented the old one. We used to burn coal in it, but in his opinion, coal was too expensive, so he converted the coal furnace to a sawdust furnace. Everything he did to that old furnace made it dangerous, and with every conversion, it became yet more dangerous. He burned it low, so our house was always cold, and one night when there was no sawdust in the middle of the winter, Mom and one of Dad's brothers and Jackie went to a lumber company with gunnysacks and stole some. Even sawdust wasn't something Dad felt he needed to keep buying.

One night that same winter, I awakened in the middle of the night to so much smoke I couldn't see. Everybody was sleeping, so I made my way to the steps and woke up Mom and Dad, and Dad ran downstairs to see that some gloves lying too close to the furnace had caught on fire. We ended up opening all the doors to get the smoke out. It was cold outside, but the smell of the smoke was nauseating.

Dad managed to put the fire out and then blamed Bob for leaving the gloves too close to the furnace. We all could have died that night, but Dad still refused to replace that furnace.

During this period, Mom seemed to hate me, and I didn't understand why. In retrospect, I can safely say it was because I was the one who told her about Dad. She says she has no recollection of me telling her, but she seems to have convenient memory loss about this subject, especially since she's told me later on in life that she knew he was doing something with Jackie. Jackie was too young to have a period, and she'd found blood in Jackie's underpants that tipped her off he was making her have sex with him and confronted Jackie also. But she later said she didn't think he would have done anything with me. Then, she adds, Dad must have convinced her I'd lied.

I will never accept this. How a little girl describing oral sex and her dad peeing in her mouth at the end of the sessions could not be credible or memorable is beyond me. It could never have been misconstrued as a lie. Likewise, I cannot comprehend what Dad possibly could have said to convince her he wasn't having sex with us. A little girl of seven or so would know nothing about orgasms or sperm. Nobody on earth could convince me my child was lying, given those facts, and nobody will ever convince me that most moms don't know when these things are going on in their homes. They just choose to pretend it's not happening, or, worse yet, they love their man so much they choose him over their own children and climb back in bed with him.

Today, it seems clear to me that Dad didn't have a preference for boy children or girl children and I suspect that we all fell victim to him and his sexual deviance and perversions. We've never talked about this among ourselves, but Dad was pretty patterned in his behavior. For instance, when he would seem to be kind to one of us and take us with him someplace, I knew what that meant. He was not a nice man, nor did he enjoy his children. We all knew that, even though we all wanted him to love us. If he isolated one of us from the rest of the fold, he was up to no good. For her part, I'm sure Mom was delighted to see him "showing interest in the family" and saw what she wanted to see. However, I know what he did to me when I was alone with him, and I know what he did to Jackie, so I've always felt safe drawing that conclusion.

Nonetheless, in spite of Dad, the older we got, the more rebellious we became. We were becoming especially mouthy with Mom, and I think this is when Dad decided to start covering his tracks. I was nine or so when one day he told Mom we were always peeking through the keyhole at him while he was going to the bathroom. He told her he was going to put a stop to that, and he convinced her that if we wanted to see what a grown man's "wee" looked like so badly, he needed to show us.

That he induced Mom to go along with this is beyond belief, but she always did whatever he wanted her to. Dad gathered all six of us kids into the hallway outside the bathroom door and said, "Since you kids keep peeking through the keyhole of the door when I'm in here peeing and you want to see what a grown man's 'wee' looks like, I'm going to show you."

With that, he pulled his pants down to his knees and forced us to look at his penis without looking away. He kept saying, "Look, look ... This is what you're trying to see, so look." Imagine that! A family viewing of our dad's penis. I didn't want to look at his penis. I wanted to turn away, but I knew I'd be in trouble if I tried. I already knew firsthand what that penis looked like, and I hated it.

Mom stood right there and witnessed all this. How clever he was. He had probably raped us all by then, and he didn't want to get caught. Given that a grown man's penis could be described differently than a little boy's, he'd created the perfect alibi with Mom as his witness so she could stand in his defense. I'm sure he did that just in case we told on him to anybody important enough to get him into trouble.

But how any man on earth could convince a mother to allow him to do that is beyond me. By the same token, Mom wasn't a rational person, and if she did anything other than agree, she might just lose this man she loved so much. Any defiance from her would surely have cinched his leaving, and then she would be left alone, with six kids to raise no less. The basic welfare of her children was far less important to her than Dad, and so her compliance and participation in our abuse continued.

Chapter 3

><

Middle Childhood— Learning to Cope

From the time I was a little girl, I have loved horses. I used to draw them all the time, even before I was old enough to go to school, and my dream was to own horses someday. In fact, I was going to grow up and have a big ranch, and I used to run out to the road anytime someone would ride by and ask if I could have a ride.

But horses were more than something I merely "wanted." They were the only dream I dared to dream. I lived, slept, ate, and breathed this dream, for to me horses represented calmness, serenity, freedom, and love—all the things I didn't have in my life.

I used to pretend the old tree that had fallen near our house was my horse, and I would go out and "ride" it. I'd take the pillow off my bed to use as a saddle and find some kind of rope to make reins with. I loved playing on that old tree. I dreamed I lived back in the olden days in the Wild West and that I was a cowboy. I blazed a lot of imaginary trails back then and fought many Indians. Sometimes I was one of the Indians, as I always felt so sorry for them, but I was always a good guy, whether I was a cowboy or an Indian, and I always ended up riding off into the sunset. This was my escape from the hell of my life, for only in my imagination could I get away from the abuse and torture I endured daily. The stories playing out in my head sometimes went on for days, and I was happy and at peace only when I was out there riding my "horse."

Once in a while I had to fight Rod for my tree. He didn't really want to play on it; he just wanted to cause trouble, and this was the only place I played that I truly loved with all my heart. Rod did what he did to be mean, and he truly seemed to enjoy being my tormenter. This gave him a rare sense of power in an environment where he otherwise had none.

Jackie loved horses, too, and the summer we were nine and ten, we started baby-sitting for the town locals, and we decided to save our money to buy a horse. We made fifty cents an hour and put all the money we saved into a jar. To earn more money, we pulled our wagon down the sides of the road and collected bottles. Gramma also gave us silver dollars for the little chores we did when we went to her house. I think she made things up for us to do just so we could earn extra money. We also picked cherries and strawberries that summer. We weren't that good at it, but we tried our best. Because people used a lot of silver dollars back then, we could plainly see how much money we were saving.

I'm amazed to this day that somehow, in the midst of all of the horrific things we endured at home, Jackie and I managed to maintain our focus to save enough money to buy our own horse. We saved our money for two whole years when it would have been so easy to spend it on other things. We could have bought clothes, toys, candy—all the things normal kids had that we didn't—but we sacrificed all that to attain our goal.

Together, we dug all the fence holes we needed for a pasture, bought and strung the electrical wire, and made a lean-to for shelter, that part with Dad's help. Our childhood dream came true, but the only reason it came true was that we relentlessly pursued it and paid for it on our own. I also think Gramma might have said something to Dad, as she understood our goal. As an adult, looking back on this and wondering why our parents agreed to let us buy a horse when they were so inhuman in every other regard, I think it's because Dad wanted to keep us pacified, and he knew he was beginning to lose his grip on us. In his mind, if he did this for us, we would still be under his thumb. We were getting older and smarter, and we knew that what he was doing wasn't right, and I'm sure he didn't want us to tell on him. The only time he was ever nice was when he had something to gain, and this situation would have been no exception. When Dad got nice, it wasn't necessarily a good thing, but we didn't care about that right then. All we cared about was our horse.

The day finally came when we got to go choose our dream horse, and we were so excited we could hardly contain ourselves. I felt as if I were going to explode from all the excitement, one of the only joyous occasions I can recall from my childhood. When we got to the nearby ranch, the owner seemed to know just which horse we should pick. There were at least fifty horses in that pasture, but he went straight toward Sox. Now I know he was trying to unload a hard-to-sell horse on novice buyers, but Sox was beautiful, and Jackie and I were beside ourselves with joy. We had dared to dream, and that dream was coming true!

When we got Sox home, Jackie rode him first and had a lovely ride. When I got on, he went berserk and tried to kill me. Almost immediately after I mounted him, he took off through the trees bucking, rearing, and twisting. He even tried running me into trees to get rid of me. I blacked out while I was on him and was completely dazed, but somehow I managed to continue gripping the saddle horn. My foot slipped all the way through the stirrup, and had I fallen off, I would have been kicked by his back hooves. Even though everything turned black, I was aware of what was going on, and it was sheer instinct that kept me holding on for dear life. After all, I had practiced riding bucking broncos hundreds of times on my imaginary horse.

But this was the very first time I'd ever ridden by myself, and it was some introduction. Unfortunately, there were a few things we didn't know about Sox. The biggest was that he was definitely a one-person horse, and I was not his person. This was a hard lesson to learn, and I was devastated — the one dream I'd had that had ever come true was turning into a nightmare. It was simply awful, and to my dismay, I never got to ride Sox again.

Fortunately for Jackie, she was his person. She could ride him with or without a saddle, and he was a perfect gentleman, but he never let me on his back again, not even to ride double in back of Jackie, without trying to buck me off. Dad returned to the owner and made some sort of deal with him since Sox couldn't be ridden by anybody but Jackie, and he brought over several other horses for me to try. The first was a dying bag of bones we immediately rejected, and the second was a big bay gelding who was beautiful but had such a rocky, choppy gate that he gave me and everybody else who rode him a headache. He was a huge letdown, and though he was one of the most beautiful horses I had ever seen, his gate was so rough I could barely ride him. Sending him back was devastating to me, as hard as he was to ride, and I couldn't help but think that Jackie had convinced Dad to send him back because he was more magnificent looking than Sox.

The man from the ranch came and took him away, and I could tell there was friction growing between him and Dad, but it wasn't but a day or two before he returned again, and this time Dad settled on a red and white pinto gelding named Toby. The owner of the ranch said this was the final horse he would bring over and that this was a take-it-or-leave it deal. We took it, and Toby became my horse. He was very smooth gated and was a gentle horse anybody could ride. The only problem was that he was swaybacked and must have looked pitiful to other people, but I didn't care. Toby was beautiful to me, and I rode him all the time. I was so proud of him that I rode him in the Fourth of July parade in a nearby town. Even better, Jackie and I soon knew how to get everywhere through the hills, and finally we could *escape*. We rode for hours at a time and our home life didn't seem to matter as long as we were out in the hills. We were free for that time, and riding Toby soon meant more to me than anything ever had.

That winter, to get hay, we pulled our sled to the farm down the road and back, hauling maybe three bales at a time. We made a lot of trips up and down that road to get the hundred bales of hay we needed. We also carried all the water the horses needed one bucket at a time from the house. It was very cold at times, and we occasionally argued about whose turn it was to carry the water, but the chores always managed to get done. We also bought grain and all the brushes we needed to keep them groomed. It was hard to keep up on all this, and we paid for everything with our own money, but we were determined to care for our horses properly.

We had a lot of fun in the bigger scheme of things, but after we'd had them a year and a half or so, Sox came up lame with a lump on his front leg, and Jackie couldn't ride him much anymore. It was almost winter again, and Dad told us he was going to sell the horses and that we would get more in the spring. Jackie and I nearly went out of our minds. We felt terribly betrayed, but somehow we weren't surprised. Dad never let us be happy for too long, but we had fallen in love with the horses and didn't want to sell them. We loved them, and in a strange sense, they were more than just our pets. They were our friends, and I know they sensed how much we needed them. We felt peace and contentment caring for them, riding them, and even just walking in the pasture with them. We had definitely bonded with them and they with us. I didn't want any other horse but Toby, and Jackie didn't want anyone but Sox. The concept of us loving our animals as we did, not surprisingly, wasn't something Mom or Dad could relate to, and one day we came home from school, and they were gone.

There was screaming, crying, and near hysteria when we discovered this, and we felt even worse that we hadn't gotten to say goodbye to the friends who had eased our burdens and taken us on countless journeys. We hadn't even gotten to thank them for the hours of happiness and joy they'd brought to our otherwise dismal and nightmarish lives. To calm us, Dad immediately got on the phone and called every horse ad he could find. He had no intention of replacing them; he just wanted an end to the immediate situation at hand, and he used the fact that Sox was lame as his excuse for selling them. All that time saving our money picking up bottles, picking cherries and strawberries, and baby-sitting and now the horses were gone. There is no way I can adequately describe our devastation. We didn't trust or believe that Dad would try to get us more horses, and our dreams were squashed. All the love and work it had taken to get them and he had sold them right out from under us. My heart was simply broken, and I felt I would never be happy again.

My heart was broken again the following year. I was in the seventh grade and had begun cheerleading for the junior varsity basketball team. I took a lot of pride in being a cheerleader, and not only was I good at it, but it also gave me a rare sense of belonging. For the first time in my life, my clothes were exactly the same as everybody else's. For the first time in my life, I felt important. For the first time in my life, I had been chosen to be part of something. Most important, for the first time in my life, I fit in with the other girls in my class.

Mom and Dad didn't care whether I was a cheerleader, as long as it didn't involve their participation. As usual, they just didn't want to be bothered. The problem was that, it was up to me to make my own arrangements for rides. Getting to the away games was easy. I just stayed after school and rode the bus, but figuring out how to get home at night after the games was very stressful. Ultimately, I had to drop out because I couldn't always find a ride. It may not sound like a big deal now, but at the time, having to quit was overwhelming.

I believe it was around this time that the police came to our house and accused Dad of making obscene telephone calls to various women in town. He denied this and then called Bob into the kitchen where he and the sheriff were talking. Dad in turn accused Bob of making those obscene phone calls. Bob told the policeman he didn't do it, but Dad kept right on accusing him. Dad argued with the policeman for quite a while about this, but the officer stood his ground and told Dad the phone calls had not been made by a young boy. The woman had heard a man's voice, Dad's voice. Whoever that woman was, she knew it was Dad making those calls.

I was proud of Bob for holding his own against Dad. This was a huge step for him, as he already knew the consequences of not doing what Dad said. I'm not sure what happened to Dad after this, but I think he may have gone to jail. He was still driving a truck then and was often gone, so if he'd gone to jail, we wouldn't have noticed anything unusual in his absence. We knew he was arrested for something back then; we just didn't know what for. We asked Mom about it, but she refused to talk about it.

Time passed slowly, but soon I was close to twelve or thirteen years old. That summer, I started baby-sitting for my dad's brother and my Aunt Ester to earn money to buy new school clothes for fall. It wasn't a hard job, but it involved my constant attention. My uncle was a retired Navy man and had an over-the-road trucking job, so he was gone most of the time, and Aunt Ester cleaned rooms at a nearby summer resort.

I never liked this uncle; he reminded me too much of Dad. He looked so much like him that my younger sister Tay once thought it was him and began hanging on his leg. When she realized who it was, she took off running. There was just something about him that made me nervous. His demeanor was the same as my dad's, and I tried not to ever look at him or talk to him.

One day as I was baby-sitting, my uncle came home from the road early. He followed me out to the backyard and pushed me down to the ground and lay down on top of me and tried to kiss me. I didn't know what to do. I didn't want him to kiss me, but he was so forceful I had a tough time pushing his face away from mine. I told him to leave me alone and get off me and he replied, "Why don't you let a real man fuck you instead of one of those sixteen year olds?" I was only twelve years old; what was he thinking? Maybe Dad had filled my uncle in on what he did to us. Maybe that type of perversion just ran in the family. I knew I could never tell my aunt; I'd learned from telling my own mother this wasn't a safe avenue. Plus, I loved my Aunt Ester and didn't want to hurt her. Aunt Ester was one of the few people who actually cared about me, and I didn't ever want her not to love me. The thought of losing her in my life was more than I could bear.

At the end of the summer, I was invited to go to New York with Aunt Ester and my uncle to a wedding for their oldest son, John. I didn't want to go with them, as I was deathly afraid of my uncle, but they desperately needed help with the kids, and I didn't know how to say no to my aunt. Unfortunately, I was so fearful I don't remember much of the trip, nor do I remember the wedding. Being near my uncle was so stressful it clouded up anything that might otherwise have been fun. After we got home, my uncle said to me, "There, you see, I can be trusted. I didn't touch you." Needless to say, I never baby-sat for them again.

I was growing up, and that fall, shortly after my eighth grade year started, I stood up to Dad for the first time. It wasn't premeditated, but Dad was going to beat me for something, and I knew that whatever I was getting a beating for, it wasn't good enough. I remember that he took his belt off and grabbed my arm abruptly to start the whipping. I remember thinking, "I'm not going to put up with this anymore," and somehow I reached into myself and mustered up the strength to fight back. I jerked my arm out of his grip with all my might and stepped back, looked him square in the eyes, and said, "You're a bastard."

He laughed and said, "You don't even know what that is."

I said loudly and firmly, "I may not know what that is, but I know that you are one." I never looked away from him, and I think this was when he realized he wasn't going to get away with abusing me anymore. He just looked at me and laughed a non-laugh and turned and walked away. When he left without beating me, I knew he'd lost the control he'd once had. For once, I had victory over my dad.

Not long after this, he left Mom and moved out. That was fine with me, and besides, we later learned he'd been planning for this day for a long time. As a matter of fact, Dad already had another life that Mom didn't even know existed. He'd begun sleeping with one of our old baby-sitters when she was in high school, and back when we'd lived in town, Mom had even caught Dad having sex with her. Being Mom, she'd accepted whatever his excuse was and chosen to keep this jewel of a man and have three more kids with him. This old baby-sitter and her sister were both a little slow and easy to manipulate, and Dad had programmed them to think his way and only his way. He'd managed to keep this up even after we'd moved out of town, and by the time he finally left Mom, he was already set up with them. With his truck-driving money and a little help from one of his family members, he'd bought two additional homes in Traverse City, the large resort community about a half-hour away, and these two sisters were his business partners, and rented rooms on a weekly basis.

If you think life improved with Dad out of the house, think again. Oddly enough, in many ways, it became worse because Mom's mission became to make us all hate Dad as much as she did. This is why she told us about the two sisters in the first place, but this in no way made her like any of us. The bottom line was, that life with a woman who was completely resentful of us was pure hell. Mom felt no sympathy for any of us and never had. It was all about her, while her six kids paid the highest price for her husband's evil, selfish, and sadistic ways. In spite of this, in her mind, she was the only victim. In fact, she felt we were the reason Dad had left. She felt he didn't want to be a dad or have the responsibility of raising kids. This was probably the real reason Mom treated us so horribly herself. After all, her one goal in life had always been to hold onto her man.

Ultimately, she grew so resentful of us that one time she didn't come home for more than two weeks. We older kids had to hold down the fort and take care of the family. At that time, Bob would have been about fifteen, Jackie would have been around thirteen, and I was around twelve or so. Mom's sister's husband came over about ten days into her strange disappearance and said, "Look what you kids have done to your mother. You ought to be ashamed of yourselves; she just had a nervous breakdown." To my knowledge, this certainly hadn't happened. She wasn't in the hospital; she was just at their house, and was crying on their shoulders. She somehow convinced them it was her kids who had pushed her over the edge, and she never told them how bad things were with Dad.

Mom simply had an insatiable appetite for attention, and this was just one of her big pity parties. She felt sorry for herself because Dad had rejected her, and she was just trying to make him feel guilty by saying she'd had a nervous breakdown. As usual, we big kids took care of the little kids, but we were hungry, and there was no food in the house. We were not grown-ups with jobs or resources, so we called Aunt Ester, and she brought over some food. It still amazes me that Aunt Ester was the only adult who assisted the six children who had been abandoned, as there were other members of Dad's family in the area who knew what was going on and could and should have helped.

Soon after this incident, Mom started to drink and wear trashy clothes and cut off her long brown hair. This was also done to get back at Dad, as he loved her hair long and had always made her wear it this way, as well as dress the way he preferred. Then there was the makeup. Oh, Lord, did she wear makeup. She also started wearing cheap blonde wigs. She had two foam heads she rested them on at night, and she took a lot of time putting rollers in those wigs and styling them so she could look beautiful. Unfortunately, by the time she finished dressing, she always looked like a half-witted hooker. She wore cheap vinyl "go-go" boots that she had to buy larger than her foot size since her legs were so thick through the calves, and I know it sounds mean to say this, but she looked like some kind of clown. Then she went out to the bars. Along with her day job, Mom then took a nighttime job working at a bar, and soon we never knew whether she was going to come home. Her usual arrival time, if she came home at all, was 6:00 a.m. Mom felt so sorry for herself about Dad leaving her that she went out of her way to reinvent herself to be the exact opposite of what Dad had wanted her to be.

For our part, it seemed this was just another ploy to get Dad's attention and to get him to come back. She also used to call and ask him to come all the way from his new home in Traverse City just to spank us, but eventually he stopped coming, thank God. It was amazing to me even then what a desperate woman would do to try to keep a man. I can say with some certainty that Mom would have done anything for Dad, and I mean anything. She never did grasp that there were children in the picture, and she later disclosed to me that when Dad left her, she got down on her hands and knees in tears and begged him to stay.

But Dad would have nothing to do with her, and with the divorce in full force, Mom and Jackie began to have some major conflicts. Dad was no longer present to protect her from Mom, and Jackie, ever the rebel, began rebelling even more. They fought continuously, and Mom did everything in her power to take Jackie down a notch or two. One time after Jackie and I cleaned upstairs, Jackie left the mop water in the bucket. Mom didn't come upstairs more than once or twice a year, but she could see the bucket at the top of the steps. She told Jackie to dump it out, and Jackie didn't do it in a timely fashion. They got into a fight, and Mom went upstairs while Jackie started back down. Then Mom took the mop and squeezed the water over Jackie's head. It was filthy water, and since there was never any floor cleaner in our house, we'd used ammonia in it. This mess dripped down Jackie's face and ran into her eyes and burned them. She could have been blinded, but Mom didn't care as long as she got her point across. Soon, she became even more physically violent with Jackie. She would get Jackie backed up against a wall and hit her over and over with a hard straw purse with metal ends on it. It was only out of a belief that we shouldn't hit or shove our mother that she wasn't hurt in retaliation, but that lasted only so long. When your back is up against the wall and you're being hit with whatever's handy, there are bound to be repercussions sooner or later.

Finally, Jackie called Dad and told him what Mom was doing and asked what she should do to get her to quit. Dad told her, "Just cover your face." In other words, let her hit away. Mom did a lot of other things to Jackie, too. One day she got mad because Jackie's bangs were hanging in her eyes. She took her into the bathroom, sat her on the toilet, took a razor, and at first started with her bangs, razoring them off, and then she started chopping off her beautiful long blonde hair. When I say chopped, I mean chopped. When she finished, Jackie had short, choppy hair, and the fighting between those two became worse.

Ultimately, Jackie began running away from home, and Mom quickly sent her to a psychiatrist. She just knew it was Jackie with all the problems, not her. Finally, Jackie ran to Dad's and moved in with him. As awful as this sounds, he was the lesser of two evils for her, and at least he treated her as though she was special. But since Mom had found out about Dad's two sister-lovers and had gotten everything in the divorce, she had bargaining power. Infuriated that Jackie had moved in with Dad and had gotten her way, she offered to trade Dad his airplane for Jackie. Jackie might have been Dad's favorite, but he liked his airplane even better, and he jumped on such a trade. Soon, Jackie was home again with the rest of us. She wasn't very happy about this, and the tension between her and Mom grew.

The next summer, two years after Dad had left, Jackie and I ran a baby-sitting ad in the paper for a summer job, and one day a man came over to our house on his motorcycle and said he was answering our ad. God, I remember him well. He was tan and wore sunglasses and was probably in his late thirties or early forties. He said he had two daughters and was willing to pay $145.00 for a three-day week. Thirty-some years ago, that was a lot of money. He noticed we had a fence and asked why we didn't have horses. We told him the sad story, and he sweetened the deal by throwing in that he had horses and would be willing to pasture ours with them and, better yet, he would get another horse or two for us.

This was just one of those too-good-to-be-true, once-in-a-lifetime jobs for girls who were just fourteen and fifteen. He asked if we wanted the job, and we told him we had to talk to our mom when she got home from work and that nobody was allowed to come over about the job unless she was home. We already suspected he was another pervert, but we naively told him her hours.

The next day, he showed up around noon. That's when Jackie and I started getting scared. He knew he wasn't to come back until Mom was home, but he came anyway. We told Mom about him as soon as we could, but she didn't seem concerned. Besides, she had her own plans for Jackie. She had just made arrangements with Aunt Jane to take Jackie downstate for the summer to baby-sit her kids, and before I knew it, my sister was gone.

I knew Jackie didn't want to be home and that this was a good move for her, but I was abandoned again, alone with Mom who seemed to hate me so much. I felt like a "Joe Smith" once again. I was isolated from the only comfort I had in the whole world, and this impacted me tremendously. I felt like I'd lost part of my own identity, and making matters worse, now I was home alone with this weirdo around. The little kids were home, but Bob was working on a garbage route and was gone a lot. Not since Dad had given away our horses had I felt so low.

Mom herself never seemed to be home back then. She would appear to change her clothes and then take off again, but when she was around she was unbearable. She not only continued to be meaner and meaner to me, but she also began using Bob as her disciplinarian. She had learned with Jackie that she wasn't strong enough to push her bigger kids around, and with Dad gone, Bob became her solution to the problem. If I did something she didn't like, she had Bob hit me. One day she was screaming and yelling and called Bob into the room and told him, "Hit her, Bob; hit her!" I was on the floor, and he just kept slapping me over and over again. When he quit, Mom looked at me and said, "I know, you're crying because you miss your sister, don't you?"

I did miss my sister, but I was crying because I was in pain from being smacked around by Bob. Another time Mom was going to have Bob beat me up, so I ran away through the field and came out on a road in front of a family I used to baby-sit for. Bob had just gotten his driver's license, and he drove up and grabbed me and smacked me. Then the father came out of his house and told Bob to let go of me. He added that if Bob hit me again, he was going to show him what an ass whipping felt like. I was saved by a person who barely knew me other than as his baby-sitter, but I was grateful.

In another incident that summer, we were all sitting down at dinnertime when our black and white cat tried to climb up on the table. Mom looked at Bob and told him to get rid of the cat and shoot it. He threw the cat on the front porch while we all screamed and cried, and then he grabbed the .22 rifle and shot that cat twice right then and there. He didn't kill the cat, and it ran into a bush, making all kinds of suffering noises. Trying to get the wounded cat out of the bush was dangerous, and if I'd succeeded, Bob would have just shot him again. Mom, being the good little victim she was, called my perverted uncle and had him come to her rescue and finish the job. It was all so uncalled for and was far too much drama for young kids to witness. We were simply horrified at the sight of our older brother shooting that cat, and to have our creep of an uncle come and finish the job was devastating.

I just couldn't stand living at home anymore. I hated everything about it, and I didn't want to feel this awful turmoil inside anymore. I hated the fact that Mom needed to be saved so much that she used Bob to defend her. In her mind, she was replacing Dad with Bob. After all, he was the oldest son. Mom wasn't that much of a deep thinker; she was unpredictable, but she always went for the immediate gratification. As long as she felt somebody male was on her side, she was satisfied, but what she was really doing was dividing us kids. She just picked up where Dad left off, pitting us against one another. Bob was simply her male enforcer, and he hated her for making him do the disciplining for her.

I do consider Bob a victim of circumstance. Here was this young man who had been tortured and ridiculed his entire childhood put into a position of some authority. I think he did what he felt he had to do in order to keep surviving. I don't hate Bob for any of this, and I'm so grateful that later in life he didn't become a gruesome abuser or worse yet a serial killer.

But with Jackie gone, I had no one to talk to, and I hated my life even more now than I had before, especially since I had no protection from Mom or Bob. In response, like Jackie, I started to run away from home. I was fourteen now, and at first I just stopped coming home at night. I stayed mostly with Debbie, one of the few friends I had from school. We were sitting around one day when I had a brainstorm to really run away. Right after Dad had first left, with Mom always gone anyway, Jackie, Debbie, and I used to sneak off to Traverse City, and we'd made many new friends there. I'd even met my first boyfriend at a party in Traverse City, and he used to take us back to town to hang out with the "cool people" we'd met, basically hippies who accepted us. This boyfriend was nineteen, and he was the first guy I was sexually active with. In this group and in this day and age, having sex was cool, and I did whatever it took to be cool. Even with Jackie out of the picture, Mom didn't know I was gone all the time. She was busy soothing her own wounds, and her selfishness and neglect of her family made her oblivious to what I was doing. This gave me the first real freedom I'd ever had, and when I wasn't hanging out with my boyfriend and new friends, Debbie and I would meet some of the local boys on the road and drive around with them and drink.

With our minds made up, Debbie and I ran off to Traverse City to see our friends. We stayed at various houses for about four days, and they hid us the best they could, but pretty soon the cops saw us walking downtown and picked us up. This was humiliating, but cool at the same time. We were a good half-hour from home, so we had to wait for somebody to come and get us. Debbie was picked up immediately, but I guess my mother wanted to teach me a lesson. I had to sit at the police station for quite a while before Mom finally came, and it seemed that she was more put out with having to interrupt her day to come and get me than with the fact that I'd run away. We had to go to court after that, and Mom was insistent that I'd had sex with boys while I was on the run. She tried to force the judge to make me admit this, as she wanted to put all the boys she could in jail, but she had to finally give up on that idea, as I wasn't going to tell on anybody and neither was Debbie.

Since it didn't work to get the boys into trouble, Mom decided to try to convince the judge that I was insane. Even though the judge gave me probation, my mother insisted I should be locked up in the nearby state mental institution or in an institution downstate where they sent hardened criminal young women. She didn't want me to come home, that was for sure. She was so convincing that the judge ordered a psychiatric evaluation and an EEG to see whether indeed I was crazy. He also added into my probation clause the stipulation that I not cross the county line into Traverse City.

I just barely remember going to the court-appointed psychiatrist, but I do remember that he was very nice. We talked about a lot of things, and I told him I was unhappy and that our life hadn't been easy. I discovered that I really liked talking to him. He was the first person in my life who listened to me, but I never mentioned the abuse to him, especially the sexual abuse. I was still afraid of what Dad might do if I told. Plus, I was ashamed of it and somehow felt I was at least partly to blame.

The EEG was done at the state hospital in Traverse City, conveniently across from the psychiatrist's office, and I was terribly frightened that my mother was going to pull this off. She had managed to convince everyone else so far that her kids were horrible monsters and that I was crazy, and it would have been one of her biggest conquests to successfully commit me.

The test itself was terrifying. As soon as they stuck wires all over my head, my mind started racing with worrisome thoughts. Then they told me to lie there and think of nothing, so immediately I started thinking, "Oh, my God, I can't think of nothing." I simply couldn't stop thinking, and most of all I couldn't stop thinking that Mom was going to succeed if I didn't stop thinking. Though the test lasted only twenty minutes or so, I was sure I hadn't passed, and I wouldn't know for certain until my next visit with the psychiatrist.

Mom was haughty all that week. I know she thought she'd won this battle, and I was miserable because I figured she was right. All week I had terrible diarrhea and headaches and could barely sleep, and all that time she rolled her eyes at me and treated me like a "Joe Smith" and whistled whenever I tried to talk to her. I could tell she thought she was about to get rid of her biggest problem, but I wanted to make her like me that week so I wouldn't have to spend the rest of my life in the state hospital. I was in sheer agony. Finally, after the longest week of my life, the psychiatrist looked at me at our last appointment and said, "Rhonda, you are not crazy; you are just a normal teenage girl." I was so relieved; I felt like a boulder had been lifted from my shoulders. I felt more than just relief, though I'd been terrified I would be committed to the state hospital. I didn't feel I'd outsmarted my mother in any way; I just felt incredibly lucky to have escaped the torment she'd planned for me.

With that, the psychiatrist called my mother into the room and told her the same thing, and she instantly became furious. The psychiatrist then suggested that she see somebody because the problem didn't lie with me, and he also suggested that a little mother and daughter counseling might help.

Mom looked at him and said, "How dare you accuse me of being crazy? How dare you; just who do you think you are? She's the crazy one, not me. I don't know what she did to convince you, but she's crazy." She was one livid woman, and I thank God she didn't succeed in dumping me in the state hospital for the rest of my life. The sad thing was that I didn't get to go back to counseling. There was so much more I needed to talk about, but of course Mom hadn't done any of this to help me. She wanted only to hurt me and cause me to fail. I could tell the psychiatrist thought she was crazy, but his hands were tied—she wasn't the one who had been court-ordered to get help, so he couldn't do anything.

The next school year was hell. I was now a freshman, and Mom made sure my probation was enforced to the fullest, which meant I couldn't talk to my friend Debbie and I was set apart from the rest of the class. I felt abandoned, alone as usual, and it became a burden just to get up and go. I became an outcast yet again, and my probation officer herself started a rumor that I never wore underwear under my skirts. I met up with her later in life, just before she died, and she apologized for perpetuating that rumor and also for ignoring the abuse that was going on. She told me that in those days, probation officers were taught to believe the parents, not the children, but she'd known what was really going on, and she'd always felt sorry for us.

The highlight of the year was the shop class I took. We all had projects to make for our test at the end of the year, and I decided to make Mom something since we never had anything nice in our home. I spent many painstaking hours making her a beautiful mahogany coffee table with a matching shelf, and she didn't seem to care at all. Indeed, her feelings of resentment toward me superceded any feelings of appreciation she might have had. She didn't comprehend the numerous hours of hand-sanding and staining and varnishing that went into that project I got an "A" on, and ultimately I realized she really didn't want such efforts from me. I was probably just trying to get her to love me anyway, but at this point, I realized it was time to give up on that idea.

That summer, Mom's friend Marsha once again baby-sat for the kids and me each day while Mom worked. It was humiliating to be fifteen years old and have a baby-sitter, but I guess that was the point Mom was trying to make. Whenever she wanted me to take on extra chores around the house, she would tell me that if I didn't do what she wanted, she would call my probation officer and have me sent away. I was fearful of that, so I obliged her in whatever she asked of me. Jackie hadn't come back to live with us that school year; she'd ended up living downstate with our aunt and going to school there and had been back only for a short visit, so I not only knew Mom meant what she said, but also I was still alone. Even Bob was gone now. He'd hated the position Mom had put him in with me and had moved out to get away from our home life from hell.

One day Marsha hadn't gotten to the house yet, and guess who showed up? The same man who'd answered our baby-sitting ad the summer before. I managed to send him away by telling him Marsha was on her way, and that night I told Mom he'd come back and that I was afraid of him. She wasn't concerned and just told me that if he came again, I should call Marsha. I knew this man had evil intentions toward me, and sure enough, it didn't take him too many days to return. This time he walked right into the house without knocking. He saw my two younger brothers and sister and told them he would give them each $20.00 if they wouldn't tell Mom I went for a ride with him. He then added that he wanted to go to the store and get them some ice cream. So, of course, my brothers began jumping up and down, saying, "Go, Rhonnie, go."

I was scared. I tried to get him to leave the house, but he wouldn't. He grabbed my arm and said, "Let's take a walk outside, and you can show me around the other side of your house." I was so afraid; I was speechless. I knew by the grip on my arm he wasn't trying to be nice. I told him he could walk around the house himself and see the yard, not that there was anything to see. It didn't help that my brothers were still telling me to go. They wanted the money, and getting ice cream would have been a huge bonus.

His grip tightened on my arm and he said, "Come on; I want you to show me around." He pulled me outside and to the back of the house and then slammed me up against it. I'd thought I'd seen a gun under his jacket while we were in the house, but now he made it very apparent the gun was there by exposing his shoulder holster. I could hardly breathe I was so frozen with fright. I remember that he put his hand under my shirt and then pulled my shirt up to expose my breast. He squeezed my breast really hard, and it was painful. I don't know how, but somehow I mustered up the courage to overcome my fear and pushed him away as hard as I could. I ran back to the house, and he hurriedly took off and got in his car and left. I called Marsha right away and told her what had happened and to come quick.

Marsha didn't believe me, which made me frantic. I was in tears and panicky, totally overcome with fear, and she told me to behave myself. Mom had never filled her in on this man coming around, and she thought I was making it up. Once again, something this serious hadn't resulted in a normal reaction from Mom, who had failed to protect me or even to think enough about the situation to communicate it to Marsha.

I was so scared I called the police and then Mom. Even though my little brothers seemed like they were going sell me out for $20.00 and some ice cream, they, too, knew something was wrong. While they were acting one way, they were smart enough to know the man was dangerous. I don't know whether they saw his gun or not, but what they did was heroic. They ran out to his car when he dragged me to the backyard and wrote down his license plate number and the make of his car.

The police came right away, and I had to go into the sheriff's department after Mom got home. The sheriff was really nice to me. He informed me they'd run a check on the man's license plates, and they were fictitious. Now he knew they had a predator in the area, and they had a description of him. The sheriff promised that all I had to do was call him if this man ever came by again, and he would send a car immediately. I think even Mom finally realized the seriousness of what this man was capable of, for she co-operated with the police one hundred percent.

Marsha apologized to me over and over. She felt really bad that she thought I'd lied, but what else could she have thought? To the best of her knowledge, I was a troublemaker and a liar, as that was Mom's synopsis of me. Marsha's reaction was a normal one under those circumstances, but needless to say, this incident didn't bring Mom and I any closer together. I don't think anything could have done that.

I did get a job that summer, working as a personal maid for an older couple in the next town over. I got up early enough to hitchhike to this job, but a lot of times I ended up walking the whole five miles. I showed up in the morning and cleaned their house, made lunch, and just kept cleaning until I went home at night. They were an odd couple and had been married many years. They never acted like they liked each other, and it put me in a bit of a predicament. The man was an alcoholic, and the woman told me to keep an eye out for hidden bottles of liquor and to tell her about it so she could catch him drinking.

I found the bottles, of course, but he asked me not to tell on him. I didn't know what to do. I didn't feel any loyalty to either of these people, but he reminded me that he was the one who had hired and who paid me. I never told on him after he shared his reasoning with me, but I didn't really like the job, and I didn't like the dynamics of their marriage. I was always under the wife's scrutiny. I felt like she didn't trust me, so after a month or two, I quit. That was long enough, considering the constant bickering those two did. I guess that just goes to show you that all the money in the world doesn't buy happiness. It certainly didn't for this old couple.

Life needed a drastic change, and it was coming. Soon, Mom started dating an extremely creepy guy. He was a security guard of some sort, and I guess Mom thought he was really something because he wore a uniform. He and another couple came to pick Mom up for a double date one night. The other couple was just as disgusting as he was. The woman had scabs on her legs, probably from shaving, with little drips of dried blood running down them that she hadn't wiped away.

Mom was still getting ready and was running fashionably late and was making them wait for her. She hollered an introduction from the bedroom and told them I would keep them company until she was ready, and then she instructed me to make coffee or tea and sit down with them at the table. Mom was trying to make an impression on them with me as her obedient, loving daughter. I really couldn't think of anything to say, so I just sort of sat there. The way the other woman's date looked at me sent shivers down my spine. I could tell right away he was some sort of lech.

Then Mom's boyfriend tried to give me a hug. While he was doing that, he reached up under my shirt very fast and squeezed my breast. I pushed him away and went into Mom's bedroom and told her this guy was trying to get fresh with me and had tried to grab my breast.

She said, "Rhonnie, he's just trying to be friendly and get to know you." I was furious. I told her, "Yeah, Mom, he's trying to be real friendly." She then told me to quit lying like that and that he was a really nice man and to stop making trouble for her.

I didn't know what to do. I didn't want him to get away with grabbing me, and it seemed that Mom wasn't going to do anything about it. Not that I was surprised by her lack of action, of course. Why would she act now when she never had before? I called Dad and told him what had happened, and Dad talked to Mom and straightened it out the best he could, which wasn't much. Mom defended her boyfriend and told Dad he was a gentleman. I'm sure she thought Dad had become involved because he was jealous!

Mom didn't value me, nor had she wanted me around for quite some time. She'd done everything in her power to get rid of me legally, and when she'd failed in that, she'd become even more hostile toward me. She just couldn't stand it any longer, now that I was getting in the way of her personal life and trying to put a wedge between her and her new boyfriend. Her solution, to my great horror, was to go back to court and change my residence to my father's. That's right, she sent me back to live with the wolf, the monster, the pedophile who had tortured and abused me my whole life. As much as I hated living with Mom, this was certainly something I never wanted to happen. I'm sure Mom knew that, but her life revolved around what she wanted. It certainly didn't revolve around any of us.

Mom simply didn't want to deal with us kids. First it was Jackie, then she'd forced Bob out, and now it was my turn to be kicked out of the house. So far, fifteen seemed to be the magic age to shuffle us out, except for Bob, who'd been sixteen. Bob was living at Dad's, too, but he was renting a room from him and working and going to school, and Dad was not involved in Bob's life other than renting to him. I felt like there would be no protection for me at Dad's from Bob, as he was the one who'd been smacking me around for Mom. Maybe he would be nicer without Mom there to goad him on, but I wasn't sure of anything right then, and I was in total despair. I just wanted to run away or die, anything other than live with Dad.

I arrived at Dad's reluctantly. The two all-important sisters lived in one house, and I lived upstairs from them and shared a room with one of the renters. Dad's girlfriend, Barb, lived across the alley from this house with her roommate. Dad spent his evenings sleeping at Barb's across the alley and his days at the house I was in.

When I saw Dad, the memories all came rushing back: the smell I hated, the voice I hated, the touch of any kind I hated. I was also nervous about going from a class of seventeen to a large school with several hundred kids in each grade. An introvert, I panicked at just the sight of such a large school. I liked to keep pretty much to myself with maybe one friend to hang out with, and never did I let any of my friends get too close. Now I had to start over in a new school and meet new people. If the truth were known, I was afraid. I never thought I'd fit in anywhere, and even though I'd made friends in Traverse City prior to this, they'd all been older than me, and none of them was still in school.

With my sophomore year about to start, Dad gave me a crushing blow when he took me shopping for school clothes. I had grown that summer and had very little to wear, but he took me to the department the old ladies shopped in, and I simply could not believe the clothing he picked out. I was mortified. There was no way I would wear such clothes anyplace, and I knew my dad well enough to know he did this deliberately to show me who was in control. He wanted me to feel the same shame I'd always felt, and this allowed him to embarrass me in a new school where I could have had a new beginning. Those clothes simply screamed, "I'm uncool!"

To make matters worse, I couldn't stand the two sisters, and the feelings were definitely mutual. They never cared how much they were taking from us when we were little, and now they were going to make sure I couldn't take anything from them, including Dad's attention. They were very pliable women, easy for a slick predator to manipulate and mold, and they worshiped the ground my dad walked on. He told them what to wear, how much to weigh, what color their hair should be, where to work, what to eat, when to shower, and what to say. In other words, he could ask them to jump, and they would ask how high! They had no identity of their own, just the one Dad had created for them, and that's exactly why he chose them. Dad had no official job; only the sisters worked. They let him handle their money, and he invested it in real estate and rental houses. He was basically a "slum lord."

I spent most of my time upstairs in my room and talked with my roommate. I never liked coming downstairs to see any of them, and for their part, they made no bones about my presence being an intrusion in their lives. In spite of this, Dad had tight reins on me and watched me like a hawk. Though I was not allowed to have any friends at all, just like when I was a little girl, I soon found that a lot of people in my new school were just like me, and I started looking at this experience in a more positive way. I learned to take my change of "cooler" clothes out the door with me in the morning on the way to school and change into them at the gas station on the corner. I would then walk right back up to the bus stop, which was at the elementary school across the street from Dad's house. It surely wasn't an accident that he found another house across from a grade school. Once a predator, always a predator.

I sneaked out one time with my older roommate and drank some wine and got drunk with her. I got sick and threw up everywhere, and I was surprised that Dad didn't punish me. I think he thought being sick four whole days was going to teach me the lesson I needed to learn. Soon after that, he moved me across the alley to Barb's house, probably because my presence was making his life with the two sisters miserable. I liked living there better. Barb was nice to me, and I liked her. She was actually too nice for my dad, and I couldn't figure out how she'd ever let herself get involved with him, but he was a master manipulator and had a very convincing manner.

Even though Mom had succeeded in getting me out of her house, she just couldn't leave well enough alone. Every so often, she popped in at Dad's on her way home from work. She worked in town anyway, so this was an easy stop for her to make, and I'm sure she had a twofold reason for doing so. One, it was an opportunity to try to get me into trouble with Dad, and, two, she wanted to see Dad and wanted him to see her and how well she was doing without him. She would immediately start in with, "Jack, look at her eyes; I think she's on something."

I'd been smoking pot for years by now, but I would never think of getting high around Dad. He would have made anyone's high a big downer, and I simply would have been too paranoid. I'm convinced Mom was just hoping to stir him up and get me in trouble. She knew that if she got Dad angry, I would undergo severe consequences, and I just wanted her to leave me alone. Every time her car pulled in the driveway, I started feeling nauseous. She never once stopped by to say hello or because she missed me. She just wanted to torment me further and hopefully make my life more of a living hell.

Like many children, I could always tell if I was in trouble with either of my parents by how they addressed me. If they called me "Rhonnie" I was okay, but if they called me "Rhonda" or "Rhonda Joan," I was in big trouble. Mom always addressed me as "Rhonda" whenever she stopped in. She didn't have to check up on me, though; I was afraid for my life while living at Dad's.

The only saving grace in staying with Dad was that I was much too old for him to be interested in sexually. He really only liked molesting us when we were little. Even though that element was now removed, he found other things to say and do that were degrading. He often called me a "slut," occasionally called me a "whore," and usually called me a "bitch." Mom needn't have worried; he was properly humiliating me just fine without her. But he was a little more careful now that Barb was around, because she defended me when she felt he was unjust.

However, Dad's perversions continued in other ways. When I needed to see a doctor, he let me go only to one particular doctor who was so fat his lap disappeared when he sat down. I didn't like him, and I told Dad I wanted to see another doctor instead of him after the first visit. He had given me a Pap smear, probably because Barb wanted me on birth control pills since sex was so prevalent in my age group, and even though the nurse was standing by my upper half, he lingered a little too long with his finger in the wrong place on my clitoris. After that first visit, he always did his exams without a nurse present. When I asked where his nurse was, he would say it was her day off. I believe he scheduled me on purpose only when she was gone.

This doctor was more than flirtatious; he was a pig. One time I had an itchy rash on my arm, and he had me lie on the examining table. He then unzipped my pants and started to pull them down. I grabbed my pants and asked what he was doing, and he said, "I just thought I would look for crotch crickets."

I was furious. I got off his table and buttoned up my pants. He then sat down in his chair and started writing a prescription to treat scabies, which were going around school. He knew it was scabies; he was just trying to look at my vagina without a nurse present. Before I left, he tried to pull me onto his lap so he could talk to me. I found this to be nothing but professional misconduct. I told Dad all this, not that I thought he would do anything, and he replied that this was a good man and a great doctor. I knew there would be no winning this argument with Dad. He simply never cared what anybody did to his kids.

Though it seemed like an eternity, I lived at Dad's only a short period of time, five or six months at most. In that time, I managed to gain forty pounds. I was depressed and felt trapped, and I hated my life. It didn't seem like I was eating much, but I was still gaining weight. No matter what I did, I gained weight. Dad was also making me bleach my hair blonde, just like he'd done with Jackie. This was certainly one of his fixations, as the two sisters had to do their hair blonde, too. When the roots grew out, he would get hair bleach and take a paintbrush and redo them. Even though I was blonde by birth, I began to hate blonde hair simply because he obsessed over it so much.

I was virtually a prisoner in Dad's house, and except for school, I was never allowed out. Something had to give, and since I'd made some friends at school, I came up with a plan. Dad loved to flirt with girls, so I decided to ask my prettiest friend to come over and ask if I could baby-sit with her. When he said yes, we'd go to a party instead. Dad took the pretty girl bait, and after a whole lot of flirting, and I mean several hours of it, he finally agreed to let me baby-sit with her that night. How predictable Dad was!

Without delay, we were on our way to the party. I had a few beers and smoked a little pot and was having a really good time. It was such a relief not to be at Dad's under lock and key. I was with the people who made me feel comfortable for a change, and I could be myself and laugh with them. It was starting to get late, and the party was in full swing when all of a sudden the front door swung open, and there was my dad standing there with a claw hammer in his hand. He just looked at me and said, "Rhonda, get your shoes on."

Oh, God, I knew I was going to get it. Everybody in that house became quiet, and no one knew what to do. No one even moved, as they were afraid, too. I put my shoes on, and he grabbed me by the hair and jerked me out the door. He then dragged me down the street by the hair. My feet never took one step. I thought that once we got to his house he was going to beat me to death with his hammer, but instead of using the hammer, he threw me up against the wall and took his belt off and beat the living tar out of me from my shoulders to my ankles, with the buckle side of the belt. I thought he would never stop. Barb was at work, and he had free rein to do what he wanted.

As bad as it was, I was happy I was slightly drunk because it didn't hurt as much as it would have otherwise. When I woke up the next morning, I felt hot from my back to my ankles, and when I looked in the mirror, I couldn't believe what I saw. I was black, blue, and bloody with giant welts. When I started getting dressed, I almost cried out while pulling my clothes over my wounds I hurt so bad. I packed my suitcase and left my room. Dad was sitting in the kitchen with Barb and said, "Where do you think you're going?"

I told him I was leaving, and he said, "I'll see you in jail by the end of today."

I replied, "I don't think so, Dad; I'll see you in jail today, you pervert." With that, I walked out the door. I was not even sixteen years old, but I knew he'd beaten me pretty severely and there were witnesses as to how he'd entered my friend's house with that hammer in his hand. They all would have gone to court on my behalf, but if leaving that house meant I had to go to jail, then so be it. I didn't care anymore. Anything would be better than where I was. I took my chances and just kept walking.

I ended up at my friend Mickey's house about five blocks away. Her mom and dad were very cool people, and they really loved Mickey. They were elderly people who'd had Mickey as a mid-life baby, and in fact she had siblings who had children older than she was. I told them what had happened, and they welcomed me into their home. Mickey's mom then called my dad and told him, "I don't want any shit from you, Jack. Your daughter is staying here with us. You don't cause her shit; I won't cause you shit," and that was it. I was finally safe from both my parents, and I had a place to stay, even if just for a little while. As good as they were to me, I never shared the horrors of my life with Mickey's mom and dad, nor did I share the whole story with any of my friends. I didn't want to be judged by them.

Nor did I want to overstay my welcome at Mickey's, so I started dividing my time between several different families. Essentially, I became a bit of a drifter. I knew a lot of these families were doing the best they could with their own children and that trying to squeeze in another mouth to feed was difficult for some of them.

Sad as it was, I was almost totally on my own. I was a young girl lost and alone, and I couldn't go home to my mom or my dad. Fortunately, there wasn't that much time left before the school year ended, and somehow I got through it, just as I'd somehow gotten through everything else that had happened so far in my life.

Chapter 4

><

*Bouncing Around, Doing My Best,
and Making Mistakes*

I was still drifting when the school year ended, and then I got a job working at a laundry. It was there that I met my friend Susan. I was working hard to save money for a car, and though it was a hot summer that year, with the folding area even hotter than the outdoors, I somehow maintained my focus. I knew that owning a car would make my highly complicated life a little more manageable. Besides, if nothing else, I could always sleep in my car.

This particular summer felt especially long, and each day seemed to drag. I spent many nights with Susan, and her home became another place for me to temporarily hang my hat. I'm sure that the uncertainty of my life at that time, combined with my horrible, miserable job, was the reason the summer dragged so. I was supporting myself completely at this time, except for those occasions I was fortunate enough to go home with one of my friends and have a real meal. Even so, I usually tried not to eat at those homes, as I was always concerned about being a burden, but neither Susan's mother nor her stepfather ever said a word about me staying with them.

It was an exhausting time in my life, but finally the summer ended, and I had indeed saved enough money to buy my first car. It was a 1962 Volkswagen Beetle, and I paid $200.00 for it. It was a little crunched and crinkled on the right side, but to me, it was as good as a new car, for it represented freedom.

Because I was only sixteen years old, the law dictated that I had to be on an adult's insurance and that person's name had to appear on the title, as well. I hated to approach my mother about this, and I was afraid she'd say no, but amazingly enough, she agreed to do this for me. My guess is that she agreed so I wouldn't move back home with her. At any rate, now I was all set.

I had been looking all summer in the job ads, and before long I'd found the perfect job for my junior year, as a live-in babysitter in a home where the mother worked nights and needed someone home with the kids while she worked. I didn't want to float around any longer, and this job would serve two purposes: one, I would have a home and some much-needed stability, and, two, I would make enough money to pay for my school clothes, books, car insurance, and gas. The mother was on welfare, and with my income subsidized through the state and coming directly to me, the situation couldn't have been more perfect.

When I arrived the first night at my new live-in job with my meager belongings, eager to start, my perfect job began to look a little less than terrific. The house was filthy, the kids were filthy, and there was so much clutter I couldn't see the furniture. I spent my first week cleaning and organizing, but the kids were no problem at all and seemed to appreciate having me there. The mom was home in the mornings, and my job ended as soon as she came home, or so I'd anticipated. As it turned out, when she was home, she was sleeping! I soon felt as though I were back home with my own mother, for like mine, this woman didn't seem to pay any attention to her kids or to their needs.

The checks were supposed to start right away, but for some reason, they weren't coming like they were supposed to. Before long, I could no longer afford to drive to school, so I had to ride the bus. After the checks were more than three weeks late, I asked the mother where they were, and she told me she would look into it, but nothing happened. I finally called the welfare office, and to my astonishment, I was told they'd been sending the checks all along and that they'd been cashed.

To make a long story short, this woman had been stealing my money. I promptly turned her in and filed a claim against her in small claims court, but it would take time to get my money. In the meantime, my own mother was angry that I hadn't paid her the insurance I owed her for the month. She accused me of messing this situation up and accordingly took my car away from me and made me park it in her yard. I told her she couldn't take my car away like that, and she reminded me that her name was on the title and she could do anything she wanted.

I'm sure Mom didn't want me to have any success back then and would have done whatever she could to make life hard for me. I'm also sure she was still angry that I'd successfully left Dad's home without any repercussions. Though I did finally get the money I was owed, life was becoming more and more frustrating. I was now drifting again and had no car, and it was becoming harder and harder to maintain my focus and stay in school. Sometimes just keeping my thoughts straight seemed overwhelming to me.

When things were looking their most grim, my friend Susan took me home with her and told her mom my situation. Jo, a wonderfully compassionate person, invited me to live with them. By the grace of God, she and her husband let me move right in with their family, even though they already had eight kids of their own and another homeless girl was also staying there.

Jo was a small woman with crippling arthritis in her hands and feet. She was a cashier and stood on her feet eight to ten hours a day and rang up groceries the old fashioned way with her fingers. The knuckles on her hands were deformed and large with scars from numerous surgeries, as were her feet.

Her husband drove a school bus in the daytime and at night worked at the same supermarket as Jo. He was so dedicated to his family that he never seemed to notice his lack of sleep. He had a steady, easygoing manner that was very calming to me. Nothing really upset him, not even all the constant noise in the house.

Those two made a good team, and they did all they could do to sustain their family. They shared one child together out of all the kids. Although the house was two stories, it was really quite small given all the people who lived there. Despite how crowded we were, it felt like a real home to me, and these felt like real parents. I thought I'd found a gold mine.

I was treated the same as all the rest of their kids, not any better and not any worse. With so many people under one roof, it became messy and crowded at times, but to me, that was all right. As soon as school let out, we came home and cleaned the house and made dinner. After feeding eleven people, there were many dishes to wash and put away, but everyone pitched in, so it went relatively smoothly. There were no "waps" for dirty dishes in that house. Instead, there was always gratitude that dinner and chores were done. On weekends, we did laundry, and with that many people, it was never-ending. Even though this was pretty much the same as when I grew up, the difference was the correct parenting. That made an immense difference in how I felt about working hard. The abuse I'd grown up with had made everybody resentful of helping out around the house.

Though Jo was sweet and merciful, she also had a tough side. Since I'd gained weight living with my dad, she made me exercise every night before I went to bed. She knew I was depressed and didn't feel that good about myself, and she knew losing weight would help me build confidence and self-esteem. Sometimes when I was really tired, I tried to sneak to bed without doing my exercises, but she never let me get away with that; she stayed right on top of me and sometimes even got me out of bed to exercise. I sometimes hated her for doing that and grumbled under my breath, but I knew she did it out of the goodness of her heart.

There were many times when I finished exercising early and we talked for what seemed like hours on end. She told me about her problems with her first husband, an alcoholic whom she said had been inappropriate with her oldest daughter when she was little and about how at one time she had wanted to commit suicide with her kids and almost did. She then told me that somehow in all her agony and pain, both physical from the arthritis and her emotional and spiritual pain, she had found the strength to go on. She knew that bearing her burdens and getting tough with herself had made the difference in how she viewed life.

I told her about my life and about the physical, mental, and sexual abuse we'd all endured. I told her she was the only person I'd ever confided in, not counting my mother. Somehow it was a relief to talk about it. Holding it in had been harder than I'd realized.

Jo called my dad and told him I was living with her. She also told him he needed to send her seven dollars a week child support to help take care of me. She spoke to him with such authority that I was impressed, and he didn't argue with her in the least. Somehow my dad backed off completely when there was another adult in the picture. He even sent her the seven dollars a week, which astounded me as he'd never sent my mother a nickel for any of us.

Jo could have used that money to help with my keep, but I later found out that's not what she did with it. Instead, she put it in a savings account for me until I was ready to leave. This woman was a great role model. I knew I wanted to grow up to be like her, full of compassion for the less fortunate. I had a great deal of affection for her, but most of all, I trusted her. I never told her I loved her, but she knew I did. She never pushed that issue with me, because she knew it would have been hard for me to say to anyone at that time in my life. She gave me good strong advice, but most of all, I learned from her example.

Another one of the compassionate things she did was at Christmas. She knew I'd always had bad Christmases, and she also knew my two younger brothers and sister were still at home with Mom and would not be having a good holiday. She invited them to her house for Christmas, and to their surprise and mine, there were presents for them under the tree. I couldn't believe she was so thoughtful that she included my little brothers and sister, whom she'd never met.

Thanks mostly to Jo, I made it through my eleventh grade year in a satisfactory way. I knew I had a home to go to at the end of the day, which took a lot off my mind. Even though I skipped school at times, I did not miss as much school as I had the year before. I was really making an effort to keep my grades up. Other than my last year at my old school, my grades had always been good, and my English grades had always been A's.

That last semester of my junior year, Susan and I took an English class together. Our big assignment was to research and write a sixty-page paper on any subject we thought would be of interest, and we had three months to do it in. Susan worked the whole three months on her project, and I worked on mine for the three days before it was due. When we finally got our grades, she received a "C," and I was given an "A+."

Susan was livid. She had always been jealous of anyone who could do any-thing better than she could, and this was the straw that broke the camel's back. She went to the teacher and told him I'd worked on my report for only three days and it had taken her three months. How could he have given her such a low grade when my paper was done in haste? The teacher told her that my report was done very well and deserved the grade it had been given.

This didn't sit well with Susan, and complicating our relationship was my drinking problem, which had started long before I'd moved in with her family. I also did some drugs, like most of my friends, but my drug of choice was alcohol. Drinking was becoming a hard habit to break, and I was having a hard time admitting it. I had never discussed this with Jo, nor did Jo know that Susan also had a drinking and drug problem. She'd always been disrespectful of her parents and was sneaky, and I unwittingly became her partner in crime. This wasn't neces-sarily because I wanted to be; I just felt an obligation to go along with her. I became her constant alibi, and in the same sense, she became mine. I wasn't sure I liked that, but if I kept my mouth shut about her, she wouldn't tell about my drinking.

Susan was hard to get along with, one of those people who was always right no matter what. I just found it easier to go along with her than to disagree with her. Like my father, she seemed to have a deficit when it came to having a conscience. As long as she was having a good time, she didn't care whose toes she stepped on, nor did she care if she hurt people. She lied all the time to her parents, which put me in an awkward position. I should have stepped up to the plate and told Jo about my alcohol problem, but Susan forbid me to tell about the wilder side of her life, and I felt I couldn't say a word to Jo. If I leveled with her about myself, I would be disclosing the truth about Susan.

In addition to her drinking and drugs, Susan also slept around a lot. She got a lot of pleasure stealing other girls' men from them, even if it was only for a night. If I had a crush on somebody, she'd hurry and sleep with him so he'd lose interest in me. She even slept with her sister's boyfriends. Every guy in town knew she was easy, including married men, whom she likewise had no qualms about sleeping with.

In contrast, although I'd started having sex at age fourteen, as well as drinking, smoking, and doing other drugs, I decided to clean up my life at this point concerning sex. I didn't want guys to like me just because I had sex with them; I decided I'd rather be respected by guys. This was a major accomplishment for me, and I became every guy's "friend" at that point. This got really old if I had a crush on someone, especially since he seemed to want girls who would have sex with him, but I stuck to my guns about sleeping around.

Our biggest problem was that Susan became increasingly jealous of my relationship with her mother. Since she was covetous by nature, she wanted everything the people around her had. She hadn't really wanted a close relationship with her mother before I'd arrived; she just didn't want someone other than herself to have one. I was wearing thin on Susan's nerves, and she'd definitely worn thin on mine. I didn't want to leave the home I'd found and was happy in, but Susan was getting more and more uncomfortable with my presence. I loved Jo. She was the caring mother I'd never had, and to this day, I can honestly say she helped me more than anyone ever has, but by the time that school year was over, Susan had decided she'd had enough of me. She did more than ask me to leave; she said she'd make life so miserable for me if I stayed that I'd find it unbearable. Susan didn't care about my problems or me; like my mother, she was self-centered and saw only what she wanted.

I didn't want to leave, but I felt I had no choice. I thought about this long and hard, and one day I packed up my clothes with a very heavy heart. I couldn't tell Jo what was going on, but when I told her I was leaving, to my complete surprise, she got all the money my dad had sent her out of the bank and gave it to me. I will never forget her kindness to me, and remembering what it felt like to leave that home is still painful. I really wanted to stay in this place that finally felt like home, but at least this time I knew I wasn't homeless because no one wanted me, for I knew Jo really cared.

I stayed with my old friend Debbie for a few days but soon realized we'd grown so far apart that we had nothing in common anymore. Hard as we tried, we just couldn't strike up our old friendship. In desperation, I moved back home to my mom's. This was one of the last things I wanted to do, but she was never there anyway, and it seemed pretty safe at least for a while. She didn't even know I was there at first, and when she did realize it, she just ignored me. Besides, my brothers and sister were home alone most of the time. My job was still in Traverse City, and since I no longer had a car, I hitchhiked to work and back every day. I was cleaning motel rooms now and working the second shift as a waitress at a small, all-night diner, and life was beginning to feel very complicated again.

Sometime that summer, I ran into an acquaintance from school named Terry. I didn't know her all that well other than from the parties we'd both attended, but she invited me to stay with her for a while. She lived in a little town about twenty-five miles north of Traverse City, and she had horses, which cinched the deal. I moved in with her, and one night she suggested we go to a bar in a nearby town where she knew the band. Meeting new people made me edgy, but I was okay once we got to the bar. We both started drinking, as the drinking age back then was eighteen. We were just seventeen, but they didn't question us as we were with the band. Drinking relieved my anxiety about being around new people and was truly a crutch for me at that point.

The next day, Terry asked if I would hitchhike downstate to Ann Arbor with her to a big party she'd been invited to. Not only did the mere thought of hitchhiking scare me, but also this meant being around more people I didn't know. The biggest part of me didn't want to go, especially since I was hung over and tired, but Terry persisted until I said yes. Ann Arbor was two-hundred-some miles away. I wondered how safe it was to hitchhike that far, but I figured we were big girls and between the two of us we'd be safe.

We arrived in Ann Arbor in one piece and went directly to her friend's house. Terry started smoking pot right away, but I didn't want to smoke. Pot always made me paranoid, and since I was already feeling that way, pot would have only intensified the feeling. I soon found out this was a really big party, one of the biggest I'd ever been to. It was outdoors, with at least a thousand or so people and live bands playing, and everybody was either getting high or drinking.

Terry ran into a couple more friends and told me to stay with a guy named John who would take care of me. I didn't want to be left alone with someone I didn't know, and I told her that, but she assured me he was really sweet and that she would meet up with me later that night at his apartment. With that, she was gone. We'd only been in Ann Arbor two hours, and my biggest nightmare was happening: I was deserted with somebody I didn't know. Terry was whimsical in nature, but I wasn't. I was afraid, too upset even to drink a beer. Besides, I wanted to be alert and on my guard. I didn't really like this John guy, even though I didn't know him well enough to make a judgment. I just had an uneasy feeling about him, even though he was nice to me at the party.

After we left the party, we went to his apartment, and he told me to make myself at home. It was about four in the morning by then. He started telling me how rude men could be and how most men would take full advantage of this situation. He rolled a joint and started smoking it. He said, "For instance, I could tell you right now to fuck me or get out of my house."

I looked at him and started to feel really nervous. I said, "I suppose you could, but I'm glad you're not telling me to do that."

He just looked at me and laughed and said, "No, I mean it. You either fuck me or get out of my house right now."

I couldn't believe Terry had said this guy was so sweet. He was a creep, but this was a big city with lots of rapes and murders. I knew that if I left I probably wouldn't make it far before something horrible happened. I tried to talk my way out of it, but I couldn't. I had to make a choice right then and there: either the big, dark city streets where there could someone much worse lurking about or him. I made what I thought was the safest choice between the two, and when it was over, I just lay there looking out the window and praying for daylight.

I was terribly upset. This was a hippie, and hippies weren't supposed to do these kinds of things. Hippies were supposed to be peaceful and kind. Terry never showed up, which made matters worse, and I was furious that not only had she left me, but she'd also left me with this appalling man she'd insisted was so nice. I finally dozed off, and when my eyes opened, the sun was shining. I got up, grabbed my backpack, and started walking. I knew I was only blocks away from the freeway, but I couldn't remember how to get there. There was a lot of activity in the city now, and I stopped at a store and asked for directions. I made my way to the freeway and started hitchhiking home. At that point, I was too mad to be scared.

I got a ride right away with a man in a suit who said he was going to work twenty miles or so up the highway. I knew we'd gone further than twenty miles when he looked at me and said, "It's a beautiful day, and I really don't have anything else to do, so I'll drive you a little farther. I need to stop and get some gas first." I felt pretty uneasy, but this man kept talking like he was just trying to be nice. I should have listened to myself in the first place about the whole Ann Arbor trip, but now it was too late. He found a gas station ten or so miles farther up the road and pulled in and gassed up his car. He paid for the gas, and then we were off again. Despite my unease, I was thinking how lucky I was. He had told me he was a family man and hated to see girls hitchhiking, as it really wasn't that safe. We drove for an hour or so and passed through the next several big cities. At first the freeways were teeming with commuters going to work, but as time passed, the cars became more scarce. He chose this opportunity to make his move and began talking suggestively to me.

I told him he needed to stop and let me out, and I thanked him for the ride. My voice remained calm and steady, but inside I was terrified. He apologized quickly and said he wouldn't talk to me like that again, but neither would he pull over and let me out, and it wasn't long before he wasn't just suggestive anymore. He started talking very graphically to me and told me how nice my "tits" were and said my nipples were hard.

I was very frightened and asked him again to please stop and let me out. He once again apologized and said he was sorry for making me so nervous, but still he wouldn't pull over and let me out. I knew he wasn't sorry, and I also knew he wasn't going to stop, so I started looking for a way out. I kept scanning the area, looking for more traffic. There was traffic, but it was going the other way on the other side of the median. I looked to see how fast the man was going, and it was too fast for me to jump out. I didn't know what to do, so I grabbed hold of my backpack and pulled it up to my chest so he would stop looking at my breasts. We were about an hour and a half from Traverse City when we came to an exit. I planned to jump out at the stop sign at the end of the ramp, but when we got there, instead of stopping, he pushed on the gas and floored it and went right through the stop sign. He had guessed what I was thinking, and he had obviously made his mind up about what he was going to do. I once again pleaded with him to let me out and told him I'd make it the rest of the way home by myself, but he just looked at me strangely and said, "No, I don't think so."

I thought for sure this was going to be the last day of my life. The landscape was desolate now, and even though we were on a two-lane highway, the houses were miles apart from each other. I was so frightened I was no longer able to hide the fear welling up inside me. I couldn't look at this man anymore; he wore a frightening expression I'd never seen before. It was sheer determination to perpetrate an evil act. All of a sudden, he whipped his car down a gravel road, just barely braking, and said, "This one is as good as any." He accelerated as we fishtailed, his face fixated forward, and started to reach under the seat. I don't know what he was reaching for, but I could only assume it was a gun or a knife.

I didn't want to be raped again, and I didn't want to be murdered. I looked at him in pure panic, touched his arm, and said, "Please, I'm not that kind of girl, please." I was frozen with fear. He looked at me and said, "You don't really think I drove you all this way for nothing, do you?"

I don't know how I mustered the strength; I have to say it was God-given. I wrapped my arms around that backpack, opened the car door, and just rolled out onto the gravel. I rolled and rolled, and when I finally came to a rest, I gathered myself up as fast as I could and ran like my life depended on it, because it did. I never looked behind me to see whether he had turned around to come back and get me. I remained focused on the main road, as I thought this was my only hope of surviving. It seemed like that gravel road was never ending, and even though I was out of breath and my legs felt numb and drained of strength, I never broke stride. It was a perfectly isolated gravel road in the middle of nowhere, the ideal place to commit a crime. There were woods on both sides, no houses in sight, and best of all for him, there was no traffic.

I finally made it to the main road and kept running until I was in front of the first house I came to. I was grateful to see there was a car in the driveway. I stooped to catch my breath and felt stinging pain in my arms, legs, and rear end. My arms had road gravel embedded in them, as did my legs. I tried to pick the gravel out of my skin and wipe off the blood as best I could. I knew I looked like a wreck, but in the distance I saw a car coming down the road. It wasn't red, but still terrified that man would find me, I jumped up and down and flagged down the driver. I didn't care if I looked stupid right then; I needed to get out of there quickly. It was another man with two small children in tow. He asked me where I was going, and I told him. Luckily for me, he was going right into Traverse City. I was visibly shaken and sweating as well as dusty from rolling on the gravel road. He asked why I looked like

I'd seen a ghost, and I started to cry and told him what had just happened. He told me the same thing the other man had said, that it wasn't safe for girls to hitchhike alone because you never knew who was picking you up. Then he added, "It's your lucky day. I have my kids with me, or I'd be doing the same thing to you right now."

This statement horrified me, and while I couldn't believe my ears, I knew I was fairly safe with those kids in the car. They were both old enough to talk, and I figured he wouldn't want them to relate any bad stories to their mom. They were friendly, and even though I didn't feel like it, I talked to them all the way to Traverse City. The driver let me out once we got in town, and I thanked him. I think he was just trying to make a point saying what he did. I already knew it wasn't safe for girls to hitchhike alone, and I also knew I would never do it again.

I was finally safe, on familiar ground, and as I started walking and reflecting on my last twenty-four hours, I broke down and cried. I knew angels had surrounded me in that time frame, and I realized that no matter what had happened to me up until this point, there was value in being alive. It was a huge deal for me to acknowledge this to myself, as most of the time I wasn't sure life was worth living. In spite of what seemed like constant turmoil and pain in my life, I was glad to be alive, and I thanked God for it right then.

Shortly after this incident, my sister Jackie moved back to Traverse City and got an apartment with a friend. It was nice to have her back, and sometime that late summer I stayed with her briefly. I'd gone back to Mom's after my traumatic incident, but I'd never told her about it as it wouldn't have done any good. She didn't care about my welfare and probably would have said I deserved everything I got. She also would have told me how stupid I was, and that I already knew. It almost felt like old times, being with Jackie, except that we were older now. We often hung out at the bars and played pool, which was always fun. I tried to spend as much time with her as possible without being a burden. She was working someplace at the time and had not finished school to my knowledge; she just wanted to be back in northern Michigan.

When my senior year started, it was more difficult than ever to get a ride to school, then to my job, and then back home to Mom's, but I tried hard to find a balance. I had only until January to go, as I'd have all the credits I needed to graduate mid-year, but I also had to work. Although I was living at Mom's, that in no way meant she was supporting me, nor as usual was she home enough even to know I was there. I don't know whether Rod, Tay, and Roger were even going to school then. I was oblivious to what was going on in their lives, but if they were attending school, it wasn't often.

I finally quit school in October. I had only two and a half months to go, but I felt as though I didn't have any choice. I had to work, and I couldn't manage to get to both work and school. I was exhausted all the time, and it was more than I could handle at age seventeen. I told myself I would go back later and get my diploma.

In my spare time, I began hanging out with a girl from a town about twenty miles north of my hometown. I can't recall how we met, but I'm sure it was while I was visiting my sometimes boyfriend, Harvey, whom I'd dated off and on since I was fourteen. Cheryl and I had both dated Harvey, though of course not at the same time. This was a strange sort of bond, but it seemed to work for us. Cheryl was a fun-loving person, and she made me laugh. She also loved the boys; oh, boy, did she ever! This didn't bother me, since she wasn't sneaky about it. I wasn't interested in getting involved with a guy at this time anyway; I just needed someone to hang out with. We both worked in Traverse City and loved horses, and soon we had a brain-storm to buy a couple of horses and keep them at Mom's. Since Mom was gone most of the time and didn't care whether we were there, Cheryl started staying with me, and we hitchhiked back and forth together to our jobs. I never did hitchhike alone again, and we saved as much money as we could to buy horses.

We kept looking in the paper for the right deal, and finally, we got a ride to see a couple of horses that were for sale. They were in good condition, though older than I wanted, and the price was right. We rode them and liked how they handled, and we purchased them that day. Sam was the big cream-colored Tennessee Walker that Cheryl bought and my horse was Ty, a chestnut pinto. We bought only the two of them, but they made us take a buckskin pony with the deal. His name was Smokey, and he was really cute. We didn't want three horses, but I thought Smokey would be fun for my younger brothers and sister.

After we got Smokey settled in, I saw why they made us take him. What a stinker he was! That pony could get out of anything and did. I didn't have a fence that could hold him, so I was forever chasing him after he'd gotten loose. He would either run full tilt through the fence or dig under it. Truly, before Smokey, if someone had told me a horse would dig under a fence, I never would have believed it. I found him a new home as quickly as I could, but in the meantime, he was teaching the other two horses bad habits. Cheryl and I had a lot of fence mending to do, and we did the best we could with the little bit of money we had.

It was getting close to the end of summer now, and we needed to buy hay. About this time, Cheryl informed me she was going to Florida for a few weeks. At that, she took off, and I was stuck with her horse to take care of, with her hay bills, with finding people to help haul the hay to my house and stack it, and with hoof care. I wasn't happy about this situation, but sometimes Jackie came out and rode Sam, and it was nice just spending time with my sister. Jackie stayed around through that winter and into the summer of the following year. She even stayed at Mom's for a while that summer. It was a good thing she did, as she bought groceries for all of us with money from her job. Otherwise, there often would have been no food in the house.

That fall, to my dismay, Jackie moved back downstate, and I was again alone. At that time, I traded both horses for a younger horse who'd just turned two whom I named Chelsea. Cheryl had not come back to take care of Sam, nor had she made good on her hay bill. She'd been gone over a year, so I didn't feel a bit guilty about getting rid of her horse, even though she made a big stink over it when she finally did return, which effectively ended our friendship.

Chelsea was a much better horse for me than Ty. She was young and fresh and would be the first horse I'd had that I could keep for thirty years. That was the plan I had in mind when I bought her. She was also the first horse I'd had that I would get to train myself. She hadn't passed through a lot of hands and wasn't ruined by other people's mistakes. She also had a pliable disposition, which was another bonus. She didn't come problem-free, as she had a quarter crack in her back hoof that required special shoes until it healed, but that wasn't a big problem. She was still too young to ride, I wasn't in a hurry, and I had a lot of patience. After all, this was the horse of my dreams. She was sweet, though a little on the thin side, and she was really pretty when I'd brushed and washed her. We became friends right away, and I guess you could say I fell in love with her.

It wasn't long after I'd purchased Chelsea that Mom and I were at odds again. I don't recall what the specific problem was, but I think it had something to do with my friends or with Harvey, the guy I was dating again. I was now eighteen, and one day she came home from work and said, "Don't think now that you're eighteen years old that you are going to do anything you want. While you're living in my house, I want to know where you're going, when you're going, who you're going with, and when you're coming home!"

I can't imagine why any of that concerned her at this point. She'd never cared before, but I guess it was a power play to get me to leave. She was dating an older guy named Arnie at the time, a very nice man, an old cowboy. He liked her a lot, and he liked all us kids. One night my friend Lenny, whom I'd known for years, called to see if I wanted to play pool down the street with him and his brothers, and I told him I'd love to. He told me they'd be by in an hour to pick me up. I'd known these guys a long time. They'd been over to the house many times, but for some reason, this was the night Mom was going to make trouble. I figure she didn't like them because they were Indians, but whatever her reason was, she told me I was forbidden to play pool with them. I had no way to call them and tell them not to come. They lived on a reservation with no running water or electricity, and I knew they'd had to have used a pay phone to call in the first place.

I was in a real dilemma. Arnie had stopped by to pick Mom up, and she left for a brief period of time. While she was gone, Lenny and his brothers pulled in. I went out to their car to tell them Mom was on a rampage and to leave, but I wasn't fast enough, and Mom soon pulled up and parked at the end of the driveway and blocked their exit. I walked to her car and found her sitting there writing down their license plate number. She told me she was having them arrested for trespassing on private property, and I told her to move her car and they'd leave. She ignored me and kept writing, and when a friend of hers pulled up, I ran to him and said, "Benny, why won't she move her car? She's going to put my friends in jail for trespassing, but they can't leave." I was frantic. "She can't do that, can she?"

Benny told me she'd come to his house for assistance and that she'd already called the police. He also told me to tell my friends to find a way out of the driveway as fast as they could. He then told me Mom was too unreasonable to talk to and she'd asked him to bully my friends so she could try to put them in jail. My poor friends; what a nightmare! I was so embarrassed. They didn't know anything about this; they were just coming by to pick me up to play pool like they'd done so many times before.

I told Lenny what was going on, and he maneuvered his car over the yard and out past the deep part of the ditch where it leveled off. Seeing that he'd escaped, Mom huffily stomped into the house on her stumpy legs and told Arnie, "Let's go!" He looked at her and said, "What you just did was wrong, Betty. Those boys weren't doing anything wrong, and your daughter is eighteen years old!"

Mom replied, "I didn't ask you how to be a mother, and I never asked for your opinion." Arnie just shook his head and told her again how wrong she was, and then he left. He never dated her again, having gotten a glimpse of what little Betty was really like. Of course, Mom's solution to this was to throw me out. I had to leave immediately, and I didn't have a place to go or a way to get there. I was so idealistic when buying my horse that it hadn't occurred to me I should have bought a car instead. I knew Mom, and I should have guessed she'd throw me out without any thought whatsoever, but now I was really in a predicament. I was slowly learning that you can't make a silk purse out of a sow's ear.

I learned that Rod and Roger were shipped off to Dad's soon after this. I guess Mom just couldn't stand any of us after we reached a certain age, even the little kids. Of course, they became drunks while at Dad's. He put them in one of his rooming houses, down in a grungy basement, and brought them food once a week, never checking on them other than that. He didn't want to be bothered with them either. From what I understand, they just had one continuous party, and all the other lost kids they met ended up partying with them down in that filthy basement. I don't recall for sure where Tay was while all this was going on, but I think she stayed with her friend most of the time.

Luckily, this same friend found me a place to temporarily put my horse down the road a mile or so, which bought me a little time to get on my feet and find a boarding stable. I was determined to keep Chelsea. She was my dream, and losing her would mean losing everything I'd ever hoped for. Then I went to Harvey and asked if I could stay with him. He still lived at home, and of course his mom wasn't at all thrilled with the idea. Ironically, our mothers shared the same name and the same temperament, but Harvey was a mama's boy. Betty loved him to pieces, and she wasn't about to let him go. He was nineteen years old and old enough to be out on his own, but she didn't want him to leave her. I guess that was the big difference between this Betty and my mother. She wouldn't let go, and my mother seemed never to have had an attachment to any of us. The result of Betty's coddling of Harvey was that she chased people away from him, which got in his way of growing up and was just as damaging in its own way as what my mom did.

I was really not in a good position. I knew in my heart it would never work between Betty and me, and I was tired of settling down someplace and then having to move on. Complicating matters was that Harvey was a half-breed. He didn't really fit in with the Indians or the whites. Plus, Harvey not only lived with his mom but also his grandmother and great-grandmother. The great-grandmother, who was in her nineties, still spoke mostly in her native tongue, and none of these ladies liked the idea of Harvey dating a white girl.

I think it's safe to say that the glue holding Harvey and me together was that he was a misfit in his community and I was a misfit in general. Strange as it sounds, there was some sort of comfort in this kind of relationship. Harvey's mom hated me, and my mom hated Harvey. That just made us more determined to be together. I never really thought of Harvey as a permanent fixture in my life, and he felt the same way about me. It was more like we were buddies hanging on to each other, with neither of us really understanding why.

Harvey had a reckless nature and drank a great deal, and when I was with him, I drank, too. We never drank to have cocktails; we drank to get drunk. He was a total maniac behind the wheel of a car, and we got into many fights. I am so grateful God spared my life, as this was the year I started to drink continuously. I knew alcohol was just a quick fix to the situation at hand, but it seemed to numb the ache and pain inside my heart, and I was willing to take anything that eased my pain. I felt like I had nothing, and having nothing with somebody felt better than having nothing alone. I guess that is what Harvey and I as a couple amounted to.

Because his mother was so dead set against us and staying there became more and more uncomfortable, we started drifting. With no place to call home for either of us, we stayed at his mom's house in the daytime, and at night we walked or hitchhiked to his sister's or my mom's and slept in the leftover hay in the garage. Sometimes this entailed miles of walking, anywhere from ten to eighteen miles a day. I wasn't eating much at the time, and soon I became really skinny, but as far as I was concerned, this was a bonus. In the meantime, I continued to work at getting Harvey's mom to like me. I tried being a slave at her home, cleaning, cooking, and doing her laundry, and for her birthday, I bought her a Charlie Rich album. That seemed to be the icebreaker, and soon she decided she loved me, and suddenly, I could do no wrong.

Unfortunately, Harvey wasn't much of a worker. He would work a little, get paid, and drink for a few days until the money ran out, and then he would work more. I can't say too much about this, as I drank with him, but I also needed to work so I could pay the board for my horse. I found a real nice place for her that winter not too far from where we lived, but in the winter, work was sparse in our area. As luck would have it, a cherry farmer Harvey had once worked for needed a small forest cut down so he could expand his farm, so Harvey and I became lumberjacks that winter. It was hard work, and we put in some long days, but I learned how to cut down trees and make them fall where I wanted them to. I also learned to split wood and helped stack it to make cords, which we sold for extra money. We didn't make a lot that winter, but it was enough to get by on. Even so, keeping my horse boarded was a real strain on us.

Essentially, Harvey had enough money to drink on but not enough to pay the board on Chelsea. It wasn't really the financial strain that bothered him; it was the obligation and responsibility. He was selfish about what he wanted, and my horse was something he didn't want. This strain alone caused our breakup, and that spring I had to face the fact that I could no longer keep Chelsea. With a heavy heart, I sold her to the neighbor girl down the street from my mom's house, and then I bought a bus ticket downstate to see my sister. I don't remember how long I stayed with her, but it wasn't long. I was still drinking, and we went out to the bars together a few times.

While I was there, I picked up a guy from Canada who spoke only French and took him back to Jackie's and slept with him. This was when I began using sex as self-medication. I thought this would fill the empty part of me. Some people self-medicated with drugs, some with alcohol, and some with sex. I self-medicated with both alcohol and sex. They just seemed to go hand in hand, alcohol for the numbing effect and sex for the closeness I desired.

Soon after that, Harvey came down to Jackie's to get me and told me he was sorry for making me sell my horse. I don't know what I was thinking, but I do know this was one of the first apologies I had ever gotten in my life. I felt bad for Harvey because he seemed so lovesick, and I believed him with all my heart. Even though this situation was similar to the time my father sold our horses, I forgave Harvey and decided to go back up north with him.

Back home, we both knew that if we were going to make a go of it, we had to move out on our own. We couldn't keep living the way we had in the past, so I swallowed my pride and approached my dad to see if he had anything to rent. He did, a gutted out two-story house in Traverse City with no running water. I didn't care; I just wanted to move. I got a job at a nearby cherry factory, and Harvey did odd jobs with Dad and worked on a cherry farm down the street from the factory I worked at.

I wasn't in good shape back then, although nobody could have convinced me of that. I thought I looked great, but I had an eating disorder and had gotten so skinny I was down to a size two, which for somebody medium boned is terribly small. I was throwing up regularly, and it seemed like I didn't have to even make myself. I'd convinced myself food was so bad for me that I would throw up automatically, and soon I ate barely enough to sustain myself, as I couldn't see the point.

After working at the cherry factory for a week or so, I developed a crush on a young guy named Bruce. He was blond and blue-eyed and liked me, too, and I started to cheat on Harvey with him. I told Bruce only a little about Harvey; I certainly didn't tell him we were still together. I just told him that Harvey was still sort of in the picture because he wouldn't let go. Plain and simple, I lied to Bruce because I didn't want him to lose interest in me, but I felt guilty, so I decided to break up with Harvey for once and for all. We parted ways, or so I thought. In reality, he was spying on me and had been spying on me all along, as he'd suspected I was interested in someone else. I was none the wiser to this. After breaking up with him, I thought he went his way and I went mine. It consequently didn't take him long to catch me with Bruce, since I saw him as often as I could.

To make a long story short, my brother Rod led Harvey right to us. What a traitor he always was. As usual the master troublemaker, he made as much trouble for me as he possibly could. They walked in on us while Bruce and I were having sex, and Harvey took one look and began beating the hell out of Bruce. He kicked him in the head over and over again with his hard-soled shoes, making a dull thud each time he kicked him, and when I finally got him to stop, he slapped my face and called me a whore.

My brother looked at me and said, "You're not my sister anymore." What a creep he was. Then Bruce's mom got involved and wanted us to file a complaint against Harvey. We went to the police station and told them what had happened, but they wouldn't process the assault because of the circumstances. I was furious. It wasn't Bruce's fault Harvey couldn't get a grip on our breakup, and I was seriously traumatized by this entire situation. Bruce didn't deserve this, and he was noticeably beaten and bruised, with two black eyes, knots all over his head, cut lips, a broken tooth, and a swollen face.

Needless to say, Bruce couldn't distance himself from me fast enough, and I never saw him again. I felt sad about that, but mostly I felt ashamed. I had acted totally selfishly when I was seeing Bruce; I'd thought only of what I wanted. I'd wanted to see him so badly that I'd put him at risk, and I knew that in his mother's eyes, I was a common slut. Frankly, I agreed with her. Even though I hadn't known Harvey would go to this extreme, I should have guessed he'd do something, as he'd been violent in the past when drinking. I knew he would be out getting drunk after I broke up with him, which would make him unpredictable, and I hadn't been brave enough to break up with him until I had somebody else to lean on. I had a lot to be ashamed of in my own eyes.

I ran into Mom someplace back then, and she must have had a human moment at the sight of me. I must have looked horrible, so thin and with my face swollen from an abscessed tooth. She had moved into a new trailer in Traverse City, and she asked me to come stay with her. I didn't really want to because of her unpredictable behavior, but she kept coming around and then told me she would get me to a dentist and help me get back on the road to good health. I think at first she thought I'd been beaten up, though after she saw the inside of my mouth, she believed me.

I was nineteen and floundering, but she was the last person I ever would have admitted this to. After she'd thrown me out the last time and I'd ended up selling my horse, I didn't want her to ever again think I needed her. Plus, I didn't trust her. I didn't want to lose the place I'd shared with Harvey, but I was in a lot of pain. I also thought that maybe she was a little jealous because I was thin and she wasn't. She finally convinced me this was the right thing to do, so I moved in with her. At the time, Roger was back living with her, too. I guess inside my innermost being, I felt like maybe she loved me after all, but I never would have shown her that side of me. That would have been like bellying up so she could go for the kill.

I found a dentist who did some wonderful work on my tooth, and then I went to my dad again and asked if I could have a job at his bar. He put me to work as a waitress at first and then as a bartender. Initially I caught rides with whoever would take me to and from work, and then I started riding home with one of the band members. He was twenty years older than me and married. He became my steady ride, and we often stopped and had sex on some two-track road before he took me home. I didn't really care about the wife or kids he had at home; I needed the ride, and that was all I cared about, though I know now that was pretty awful of me.

After saving some money, I began actively looking for a car. I planned to ask Dad for the money I didn't yet have, knowing I would be able to work off what I owed him, but things weren't going to go as smoothly as I'd thought. One night when I got home from work, Mom was waiting up for me. She came flying out of her bedroom and shoved me into the wall and spitefully told me, "I never wanted you; you were a mistake." Then she added, "I hate you, I hate you, I hate you!" This went on for what seemed to be an eternity, and she was so loud that she woke up Roger, who came out and said, "Leave her alone, Mom."

It was hard to get away from her, but I left her home that night. I didn't know then what had inspired her anger, but I later learned she'd been stewing over me staying at her house while working for Dad. She felt like this was some kind of betrayal on my part, but as far as I was concerned, the only person being betrayed was me. I was betraying myself by continuing to go back to Mom and Dad, thinking that maybe someday those ogres would become human. By the same token, I don't know what other options I could have explored. There were no women's resource centers back then or halfway houses or safe houses. I wouldn't have known where to begin looking for help.

I have to give myself some credit, though. Through all my fumbling, stumbling, and falling, I kept learning, and each time I fell, I got just a little stronger. But I wasn't quite ready to give up on the fantasy that my parents had a human side to them, and I had incredible sadness inside myself. I didn't understand that I needed help to start feeling differently than I did. I stayed with friends occasionally, but mostly I found myself staying here, there, and everywhere. Eventually I found a rental efficiency cabin to live in.

Making matters worse, I was "looking for love in all the wrong places," as the song says. I grew up in the free love generation, so I thought sleeping around was going to help. I did that for a while, but the only thing I felt afterward was empty and alone, just like before I climbed in bed with the guy. There was just a whole lot of nothingness that came with sleeping around. Instead of feeling better, I felt worse, and I didn't want to be that kind of girl. I wanted to be somebody's special girl, and here I was sabotaging myself. I most certainly didn't want people talking about me like I was some kind of a slut, even though to all appearances I was. That was something my dad had always called me, and I didn't want him to ever have the satisfaction of being right.

I needed to start changing my life, and after a brief time had passed, I decided to stop the slut behavior first. When I did this, I felt better about myself, but I wasn't quite there because there was an even bigger issue I needed to face before I could move on. Of course, that was to confront my drinking, but I didn't yet think I had a serious problem, nor could anyone have convinced me that

I did. Young people couldn't be alcoholics, could they? I was maintaining my job, so I couldn't have that problem, could I?

I wish I'd known more about alcoholism then. It would have given me a big push in the right direction. Maybe having better quality friends would have helped, too, but instead I wallowed with some of the worst of the worst and kept the drinking part of me intact. I felt I needed to fit in with the people I hung around with. I didn't think anybody "nice" would like me, and I felt unworthy to be around nice people. I guess I just had to keep going to that school of hard knocks a while longer. I was obviously trying for a master's degree, and I didn't really have anybody to support me in this area. Everybody I knew was drinking or doing drugs or both. I even let Susan back into my life at this time. When she came to me and apologized for making me leave her mom's house, I forgave her. I should have known better, but I was obviously confused about people and about life.

Chapter 5

*Marriage and Motherhood
and the Mistakes Multiply*

Because I'd had to borrow money from my dad to buy another car, I was still working for him at the bar. As unwholesome an environment as this may have been, it became like a home to me. I made some friends there, and I enjoyed some of the regular customers who came in night after night. Even better, I seldom had to see Dad, because he came in only after closing to count his money and help clean up.

One night at work, I was introduced to a very handsome young man named Jack by one of my coworkers whose husband was his friend. Jack was from Texas, so I naturally assumed he was a cowboy. Wasn't everybody from Texas? Since I'd always had a fixation on cowboys and Indians, I became mesmerized by him and his beautiful blue eyes. He was also very taken with me. He was a tough guy who seemed shy and polite, even tongue-tied around me, and I'd never had any man this good looking interested in me before.

Jack and I started dating right away and continued to date for several months. I was nineteen years old and until now had felt I had no direction. Since I was still homeless, it seemed only natural for us to get a place together, but I soon found out that Jack wasn't very smart. In fact, he was almost totally illiterate. Although this would have been a warning to the average person, it wasn't to me. It awakened only compassion in me, as I felt sorry for all underdogs. I should have looked a little deeper at Jack, but all I knew at the time was that he seemed to like me an awful lot, which made me feel good. He was the first guy who pursued me aggressively, but he wasn't really after sex; he just wanted to be with me. Having somebody want to be with me just because he liked me was wonderful, a first in my life, and I was flattered, especially because he was so handsome. All the girls used to look at him, and I was so caught up in the fantasy of it all I never bothered to look at the reality. After my whole life of being rejected, this was a glimmering moment to me.

He took me to dinner one night and presented me with a beautiful card. Inside he had written, "I Luv u mor thin emybobby Ronnine." Then he asked me to marry him. This had never happened to me before, and I said "Yes" without thinking it over. That he'd tried so hard to write something nice touched my heart. I wasn't in love with him, nor did it occur to me that I was supposed to be. I felt sorry for him, because you can't fault a guy for not knowing how to read or write. I just knew my life would magically become wonderful with Jack, just like in the fairy tales. We would get married, move to Texas away from all my sadness and misery, and live happily ever after. After all, there was nothing holding me in Traverse City.

We started planning for our wedding right away. We picked out rings together, and Jack put half the money down, with a line of credit for the balance. My engagement ring was stunning, and I showed it off to everybody. I felt like I needed to let the whole world know I wasn't a loser after all. I wanted to convince myself that I wasn't a loser. We picked a date in mid-April so we could move to Texas before it got too hot.

Valentine's Day came, and Jack brought home another card for me. He couldn't wait for me to read it out loud. I looked at the card, and it was to a "Niece." This was the first time he'd asked me to read something out loud, and I panicked as I skimmed over the words. I would have to completely change the wording or his feelings would be hurt. After I'd "read" it to him, he looked at me with a delighted smile and said, "Read it again, Rhonnie. Read it again."

I didn't know what to do. I knew I could never remember all that I'd just made up, so I just kissed him and told him to let me have this moment and I would read it to him later. When he wasn't looking, I quickly hid the card for fear he would make me read it again.

One night he picked me up after work with a really big smile on his face. I asked him what the smile was for, and he told me to look at how clean and bright his teeth were. I looked and complimented him and asked his secret. With all the pride he could muster, he said, "I have a secret ingredient to make them this white, and it's using Comet cleanser." I couldn't believe what he'd said. I didn't want to hurt his feelings, but I had to tell him this wasn't good for his teeth. Just what could you do with a guy like this? Though my head was beginning to tell me to run from him, my heart melted for his weaknesses. Under normal circumstances, I might have noticed all the red flags, but my life was anything but normal, so his being illiterate and brushing his teeth with Comet and even his choice of rough friends didn't seem to be warning signs. I just thought he was a guy who, like me, needed a chance to prove himself.

Jack's father lived in the area, and he liked me a lot. He liked me so well he told me I could buy his pickup truck and take over his payments. I liked Jack's stepmother, too, and the feeling was mutual. I felt like I was fitting in with that family, something that was very important to me. Jack's dad was also a tough guy with a big heart and in his day could handle most physical confrontations with other men with one hand tied behind his back. When Jack talked about his dad, you could tell how proud he was of him.

Of course, my mother hated Jack's guts, but this made me only more determined to marry him. She didn't have to worry about it costing her anything; Jack and I were paying for it. Jack worked on the oil rigs as a roughneck, which is where a lot of tough guys worked. Since my mother had a long history of going out of her way to make my life miserable, I figured Jack was just another person for her to pick on. She even told me she'd hired somebody to investigate him. As far as I was concerned, here she was, trying to tell me what I should be doing with my life, when she'd made a huge mess of her own and her kids' lives. She'd lived with the biggest pedophile in the universe, and she was having *Jack* investigated?

In my head, I knew something was wrong with Jack, though I didn't know what it was or to what extent, but my heart wouldn't let me see it. I thought he really loved me, as he was the one who had chased me. He would have fought any army that attacked me; he would have stood up to any danger for me, and I mistook all this for love. What did I know at age nineteen? Up until now, I'd never experienced love, and it felt pretty good to have someone on my side. It was the first time I knew somebody would defend me against my enemies, or so I thought at the time.

We were married on April 12, 1975. It was a big church wedding with a minister, the type of wedding all little girls dream about. I wore a beautiful white dress with a long train and beautiful veil, I carried flowers, and my father even walked me down the aisle. But as I was getting dressed in the church dressing room, I sneaked out to peak at who had come. Everyone was there, all my aunts, uncles, friends, and family, including my sister Jackie, waiting for the blushing bride to walk down the aisle.

Everything was going as planned, except that I was having second thoughts about marrying Jack. The night before, to my amazement, I'd pulled him out of another woman's bedroom when I'd gone to pick him up from his bachelor party. This really surprised me, as sex was not a high priority for Jack. In fact, I would have said it was low on his list of priorities.

I tried telling my maid of honor and my younger sister, but I didn't know what to say. Then I'd looked around and realized I'd chosen Susan of all people to be my maid of honor. Although she'd apologized for making me leave her mom's, I was still in shock that I had so few friends that I'd resorted to her. I suddenly felt panicked, but I was overwhelmed with the feeling that I couldn't let everybody down at this point.

When my dad came to walk me down the aisle, I told him, "Dad, I don't want to do this anymore; I don't want to get married to Jack." With that he looked at me and said, "Too late for that now." He put his arm in mine and down the aisle we went. I cried the whole way, though not with tears of joy or happiness. They were tears of sadness and regret. I had to do this, didn't I? I couldn't just waste everybody's day or even the expense of the wedding and reception to follow. It was horrible feeling I was trapped into marrying Jack, and even though all I really had to do was say "No," I just couldn't admit that I was wrong about this guy. I couldn't admit it even to myself. I felt like I would be letting everyone down if I didn't marry him. It was obvious how my dad felt; how could I have known the others didn't feel the same way? I knew I was making a mistake, but I felt that not following through would be just another failure on my part. After all, I had bragged about Jack to everybody, had showed off my ring, and God forbid that my mother was right about him. I was in a dilemma, and I was simply torn as I walked down that aisle.

That was all I thought of during the entire ceremony. I don't remember anything the minister said, but I do know that when it came time to say "I do," I said it, and so did Jack. However, I knew inside that I had let myself down and done something I shouldn't have done, and I couldn't even look at Jack. I noticed that his stepmother was present, but his dad was nowhere in sight. Later that night, at the wedding reception, my new father-in-law appeared to have a dance with me, and I asked why he hadn't come to the wedding. He looked at me and said, "I couldn't stand to see somebody I care about so much make the biggest mistake of her life." I certainly wish he'd said something about this to me earlier in our relationship, but maybe he was hoping I would make a difference in his son's life. My worry increased, but with the wedding over, I lay down on the bed in our motel room and fell into an exhausted sleep.

The next day, we started getting ready to move to Texas. I had barely even been downstate, and now I was moving thousands of miles away. At least we were going to a little town on an island just off the coast to help his grandparents run their motel. I was a small-town girl, so this appealed to me, and I began again to anticipate that part of my life where the "happily ever after" would begin, in spite of catching Jack cheating on me the night before our wedding.

It was a long drive to Texas, and we were on a shoestring budget, but I was finally leaving my old life behind. We had the money we'd been given at our wedding, but that needed to last until we were settled in Jack's grandparents' motel. We were planning to stop in Fort Worth and visit his mom for a day or so before heading to the coast, and we arrived in Fort Worth at about 3:00 a.m. Before taking me to his mom's, Jack drove through the part of the city he used to hang out in and immediately recognized someone and flagged him down. The man's name was Jimmy, and when Jack introduced me as his wife, this man became extremely agitated. He started acting like a jealous lover and even stuck his head in the window when he heard my name to see if I was male or female. This was when I began to realize that I would not be able to run away from my past, and it was obvious that Jack wouldn't be able to, either.

As it turned out, Jimmy was gay. Jack explained how he knew him, from hanging out on the streets himself, and he told me Jimmy worked the streets as a male prostitute. I listened carefully when they talked, and it sounded like Jack had worked those streets, too. It also sounded like they'd had some sort of relationship, and I started to feel there were even bigger problems brewing with Jack and me than I'd realized. It was at this point that I started to realize that I didn't really know Jack. This was certainly not a side he would have shown to his tough guy friends in Traverse City, nor had any of his friends ever talked to me about this side of him.

Nothing improved when we got to his mom's house. She answered the door and didn't acknowledge me at all. Instead, she fussed over Jack. It was obvious her oversight was purposeful, and I found her sickening. Completely drunk at this hour, she began slobbering all over him. Then she looked at me and patted Jack's stomach and said, "You're getting awfully skinny, Jackie. Isn't that new wife of yours taking good enough care of my baby?"

I could barely stand her behavior, and I couldn't wait to leave. That old anxious feeling was twisting my stomach again, and though I wanted to believe Jack didn't have any gay tendencies, my gut feeling was that he did. For one thing, we didn't really have sex very much. In fact, we barely ever had sex. He just didn't seem turned on by me that way. Until now, I'd just blown off his difficulty getting an erection as an unfortunate abnormality, but now the picture was unfolding before my very eyes. His problems were deeper than I'd thought, and after meeting his mother, I could more clearly see why he might be so messed up. After all, he and his siblings had been left in Texas with her when his father had moved to Traverse City.

We left Fort Worth early and finally arrived at our destination in the wee hours of the following morning. Jack wanted to take the ferry to the island, so we slept in the truck until the sun came up, when we could cross. When the ferry started moving, dolphins swam alongside the boat. They were beautiful, jumping in and out of the water next to the ferry. For the time being, the excitement made me forget all that had happened so far. Traverse City was behind me, the night before the wedding was behind me, my parents were behind me, and Fort Worth, Jimmy, and Jack's mother were behind me. My new life was about to begin.

Jack's grandparents were two of the nicest people I had ever met, but it soon became apparent that they were surprised to see us, to say the least. In retrospect, it's obvious they had no idea we were coming to stay with them, but nevertheless they were kind and hospitable. Once they realized we were staying, they showed us to our bedroom, and then we went back outside to begin unloading the pick-up truck. Outside the house, Jack unexpectedly slapped me hard across the face and said, "There, now try to run home to your mother from here." The slap was out of the clear blue and for no reason that I could see. I was in shock from him doing this more than from the stinging pain of the slap. More than in shock I was stunned. I had no idea he was capable of hitting me. In tears, I asked why he had just slapped me like that, and he informed me he was now in control of my life.

Somehow I knew that was true, and I felt completely helpless, trapped in another nightmare that was beginning to unfold. Sure enough, this was the beginning of a downward spiral that would accelerate in a fast and furious manner. That first slap was one of many to come and unexpected slaps soon became a regular part of Jack's daily routine. They were always out of the blue, and he never did it in front of anybody. They were secret slaps, hidden from his grandparents and all who knew him, but they soon escalated to a higher form of hitting with his fist, though once again never where anyone could see the marks.

Jack told me I would never be able to get away from him, and he made it very clear there was no place in this world I would ever be able to hide that he couldn't find me. He also told me that I was worth $2,000.00 to him. He told me Dad had promised him the money if he took me away and didn't bring me back. Though I wanted desperately to get away from him, there was no one I could ask for help. My older brother had joined the military, my sister was just barely getting by, and I would rather have eaten dirt than ask my mother for money, as this would have been something she would have thrown in my face the rest of my life.

The only nice thing about this time was getting to know Jack's grandma. She was very nice to me, and though she'd had a hard life, she was kind and caring. I cleaned all the cabins for her, as well as their house, and she was very appreciative. She must have known how awful her grandson was, but she was eighty-six years old and had her hands full with her own husband. Grandpa, who was affectionately called "Snippy," seemed to really like me, but I could tell he'd been a real stinker in his day. Gramma had her hands full with him even now. He had a heart condition but still drank and smoked, and I think he had a crush on me. He gave me a necklace with a starfish on it and told me not tell Grandma. I would never have wanted to hurt her feelings, so I didn't. I could almost see the life Gramma had with him and why her own daughter, Jack's mother, had ended up such a drunk.

After my work was done in the early morning, Grandma and I usually went fishing. She was interesting to talk to, and I learned just how the family had become so messed up. She and Grandpa had owned a traveling carnival, and all their children and grandchildren had traveled with them, and these kids had all learned to con people out of their money early in life. There had been no schooling to speak of, and they'd never stayed in one place more than a week. Jack had gone to school only up to the sixth grade, and because the carnival had traveled from town to town, even this schooling was not monitored. Grandma and Grandpa had finally sold the carnival when they'd become too old to run it. Learning all this and realizing I'd married a "carnie" was embarrassing to me.

In the afternoons, I often walked down to the beach alone. Grandpa and Jack ran a super slide just up the road, and this gave me extra time to myself. I adored the beach. It was very peaceful, and I loved the sound of the waves and the salty sea air. I could have lived there forever, though not with Jack. We stayed for three months, and other than the abuse from Jack, I have to say I enjoyed it. Abuse had always been part of my life, and since my father's abuse had been far worse than what Jack was doing, it almost made his abuse tolerable.

Out of the blue one morning, Jack decided we were leaving. I wanted to return to Michigan, but the chance of that was slim as he had his sights set on collecting the $2,000.00 reward from my dad. We went on a long tour of Texas, and slept in the truck and borrowed money from his friends here and there. Eventually, we turned back to Fort Worth, where he headed straight to his mother's house. I'd hoped to never see her again, but we soon got our own apartment, and Jack took a job managing the place in exchange for our rent. It didn't seem like a good part of the city, and I was scared there.

We'd come back to Fort Worth for business reasons. Somehow, Jack and a woman we knew from Traverse City named Nancy had struck up a deal, and she was flying down to become a professional prostitute. Indeed, it was her life's ambition to do this. Jack was going to pick her up at the airport and take her to a man named James that he knew. He said James, a big pimp in Texas and Oklahoma, would pay him a finder's fee commission for her.

I couldn't believe my ears. I really didn't know this man. Jack then told me that his own sister Janeen used to work for James. I knew Janeen; she used to live in Traverse City and had even worked at my dad's bar, which is where I'd met her. To guess that Janeen had been a prostitute was a real stretch of the imagination as she was not in the least attractive, but now it all made sense. Back when I knew her, she used to ask me if I wanted to move to Oklahoma. She told me she used to work at a massage parlor where she made at least $35.00 per hour. Being the stupid small-town girl I was, I was almost tempted, but I kept telling her I didn't have the foggiest idea how to give a massage. She told me this was okay, that even during your training period, you made at least $15.00 an hour. She said it would be fun and that in no time I would be making a lot of money.

This was back in 1975, so you can imagine that $35.00 an hour was an outrageous sum of money. Janeen always told me not to tell Jack, as he would be mad at her for asking me to move away. Now I knew the real reason he would have been mad. She was soliciting me to prostitute with her, and I still can't believe I was so stupid I didn't figure it out.

As arranged, Jack picked up Nancy at the airport and brought her to our apartment, and then we all got ready to meet James at a club called the Godfather's Club. All Jack could think about was his finder's fee, which was $1,000.00. I soon realized this wasn't the first time Jack had found James girls to work for him, as Jack seemed to know the ropes and just how to contact a guy like James.

When we got to the club, James looked around and smiled at me and, with an ear-to-ear grin, told Jack he would gladly pay the fee. Jack wasn't quick enough to realize that James thought I was Nancy. I finally got Jack's attention and told him, and Jack quickly introduced me as his wife. To my surprise, I found James very pleasant to talk to. You would never have guessed he was a pimp upon meeting him, for he was well mannered and kept his cool. His wife, on the other hand, was pretty scary. She was in charge of the girls and kept them in line, and James had met her when she was released from prison for killing her husband.

That I wasn't Nancy was the deal breaker with James. Nancy was older and not that pretty. She looked rough and had the look of a woman who had been around the block a few too many times. She was sleazy looking, like most prostitutes, while I was fresh, young, and pretty. James said he would put Nancy to work, but she wasn't worth a finder's fee. He told Jack he would only pay him some sort of commission off what she made. This didn't make Jack happy, but there was nothing he could do. James was a powerful man, and Jack respected him. He knew better than to try to stand up to him or even try to put anything over on him.

However, James wanted something from Jack: his help finding Janeen. Last James had heard, she'd moved to Oklahoma and was working for another pimp, and James said she owed him something. I didn't want to know what that was all about, although I figured she'd somehow ripped him off. I didn't want to go to Oklahoma either, but Jack told James we would be ready to move tomorrow. I couldn't believe Jack was going to hunt down his sister for a man who was obviously angry at her. Though I'd briefly felt amused by the whole idea of James being a pimp, I was becoming increasingly concerned.

We got to Oklahoma City the next evening, and the following morning James found us a house to live in. When we arrived at this house, it looked as though the people who had been living there had left in a hurry, as their things were strewn about like they were trying to get out of there quickly. Then we started looking for

Janeen, and Jack knew just where to go: massage parlors. He obtained a lot of information from the prostitutes there once they knew he was Janeen's brother. Janeen was hiding from James, and they were protecting her, never figuring her own brother would be working behind her back.

One thing led to another, and we finally found her at an Army base about eighty miles away. We arrived on a Friday night, and, driving through town, Jack saw her standing on a street corner. We stopped, and she quickly gave us a key to the motel she was staying at and said, "Go on now, you're messing up my business here." We got to the motel room where she lived, and there was her two-year-old son, Michael, there all by himself. I was aghast. I was disgusted anyway, but to leave a child alone was unforgivable.

Janeen got to the motel three or four hours later. I asked how she could have left Michael alone like that, and she said she never left him too long, but Friday night was a big night for her to make money. Then she told Jack he should work the "queer" corner on Friday nights. Jack got mad at her and told her to be quiet and to quit talking like that in front of me. He really thought he was sneaky enough to have fooled me; I guess he had no idea I'd already figured it all out. He never let on that James was looking for her, and we soon left and went back to Oklahoma City so he could report to James.

James soon paid us a visit in Oklahoma, and one night I told him I didn't like Jack or the way he treated me. Jack's beatings were getting out of control, and I just wanted to leave him and go home. Maybe he was still dreaming about the money he thought Dad was going to give him, but he tried his best to control me by hitting me and threatening me, and the lifestyle he was caught up in was not for me. Living this way was a nightmare, and I still couldn't believe it was unfolding right in front of me like some sordid movie. I didn't like the people I met, though strangely enough I did like James. He was a good pimp, and he knew how to be charming in all ways. He wasn't like the pimps you saw on television. He was a white man and looked like a cowboy. He had a gentle demeanor and was soft spoken and articulate. He just wasn't what I expected a pimp to look or act like. He was always polite to me, even though he didn't have to be. From what I could see, he didn't care for Jack or for the prostitutes who worked for him.

The next morning, James said to me, "You don't belong here. You need to go home; you don't belong in this group of people." He reached in his pocket and gave me money to go home with. He told me it was really nice to meet me and wished me luck in the future.

With that, I told Jack I was going home. What could he say? I told him in front of James, but later that day, after James left, he told me I would never get away from him as long as I lived and that I would not be leaving without him. He told me he would drive back to Michigan with me, but before we left, he needed to see Janeen one more time.

I was afraid of Jack by then and of his ruthless, reckless lifestyle. This was a man who had no loyalties to anyone in the world other than himself. He sold his own sister out to a man who intended to somehow hurt her, and he convinced me that I would never get away from him. I knew he would be able to find me no matter what, as he went into a city he'd never been to and found his sister within two days' time. My fear of him controlled me, and I figured that if I were at least where I knew people, I might be a little safer. Even though my world had always been distorted, meeting Jack was the icing on the dysfunctional cake. I didn't argue with him at all when he told me was driving me back to Traverse City. I was mentally exhausted and thoroughly frightened and confused.

When she learned we were heading to Michigan, Janeen asked us to take Michael with us and said she would soon follow. I didn't want to take her son with us, but she begged and pleaded, so Jack finally agreed. I had other plans once we got to Traverse City. I wanted to find a way to leave Jack, and I was afraid taking this little boy was going to mess up my plans, but I decided I could handle it for the two weeks until she arrived. Plus, I certainly did feel sorry for that little boy.

As if returning to Michigan with Jack and facing my family again weren't bad enough, Janeen never came for her son. She was a big liar who had no interest in the child, and I didn't know what to do with him. He was a sweet little boy, but I was in no position to give him the care he needed. There was no way I was going to let on to my family that things weren't working out with Jack, but we were completely broke and had no home, so when we got back to town, we immediately moved in with friends of Jack's. That environment wasn't a good one, and Jack wasn't getting any nicer. He was now brave enough to hit me in public as well as in visible places on my body, but the couple we stayed with never said a word about Jack or his behavior. Looking back, they probably thought such behavior was normal.

Once we got on our feet and Jack started working again, we rented a little cabin for the winter. Even though he was working, Jack wouldn't help make the truck payments I owed his dad, so one day I drove that truck to his father and told him he needed to take it back. Otherwise, Jack would continue to rip him off. Jack left me shortly after we moved into the cabin and told me to stay there until he decided whether he wanted to stay married to me. As soon as he left, I packed up my bags and Michael, swallowed my pride, and went to my mother's for safety.

Once there, I began slowly losing my mind, wondering what Jack was going to do, and one night I decided I needed to get out. Amazingly enough, my mom liked Michael and agreed to watch him for me. While I was out, I ran into my old boyfriend Harvey who was out with his brother and his wife, and they asked if I would like to have dinner with them. It was late, but I decided to go. While we were eating, my brother Rod walked in. He took one look at us, turned and left, and returned a short time later with Jack. This was the second time Rod had made trouble for me, and even today it is hard for me to accept that he had no loyalties to his sister whatsoever.

Jack started to beat up a cousin of Harvey's who was sitting with us, and my brother began screaming at me, calling me a whore. I was so embarrassed; I wanted to cry. The police came and told Jack he had to leave, but he sat in his car right out the window and beeped his horn at us and gave us the finger. He had an insane look on his face that I'll never forget, and we sneaked out the back door of the restaurant. I was apprehensive about going to my mother's for fear of facing Jack in his rage, but he didn't know where Harvey's brother lived, so I decided to hide there. Somehow he found out where I was, and pretty soon I heard his car coming down the road. He made the corner, but he must have been going too fast, and we heard what sounded like his tires blowing out. Then there was no noise. It was very quiet, so I went to the unfinished house next door and hid there for the night. The next morning I was sick, from what I thought were nerves. I was throwing up and shaky, and Harvey's brother gave me a ride to Mom's. I told her Jack was on a rampage, and when I called to try and talk to him, he told me he would speak to me only at our place.

Michael and I went home to face the music. When I walked in, he laughed at me, but I knew better than to misinterpret this. He then walked over and beat the living daylights out of me in front of Michael and said, "When I tell you to stay home and wait until I decide if I want to be married to you or not, your ass better be staying here at home. If I'm gone for a year, you'd better not leave this house, or I'll kill you next time." I knew he meant just that, and I apologized to him to get him to stop hitting me.

Not long after this incident, he got a job working on the oil rigs outside of town. I liked him being gone; it gave me moments of peace when I could just sit and pretend my life was okay. One time he came home injured after a chain wrapped itself around his leg. Usually when this type of accident occurred, the person was killed, and I guess it was the devil who spared Jack's life that day. He was always a great warrior for the devil, but I hated him for surviving this accident. Finally, I thought I was getting a lucky break when I learned his whole crew was being relocated to Wyoming. I hoped he would take the offer and move to another state, and I prayed I would get to stay behind.

I'd been throwing up a lot since the incident at the restaurant, and the doctors couldn't figure out what was wrong. They'd run a pregnancy test, but it was negative. I was still having my periods, so I knew I wasn't pregnant. Besides, in my opinion, a pregnancy would have been next to impossible. We'd had sex only a total of five or six times our whole marriage. The last time had been several months earlier, and it was after a beating. I was now on medication to settle my stomach and nerves, but I was afraid of what might be wrong with me. It sure felt like something was wrong, and I was worried.

Jack's crew took the Wyoming job offer, and all the men caravanned out there while the wives stayed behind until they settled in. Michael and I gave up the cabin we lived in, and I moved in with one of the other wives. I was still so sick that my nerves were trashed, and one day I fell down a flight of steps and started to bleed profusely from my vagina. I went to the doctor once again, and he ran another pregnancy test, which again was negative, and then he gave me something even stronger for my nerves. He told me he thought I'd been pregnant all along and that, when I fell, I'd lost the baby. He assured me that many women lose babies early in their pregnancies without even knowing it. He said that even though I hadn't tested positive, it was probably just too early to detect the pregnancy and my sickness was probably just the residual effect left over from that. Reassured, I took the strong medicine to help settle my stomach and the pills to settle my nerves, but I didn't get better. Instead, I began to feel even worse, and soon I was afraid I had some sort of disease. I was lightheaded and dizzy all the time, and I lost my equilibrium. It was hard to play surrogate mom to Michael, but I did the best I could.

Jack and the crew had been gone about a month when Jack called from Wyoming and told me to buy a plane ticket and get out there. I wasn't well enough to fly, but Jack made his usual threats, so I finally bought the tickets with the money he sent, and Michael and I flew out. Jack was still living in a motel room, and when I got off the plane, I had to go straight there to lie down. I was too sick to get up for days, and Jack, who couldn't have cared less about me, was concerned enough to make me a doctor's appointment. I looked awful and had lost so much weight I was thinner than when I used to not eat. Nothing would stay down, and I was getting weaker and weaker.

The doctor I saw was really nice. I told him I'd been having this problem for several months and that I was getting worse, not better. I told him the treatment I'd been on, and he suggested we run another pregnancy test to make sure I wasn't pregnant before he gave me an even stronger prescription. The long and the short of it was that I was pregnant and had been all along. I wasn't at all happy about this news, and I left the doctor's office with a blank stare. I was reluctant to tell Jack, and when I finally mustered up the nerve to let him know I was pregnant, he flew out of the car and ran around telling everyone he knew. He seemed happy, and I wished I could have shared the moment with him, but I knew he was the wrong man to have a baby with. I knew I didn't want to be connected to him forever, and I felt this pregnancy was dooming me.

That same night, Jack decided we should have a party to celebrate the good news. All the wives had joined up with their husbands by then, and the party was at one of the other worker's apartments. The men started playing poker, and I was soon glad I'd hid some of Jack's money. I'd heard the men talking about how much they'd been gambling before their wives had arrived, and I'd felt I needed to have some money stashed away for my own safety.

Sure enough, Jack soon started gambling, and I finally asked him to please stop before our money was all gone. He told me to come outside with him, and we went to the parking lot three flights down, and Jack then grabbed my head and started beating it on the windshield of a car. He cracked the glass he hit it so hard with my head, and I begged him to stop before he killed the baby. He told me he could beat my head all night long and never kill my baby. When he finished, he said, "Get your sorry ass back up to our apartment and stay there; don't you ever embarrass me again in front of my friends like that!"

This was terribly traumatic and far too reminiscent of my childhood beatings. I couldn't make him stop, although I begged and pleaded, and I was sick, weak, and helpless in the face of his cruelty. I managed to get back to the apartment and throw my clothes in a suitcase, and then I called the two guys from Illinois who worked with Jack. They were nice men who didn't quite fit in with the rest of the group, and somehow I knew they would help me. I told them what had happened, and they came right over to get me. Michael was with Jack at the poker party since there were other kids there to play with, so for once I didn't have to worry about him. I knew I had to flee to save my own life, and I was sure the other women would see to it that Michael was taken care of.

Those two sweet guys took me to their apartment across town and let me sleep on their couch and made all my arrangements at the bus station. The next morning, I started my long journey home. I had set aside $100.00 in case of an emergency such as this, and my ticket cost $87.00, which meant I had $13.00 left for the whole four-day trip. I wasn't looking forward to the long ride. I didn't see my face until the bus made its first stop and I used the restroom, and I was shocked when I looked into the mirror. No wonder everybody looked at me like I was some sort of freak. I looked like I had been beaten senseless, and my face hurt so much I couldn't even wash it. I was swollen and puffy and had started to turn black and blue, but I certainly was happy to get out of Wyoming and away from Jack.

I didn't tell my family I was back in town, nor did I want them to see me like this, but a few days after my return, my mother was in a serious car accident. I was staying with friends of Jack's, and the police found me, as they needed someone to come to the hospital and sign papers so she could have surgery. When I got there, she was still lying in the emergency room moaning and groaning. I quickly signed the papers for her and yelled for somebody to hurry up and help her. She looked like she was near death, and I sat at the hospital all night long. Other family members eventually showed up, and though I still looked gruesome from Jack's beating, not one member of my family said a word about it.

My emotions were very mixed. I didn't like my mom, but I didn't want her to die. From what I understood, she had run a red light while driving her Volkswagen Beetle and had hit a car broadside while at the same time she was hit broadside. She was lucky to be alive. The people I was staying with must have notified Jack, for he decided to come home and be with me through this tragedy. That was just what I didn't need, but at least I got to see Michael again, whom I had not been able to stop thinking about since I'd left Wyoming. Now that I had to deal with my family again, I decided this wasn't the time to make my break with Jack. Mom was in intensive care, and I sat outside her room all day for nearly three weeks until they moved her.

Jack, Michael, and I stayed at Mom's house while she was in the hospital, but when she came home, she refused to let us stay with her since she hated Jack so much. She also said she didn't want anything to do with me as long as I was with Jack, and at this point, I knew her reasons were legitimate. Of course, she didn't remember me staying at the hospital with her for the majority of the previous three weeks, and there was no way she could understand how awful my life was. Right now, all I wanted was to get through my pregnancy safely without losing the baby. I was in a no-win situation, and I couldn't even work, as I continued to be so sick all the time.

We had nowhere to go, so we went to a place where two other couples were living and rented one bedroom for the three of us. Jack was never too big on working regular jobs, and we didn't have much money, so we went without all the time. We could barely feed ourselves, much less a little boy, not to mention what he was put through living in that house. It was a party house, where everybody got high and drank all the time. This poor child didn't stand a chance in this world, and I was forbidden even to talk about getting him a home with a decent family.

It may not sound possible, but Jack was becoming an even bigger monster than before. One night, walking home from a party store, he suddenly started beating me until I fell to the ground in a parking lot close to home. Once I was on the ground, he started kicking me in the stomach over and over again, and I tried to ball myself up the best I could. I was terrified he would kill my baby, and he told me he wanted to kill the baby. I knew he was trying his best to do just that. The pain was unbearable, and then he kicked me in the head a few times with the pointed toes of his cowboy boots before he finally quit and walked on home, and left me on the ground as though I didn't exist.

For a long time I couldn't move I was in so much pain. I lay quietly until the pain subsided and I was able to gather enough strength to stand up and go home. That night as I lay in bed, I knew I had to put some wheels in motion to change my life. I was afraid I was going to die if things didn't change. The next morning, I got up and went to a phone and called Jack's dad and stepmom. I told them the situation with Michael and leveled with them about Jack. I told them Michael needed to move to a better place, that Jack was too violent and I knew he would cross the line eventually and start hurting Michael.

They were not surprised, and while they agreed Michael needed to be removed from our care, they were not in any position to take him. They told me they'd already had Michael one time before and that Janeen had come and taken him. I told them I would call a social worker, and then I learned that Janeen had given birth to another boy before Michael and that she'd abandoned him, too. She had taken him to his paternal grandparents' house in Texas so she could go grocery shopping and had never returned. Jack's parents agreed that the best thing for this little boy was to remove him from the family completely, as there was a chance his mother could come back and fight for custody of him from a family member.

I made the arrangements, but I didn't tell Jack beforehand, as I was afraid he would take Michael and run or, worse, beat me once again for disobeying him. When the social worker arrived, Jack tried to refute everything I said, but his dad cut him off and agreed with me. I told this person my hope was that they would find Michael a loving home to grow up in. They took Michael that day and promised to let me know if he was adopted. It was a bittersweet moment, but I knew in my heart I'd done the right thing. I never saw Michael again, but the social worker made good on her word and soon contacted me with the news that Michael had been adopted. The foster family who had taken him in had fallen in love with him, and I was happy for Michael and relieved that God had worked a miracle for him.

I managed to find a doctor to monitor my pregnancy from that point on, and he told me my measurements indicated I was now eight months pregnant. With Michael taken care of, I turned my attention to getting away from Jack. When my income tax check came, I bought a 1968 Firebird and secured a house trailer to rent. Jack, of course, moved in with me. Though it was going to be difficult to get him to leave without hurting me and possibly killing my baby, a wonderful thing had happened to me when I'd learned I was pregnant: I'd realized I wanted this baby.

That may not be a big revelation to most people, but it was to me. Drinking wasn't an option for me anymore and hadn't been throughout my whole pregnancy, as I was too sick, and I was down to smoking only three cigarettes a day. I had a whole different outlook on life, and I'm not sure it would have happened if I hadn't been pregnant. I was ready to take on motherhood and ready to do it without Jack. I just needed to devise a plan and somehow put it in action, but I knew he had to think it was his idea to leave me or he would rebel and treat me even worse.

Nobody gave me a baby shower, but a friend gathered up all the baby clothes she could find. Without her, I probably wouldn't have gotten much of anything. I bought a used baby bed and painted it. My due date was June 17, and I went into false labor on that day. The doctor was increasingly perplexed as time went on and I didn't have the baby. I was almost two months overdue when I finally went into labor for real. Jack drove me to the hospital, and somebody must have called my mom, as she was there, too.

Having a baby was quite an experience. I was in unbearable pain, as most women are during labor, and I hated it. I wanted it to stop, but they wouldn't give me anything to ease my pain. I was mean to the nurses who were telling me how to breathe, and they moved as far away from me as they could get, as I'm sure they thought I was going to strangle them. I couldn't believe anyone in their right mind would go through something as horrible as this just to have a baby.

As they were getting me ready in the delivery room, my doctor asked if a few students could observe the birth. I told him *"I don't care!"* I was so delirious with pain, I didn't care who was watching. I just wanted to get this over with fast. They took me to the delivery room and put my legs up, strapped them in an ungodly position I was sure wasn't at all natural, and there I was, with my legs spread wide open for all the world to see. All of a sudden, I saw eight or ten students staring at my crotch. I thought the doctor had meant one or two students, not a whole class. I was embarrassed at the time, but now it makes me happy to think the birth of my son was part of their learning process. My little boy was born at 2:20 p.m. on August 10, 1976, and he was the most beautiful human being I had ever laid eyes on. I just couldn't stand not to look at him, and I counted his little fingers and toes a hundred times over. I was amazed that I'd done this. Here was this perfect little human I had made inside myself.

It was at the moment they handed my son to me that life finally made sense. I realized that sex wasn't just something to do; there really was a purpose behind it. It was like a big light bulb went off in my head. The nurses kept coming into my room for my baby and I would wait only minutes before going out and getting him back. I would stare into his perfect little face, at his eyelashes, his little nose, his sweet little mouth, his little ears with fuzz on them, and his fingers and toes. I couldn't stop looking at him. This precious beautiful baby had completed all things in life for me, and I was in love for the first time in my life.

Two days after my baby was born, a woman came into my room to fill out the birth certificate. She asked what I was going to name my son, and I looked at her dumbfounded. I never once thought it was going to be a boy, so I'd never thought of a male name. Embarrassed, I told her that, but she insisted I give her a name right then. I was at such a loss, I named him Jack Andrew. I didn't really want to name my baby that, but my mind was completely blank. I then realized that Jack hadn't been to the hospital once since the baby was born, but I was too elated to feel depressed about him right now. I loved being a mommy and couldn't think of anything else.

Andy and I were soon released from the hospital, and we went home to our house trailer. He was only a few weeks old, and things were going along rather smoothly when the eruption occurred. My friend Susan was visiting, and Jack asked if she had change for a twenty. She told him she didn't. He told her fine and then started carrying big garbage bags of clothes out to the car. I asked, "What are you doing?"

He looked at me and said, "I'm leaving and taking the car. I'm going back to Texas." This was my car, the one I'd bought with my income tax check. Then he told me he was taking my money for rent and that he'd intended to leave me ten bucks, but Susan couldn't break his twenty.

I told him he couldn't take my rent money and that if he did, I would have no place to live. He looked at me and said, "I'll do what I want. Get money from your dad. When I leave, you'd better not run to the neighbors and call the cops on me, or I'll turn around and come back here and kill you."

With that, he left. I was penniless with a brand new baby and no car. I heard him get out on the main road, and I started to run to the neighbor's house to call the police, and then I heard his tires screech and the car turn around. I ran back into the house and took the baby and handed him to Susan and told her to run. She said, "He won't do anything to the baby."

I screamed at her to take Andy and run. I could see Jack coming down the road, and I was panicked. She was sure he wouldn't do anything to the baby, but I knew better. I pleaded with her, and she arrogantly kept telling me Jack wouldn't hurt the baby, as if she knew him better than I did. He came in the back door by kicking it open. As he walked through the kitchen with his eyes fixed on me, he took his right hand and threw the refrigerator to the floor. I again begged Susan to take the baby and run.

She looked at Jack and said, "Jack, don't hurt that baby!" He looked at her and pointed his finger in her face and said, "Shut up, bitch, or you'll be next." I knew at that moment that Jack and Susan had been sleeping together while I was in the hospital having my baby. She later denied it, but I could tell by how Jack talked to her and the way he pointed his finger at her as well as by her arrogant attitude. Sure enough, years later, a friend of mine confirmed that she'd caught them in the act at my home.

Jack grabbed me as I was holding my precious little boy and threw me. He came at me again and threw me from one side of the room to the next. I could only hope and pray that I would fall just right so as to not kill the baby. I took a beating while he was throwing us around like we were nothing. Each time I landed, I took the full force of the fall and held tight to my little boy. I was petrified at the thought that Jack might kill my precious little boy. I held tight to my son, but not so tight as to crush his little body, and I silently prayed to God to let me take the punishing blows but to please save my son. The beating seemed to go on forever, but he finally stopped and told me that if I dared tried to put him in jail, he would come back and finish the job. Then he left, with my money and my car.

I filed for divorce two days later. My baby was three weeks old, and I needed money to pay my rent and to get another car. I knew where I could get the money, even though it meant swallowing a lot of pride, and that was from my dad. Dad agreed to help me, as long as I came back to the bar and worked for him to pay him back. I had been afraid of this, and I didn't want to work there now; I wanted to be home with my son. Nonetheless, since I had no choice, I agreed to come back and work nights. I also went to the landlord and told him what had happened and asked if he would give me another month to get together the money I owed him, and he told me he would think about it.

I was determined to pull everything together, not only for my sake but also for little Andy's as well, and I had one more problem to deal with. Right before he'd left, Jack had rented out our spare room; he'd also taken that rent money with him when he'd left. Mike, the renter, was a devastatingly handsome man, and thankfully he was also very nice. He worked two jobs, so I didn't see him much, but when he was around, he was a complete gentleman.

Because he was very handsome, Susan had an enormous crush on him. One night she was visiting, and once I'd gotten Andy to sleep, I went to bed. The next morning she told me she'd gone into Mike's room and had climbed into bed with him. He'd told her he wasn't interested in her in the least and asked her to leave his room. I guess that's when I decided Mike had a little more class than most of the guys I'd ever met.

He was always a kind man. He never left the house without asking if I needed anything, and he used to rock Andy when he cried. He made a lot of dinners and would leave notes on the table letting me know there was food in the refrigerator for me. I worked nights, and when I got home, Andy would hear my car and wake up. I would feed and rock him until he fell back to sleep, and then I would go to bed. More times than not, when Andy cried at night after I was in bed, Mike would come in and get him, change his diaper, make a bottle for him, and rock him back to sleep. He did this often, as he knew I was tired and needed my rest. He never expected anything in return, though I'm sure he would have liked me to be his girlfriend.

One night he asked whether I would like to go dancing, and I didn't know what to say. I wanted to, but I was afraid he would know I was developing a crush on him. He finally managed to coax me into it, and when a slow song played, we danced a very dreamy dance. When it was over, he kissed me softly on the lips, and then we went home.

I didn't know how to handle a date that brought you home, and he lived there, too. It was very strange, but we both went off to our respective spaces. For two solid weeks after that, I hid in my room with my son. I couldn't face Mike. I was afraid he would look at me and see how fragile I really was. One day after he'd left for work, I got up to find a letter on the kitchen table. In it he asked me not to keep hiding in my bedroom when he was home. He told me I didn't have to feel so awkward and that staying in my room was making him feel awkward.

I mustered up my nerve to come out of my room that night, and he thanked me for not being so shy. Meanwhile, Susan was starting to come around again. She just couldn't take no for an answer. Mike finally told her she was the furthest person from his thoughts at that time and asked her to leave him alone. Once again, that made me respect him. The night he asked Susan to leave, he sat down on the couch and put his arm around me and told me he was really interested in getting to know me better. Once again, I was nervous. Though it didn't make sense, I always got nervous around nice guys and bolder around guys who were creeps, but at least from that point on, I knew where Mike stood.

We went out dancing one more time, and he kissed me again. This time I wasn't afraid like I'd been before, but I still didn't want to get involved. Mike was nice, but I was afraid of him. Nonetheless, something kept drawing me closer to him. There was something safe about him, and I knew he didn't judge me for my marriage to Jack.

One night after I put my son to sleep, I went into Mike's room and lay down next to him. He told me I didn't have to do anything I wasn't ready for, but I was lonely, and I wanted to feel close to somebody trustworthy. We slept together, and it was the first time in my life that somebody treated me sensationally. Mike was gentle and sweet, and he asked me in the morning to please not hide from him. He also told me there was no obligation for me to come to his room again.

I never did go back to his room with him. We hung out together when we were both home, but I knew that once Jack found out I'd filed for divorce, he would be back. I had a restraining order stating he was not to come within one hundred feet of me, that he was not to harass me in any way, and that he couldn't come to my place of employment, but I knew a piece of paper wouldn't stop him from doing what he wanted to do. Still, I felt pretty safe with him in Texas. I didn't have a phone, so he couldn't call and threaten me. As long as I knew he was gone, I could live my life safely, at least for now.

One night I came home from work, and the doors were locked. Mike's car was gone, and my key wouldn't work in the lock, so I went to my mother's house for the night. The next day I went back to my house trailer, and there on the shed was a note from the landlord. He had moved all our belongings into the shed and said that he'd waited long enough for his rent. I'd asked him to wait a month until I got on my feet, and I thought we'd had an agreement.

When I went back to my mother's house to use her phone to call him, he said he thought it best that I find another place to live. I explained that I had nothing lined up and had no other place to go. I told him I always paid my bills, but the circumstances surrounding this situation were different. He didn't want to hear about all that again and told me he had another family moving in. I didn't have the energy to fight him in court, even though I knew what he was doing was illegal. When I'd moved into the trailer, I'd paid him first and last month's rent. I guess that once the last month's rent was used up, he'd figured he was free to get rid of me.

I explained that I would have his rent when I got paid tomorrow, but it didn't matter to him, and I was given no other option but to move. I immediately found a three-bedroom trailer in the want ads, and when I went over to my old trailer to get my things, Mike was there. He asked whether he could move on with me, and I told him that would be fine. I felt safer with him around.

Shortly after we moved, I met a man at the bar named Raully whom I started seeing a little. He was more like the tough guys I was familiar with who drank and got high, and I felt safe with him. I felt I needed someone who could handle a mishap if and when Jack reappeared. Mike was just too nice to give me much comfort.

Mike finally asked whether I were serious about Raully, and I told him I didn't know how I felt. Talking about it wasn't as bad as I'd thought it would be, and that's when I learned that communication is a wonderful thing. It allowed Mike to let go of any idea he still had about us getting together. He tried really hard to explain how he felt about me, but I was too caught up in my own turmoil to understand what he was really saying. I just didn't recognize something good when it was right in my face. I told Mike I was feeling mixed up and that I needed to decide which direction to go. I told him I needed to get this divorce and Jack completely out of my life before I could consider anything permanent. I told him Jack was dangerous and that I didn't want to involve him in my conflict. I hated to use the old cliche about needing my own space, but at the time, it was only too accurate. Raising my son, working, and divorcing Jack seemed to be all I could deal with right then. I worked almost every night, sometimes ten to twelve nights in a row, and I was exhausted. Andy kept me on my toes constantly when I wasn't working, and I was just waiting for the other shoe to fall.

Well, it did. Out of nowhere, Jack started calling the bar and harassing me on the phone while I was working. He told me I'd better not divorce him or he would come back and kill my entire family, one at a time. I told him the divorce was halfway over and I wasn't going to stop it. He threatened me again, and I stood my ground. These calls went on for about a month and then abruptly quit. I wasn't sure what to think about that, and one night in particular, I felt uneasy all evening long. When I happened to look up, there coming in the back doorway was Jack. He walked right up to the bar and said, "Rhonnie, come here." I was wiping the bar down and could see my hands visibly shake. I didn't want him to see that, so I hurried and put my rag under the bar and walked over to him. I was afraid, but I knew better than to let Jack see it. That night both Raully and Mike were in the bar, though Mike seldom came in for a drink.

Jack took my arm and said, "I have a .32 in my pocket, and I want to know which guy in here you're seeing right now." With that he pulled the gun out of his pocket just enough for me to see. I told him I wasn't seeing anybody, and he told me he was going to kill the man I was seeing. I told him again that I wasn't seeing anybody, that I'd been too busy even to think about things like that. All I could think of was Jack taking that gun out of his pocket and shooting Mike and Raully.

There are times in life when it's okay to tell lies, and this was one of them.

Then Jack grinned at me and said, "Did you miss me, Rhonnie? I'm coming home with you; I wanna see my son." I was afraid, but even more, I wanted him to leave me alone. I told him I had a restraining order against him and that he wasn't supposed to be in the bar. He told me he didn't care about a restraining order. He also told me that if I called the police, he would get out of jail and kill me. I was trapped again, and my thoughts were racing fast. He tugged on my arm and asked me again, "Which one is it, Rhonnie?"

I just told him once again that I hadn't dated anybody. He told me "Good," and with that, he went over and greeted Mike and Raully and all the other people in the bar he knew. I just wanted to run away and hide. I was petrified Jack was going to kill me this time. He had a real gun in his pocket, and I had seen it.

I told Mike to leave early, and he did, but Raully stayed and kept an eye on things. Raully and Jack weren't strangers; Jack knew Raully had already been to prison for armed robbery, and he respected him. I felt a lot better about Raully staying close and keeping Jack under wraps, but I really couldn't believe Jack was so stupid that he hadn't realized Mike and I had gotten together. It just wasn't that obvious with Raully. This was because Raully always kept his cool and Jack never would have suspected me of sleeping with an ex-con.

That night after work, Jack and his gun drove out to my house. The beautiful car he'd stolen from me was all banged up, and I was afraid, but at least he wasn't interested in sex. Mike was asleep in his room, and since he had his own bedroom, Jack didn't think to question his presence.

The next morning, Jack went out, and I told Mike I had a plan to get rid of the gun. That night when I went to work, I put the word out for Raully to come to the bar and talk to me. When he showed up, I asked him to offer Jack some money for the gun. I told him that if he didn't have the money and couldn't resell it, I would give him the money.

Later on that night, Jack showed up, and just like clockwork, Raully did, too. He played a couple of games of pool with Jack and then took him off to the side and asked whether he knew where he could get a gun. I was watching and saw Jack nod his head. I was relieved. Jack was broke, so I knew Raully would be able to buy the gun.

As good luck would have it, the furnace at my trailer soon broke. This gave me the leverage I needed to get Jack out of my house. I told Jack that Andy and I could stay with my mom until the furnace was fixed, but he couldn't. I then called my dad and asked him to offer Jack a room to stay in and to act like he was being nice to him. Because my dad isn't that nice, I told him I would pay for Jack's room as long as he didn't tell Jack I was paying for it. I just needed to get Jack away from Andy and me. Dad agreed, and Jack graciously accepted Dad's offer.

What I was really hoping for was that Jack would find somebody else and just leave me alone. The chance of that happening was slim, but nonetheless I could still hope. With the furnace broken, Mike moved in with one of his friends. He would no longer be renting from me, but I really didn't want him involved any longer. Jack was coming into the bar every night and threatening me under his breath, and I was afraid this was going to mutate into a violent eruption.

It finally did. One night he came into the bar and began hitting me in front of all the customers. He was yelling like a crazy man and was saying he was going to kill me, and he called me every name he could think of. A man who hadn't been in the bar more than a few times grabbed him and beat the living daylights out of him. I took this opportunity to run across the street and call the police. They came to the bar but refused to arrest Jack, as they said they'd seen me talking to him one day. To them, this somehow voided the restraining order.

I was furious, as this gave Jack open season on me. I was still staying at my mother's house, and I went back to my trailer to get some more things. The landlord had put a big chain over the door with a giant padlock on it. I called my dad and asked whether a landlord could do this, and he said no. I called the police, and they met me at my trailer and cut the lock for me. The police told the landlord he couldn't do that, that he had to file an eviction notice through the court. The landlord knew he couldn't evict me. I wasn't behind on my rent; he just didn't want to fix my furnace. It was cheaper for him to just close up the house for the rest of the winter. I could have pressed the issue of his fixing the furnace, but now that Jack was back in town, I no longer felt safe there.

In the meantime, I was wearing my welcome thin at my mother's house. One night, Raully called and asked whether I wanted to come over and watch TV with him. I told him I would love to. I didn't think Jack knew where Raully lived, so I felt Andy and I would be safe. I was getting ready when my mother came into the bathroom and started her old tricks. She told me that if I took her grandson over to Raully's house, she would call Protective Services for child neglect.

I told her she was crazy. She hadn't cared that I was beaten severely by Jack all the time I was pregnant, nor did she care about me being locked out of my trailer. She knew how much I loved my son, and this was the final straw for me. I told her, "How dare you accuse me of being an unfit mother! You of all people threaten to take my son away from me because you don't like where I'm going. Who do you think you are?" She tried to shove me backward, and I threw her down on the floor and pointed at her and said, "If you ever try to have my son taken away from me because you can't control my life, you will have a fight on your hands you will not be able to win."

She told me that if I walked out of her house and went to my friend's, I would not be welcome back. Needless to say, I left. Raully told me I was welcome to sleep on his couch, and I was happy about that, as now I really didn't have a place to stay. The second night I was there, while Raully was at work, Jack walked in and gave me a severe beating while the baby slept. He told me to get my things together and get out of Raully's house by morning or he would be back with more of what he'd just given me.

I didn't know what to do, but I knew I could no longer stay at Raully's. I waited until Mom left for work, and then I went to get my things and packed them in my car. I also called a man named Jim who wanted to buy the 1968 Firebird Jack had stolen from me. I knew where Jack was hiding it, so before I left Mom's, I called Jim and told him where it was. He went right over and took it to his garage to hide it until I could sell it to him. I was happy to get that car away from Jack. I figured there would be no more Mr. Nice Guy with me; I was going to play just as dirty as he did.

As far as I was concerned, Jack had beaten me for the last time, but there was only one person I could go to for help, and that was my good friend Delbert. I had known Delbert since I was eighteen, before I'd ever met Jack. I was now twenty-one years old and had been married to Jack for only fifteen months before I'd filed for divorce, but this fifteen months had felt more like fifteen years. Delbert was one of my longtime friends, one of those guys who had always treated me with kindness, just like Mike. He was sweet, gentle, and soft spoken, but he was strong, and I knew he'd be able to handle himself just fine in a fight. I'd always considered him a gentle giant. He'd come over to see my new baby several times, and he used to pick me up when he had visitations with his little daughter Marie, and we always had a good time together. He loved that little girl so much, and his ex-wife was the parallel to Jack, only in female. I was a good listener, and he told me a lot about his problems with his daughter's mother.

Despite the numerous conversations we'd had, I'd never disclosed to Delbert how tragic my life had become. He'd likewise never told me he didn't like Jack, but somehow I knew he didn't. I was too embarrassed to tell him the truth now. I knew that if I told him, he'd go after Jack. Delbert had a hero complex, but I didn't want him to feel responsible for me or my problems. It just didn't seem right. I never wanted Delbert's opinion of me to change, and if he knew the truth, that just might happen. I simply wasn't willing to lose him as a friend. I even occasionally let him take me to dinner, and he was the only man I ever let do that. I never felt he would mistake dinner for buying a piece of me. We simply had a great friendship. Even though he was handsome and women seemed to love him, we remained just friends. Our relationship was special, and that was just the way I liked it. Anything more would have ruined a perfect friendship. He scared me the same way Mike did, as he was just too much of a gentleman, even though he was strong and tough in a way Mike wasn't.

Though I was a bit apprehensive about going to Delbert for help, I was desperate. He was happy to see me, but I soon learned his two nieces were staying with him. They were too out-of-control for their mothers to handle, so instead of being on the streets, Delbert had taken them in. They immediately sensed competition and were so rude I became very uncomfortable. I couldn't bring myself to tell Delbert the dilemma I was in, so to save everybody, I told him I needed to get going. He had no idea I had everything I owned other than my baby bed and rocker in my car. I just didn't have the energy to go on a minute longer in this town. I couldn't work safely, and I couldn't live safely, so it was time to move on. I didn't want to let Delbert know anything was wrong, so I simply excused myself and left.

I had talked to my sister a couple of times, and she'd told me that if it got too tough, I could come downstate and stay with her and her boyfriend, Carl. So, when I left Delbert's, I went to a payphone and called Jackie and told her I was coming. The drive seemed to last forever, and I felt great sadness leaving Traverse City, but I had no other choice. At least in Kalamazoo I wouldn't have to worry about Jack, as he wouldn't know where I was.

Jackie and Carl welcomed Andy and me very graciously, and soon after I arrived, my car quit running. Jack had dumped sugar in the gas tank, but I was hopeful. Now that I was here, I could finally move on and do something with my life. I was tired of spinning my wheels and of being afraid, and I wanted a normal life, whatever that was.

Chapter 6

Independence Day, of Sorts

I t was a little crowded in my sister's one-bedroom apartment, so shortly after Andy and I moved in, we all decided to move. The new apartment was much larger and in a nice, quiet neighborhood, and I had my own room. The neighbors seemed friendly, and we were in a pleasant part of town, but I didn't know the city, and it was hard for me to get around.

I liked Carl. He was quick-witted and had a strange sense of humor, but he made me laugh all the time. This was something I hadn't done in years. Sometimes the three of us would get to talking and sharing stories and would laugh for hours. It was wonderful to do that, and laughter became healing to me.

I arrived in Kalamazoo without furniture, but my sister had everything I needed except a baby bed. Even though Andy insisted on sleeping with me, I felt I needed a bed for him just in case he ever wanted to sleep by himself. I wasn't working then; I was receiving public assistance. I don't think I could have worked at that time, as my nerves were so frazzled. Plus, I felt it was important to spend this time with my son. He was extremely demanding, and it seemed like I just couldn't give him enough attention. He always wanted more of me than there was to give, but I tried. I didn't want to be a neglectful mother, and we'd both been through enough drama prior to moving downstate to last us a lifetime. Though I was a little bored being home all the time, I figured I would soon find something to do.

I called Jim, the man who was hiding the car I'd stolen back from Jack, as soon as I was settled. Even though he wanted to buy it, he brought it down to me. He also wanted to be more than just a friend I soon found out. He wasn't my type, and I didn't like how he used the opportunity of bringing me my car to make a play for me. This was precisely why I never let men buy me a drink or take me to dinner. They always felt you owed them something afterward.

Just when I thought I'd die from boredom, Carl told us they were filming a Richard Prior movie called Blue Collar at Checker Motors where he worked, and they were looking for extras to pose as factory workers. This sounded like fun to me, so I applied and got a job playing a factory worker working on the same car as Prior himself. I was shocked when I found him to be a quiet man who kept pretty much to himself, as this was not the personality I'd seen on TV.

They wanted to give me a speaking line, but I didn't really want to talk. It was just like when I was in school. Whenever I was called on to talk in front of the class, I froze up. Though I declined the speaking line, I had a lot of fun going to the factory and playing my bit role. They put Hollywood spray dirt on me and never let me be clean. I guess factory workers are usually pretty grubby, and I had to look the part.

Another actor who played bit parts found my phone number on my application and began chasing me. I guess I was supposed to be impressed that he was a star. To me, he was a gross old man going after a cute young woman. He kept asking whether I would like to sit in his travel trailer. It was hot outside, and he acted like he was being generous, but I knew better. Then he called and asked me out to dinner. I politely told him no thank you, knowing he would have expected a favor in return, and you would have thought I'd done a horrible thing to him! The morning after my dinner refusal, he treated me horribly every chance he had. He was extremely rude, and I could certainly see why he never made it big as an actor.

However, when the filming was winding down, the producer of the movie asked whether I would like to have dinner with him. I told him I didn't usually accept dinner invitations, and he promised he was not making a play for me. He said he would just like to have a nice evening with somebody normal and interesting who didn't have a huge ego. I found the part about finding me "normal" intriguing. He told me he was not only married, but he was also very happily married. I told him I would think about it and gave him my phone number. He called me that night, and I broke my golden rule of not letting anyone take me to dinner. We had a nice dinner and a great conversation. He asked whether I'd ever thought about being in show business, and I told him I had no interest in it. He was a very nice man and did not make a pass at me. I was impressed with him. I gave him a ride back to his motel room and thanked him for the pleasant evening and shook his hand.

They all packed up and left Kalamazoo the next day. I was thankful for the experience of not only being an extra in this movie but also for the opportunity to watch it being made. I never did see the movie, though other people who've seen it said I appeared three times.

I also made a friend while filming this movie who was an extra, too. Evonia was a beautiful black woman, and it was a good feeling to finally meet someone other than the people my sister and Carl knew. We hung out off and on that summer. Other than her, all I had were Jackie and Carl. I figured I was probably getting on their nerves, so I tried to stay out of their way as best I could. I did a lot of crossword puzzles and tried to keep things up around the apartment, but I was becoming desperate to find something to do with my life. I just didn't know what direction to go. Jackie was a secretary, and I thought this might be something I would like, too.

Then it happened. Out of the blue, Jack called. He'd always told me I could never hide from him and that he would find me no matter what, and now he had. My dad probably told him where I was, but at any rate he said, "Rhonnie, remember when you said if I ever wanted to straighten up that you would help me?"

I had told him that. I would have told him anything to get him to leave me alone. I answered, "Yes, I remember when I told you that."

He replied, "I'm passing through with my brother, Robert, and we need a place to stay. We're both trying to straighten up, and we're on our way to Texas. I thought maybe we could stay with you a couple of days and sell my brother's motorcycle and the cap to his pick-up truck."

I didn't know how to respond. I didn't want Jack coming here. After all, I'd left Traverse City to get away from him and his beatings. He told me he knew where we were and would be there in a few hours. Because I feared what would happen if I said he couldn't come, I told him okay, but I felt completely panicked. Nobody knew how much I feared Jack.

I was on edge the rest of the day. Jackie and Carl were not happy about Jack and Robert coming, but they agreed to let them. I was glad my sister was there, as she would try to protect me if Jack became violent.

To my surprise, both Jack and Robert were fairly pleasant to be around. Robert sold both his motorcycle and the cap to his truck with no problem, and then they left, without incident and with much gratitude. I was relieved when they were gone, and I started to think that maybe Robert was good for Jack. Maybe Jack really was trying to change his ways. I hoped so and not only for his sake. The selfish side of me wanted him to change so he would leave me alone and my life would be safe again. I was hoping to never see him again. I just wanted to focus on moving ahead.

After that, things were quiet around the apartment. Life was mundane as usual, but the neighbors above us had been on a trip to California and had appeared on *The Price Is Right* show. They didn't win much, but it was exciting to see them on television. They were a really nice couple and had just had a baby. I knew they'd saved up for a long time to be able to afford this trip.

Soon, we were thinking about moving again. In addition to her secretarial job, Jackie rented out apartment houses, and one was coming up empty. It was a two-story house close to downtown with an apartment upstairs and one downstairs. I could rent the downstairs, and she and Carl could live upstairs.

I was nervous about living downtown, and though I didn't know it, we were moving into an all-black neighborhood. More than anything, I was nervous about living alone with Andy. I was still quite young, I was pretty, and I was thin, with short hair I'd dyed red as soon as I'd turned seventeen. I'd hated having blonde hair, thanks to Dad, and even though I was scared to be on my own, I was ready to move since Jack now knew where we lived. Then Jack and Robert reappeared. They showed up with suitcases in hand and lots of money and told us they'd been on a trip to New York City. Robert said he'd sold his truck in Fort Worth to pay for the trip.

I'd thought their plans were to move back to Texas permanently, but they said they'd realized they'd get into too much trouble there, since all the people they knew were criminals. Robert got a room to rent from a nice old lady right away, and that left Jack at the apartment with us, exactly what I didn't want to happen. He said he was staying just until he got on his feet, and I told him he couldn't stay long, as this was Jackie and Carl's apartment. We were still in the middle of the divorce, and then he told me he wanted to live in Kalamazoo and start his life over. It seemed like I couldn't win for anything, but I still feared Jack and was afraid to be assertive with him.

My life became something of a blur from that point on. I was extremely worried that Jack was in Kalamazoo, and when I get that way, my brain seems to blank out. He soon got a job and a place to live, and I quickly called Jim in Traverse City to see whether he still wanted to buy my Firebird. He came down immediately to pick it up, and with a sad heart, I let it go.

Shortly thereafter, Jackie, Carl, Andy, and I moved into the downtown apartment house. I was afraid in that neighborhood, even though the neighbors were all very nice. They were just like you and me, working and trying to survive, but Jackie, Andy, and I were the only white people in the neighborhood. What scared me the most was the purple Cadillac that cruised the alley every day over and over again. The driver, a black man, constantly stared at me, which sent chills down my spine. He had big gangster whitewall tires, a plush, fuzzy white dashboard, and various objects dangling from his rearview mirror. I'm sure he was a pimp, and I seemed to be of great interest to him. He was certainly consistent in his daily drive-bys.

My apartment was nice enough, though a little dark in color, which I made worse by keeping the shades pulled down. It was furnished, and Robert had given me a small television and a high chair before he'd left for Texas. He said the high chair was for his little nephew's baby gift, and he gave me the television for being nice enough to let him stay those few nights.

Andy still refused to sleep in his crib at night. He wanted to be with me always, even while he was sleeping, but he seemed not to sleep much at all. He was more than a year old now and had yet to sleep through a whole night. I tried to be everything to him, both mother and father, and I made sure he didn't want for anything, but being Andy's mommy was a very hard job. I was wrapped around his tiny little fingers, and I loved him with all my heart, but mothering him was a task.

Soon, Jackie became pregnant with her first baby, and she and Carl decided to get married. She said having Andy around made her want a baby, too. They wanted a small occasion, just something quiet. I stood up for Jackie, and Carl's brother Tony stood up for him. It was a pleasant ceremony, a beautiful day, and a very nice, low-key occasion. After the ceremony, Jackie, Carl, Tony, and I went out to dinner. Jackie and Carl must have paid for that meal, as I know I didn't have any money. I was happy for them, but after the wedding, it was life as usual, which meant that other than watching the same weary soap operas on television, I had no life.

Undeniably, I was ready for a change. I realized I was minimizing my life by sitting around watching television while the rest of the world went on without me, so I began looking into colleges. One of the local colleges was affordable and seemed small enough, so I grabbed the spring schedule and took it home. I decid-ed to enroll in secretarial classes for the spring session. At least now I had some-thing to look forward to and could maybe start planning a future. I'd never been lazy, and being on welfare just wasn't enough for me. Jackie had quit working by then, and though she was getting bigger every day and had a lot of morning sickness, she offered to watch Andy during the hours I went to school. I didn't want to do that to her, as I distinctly recalled how miserable it was to be that sick, but I desperately wanted to get on with my life, and I knew this would be only a couple of hours a week.

I started college without a hitch, though I was apprehensive, and to my surprise, I did quite well. I applied myself one hundred percent and got super grades. I was especially interested in being a legal secretary. Because learning shorthand required a lot of concentration, I stayed up late to study after Andy went to sleep, but the problem was that Andy seldom went to sleep. I would be up until four in the morning studying my shorthand, but I got really good at it. I ended up with a 3.75 grade point average, and I could write shorthand faster than I could type.

During the last few classes, our instructor told us a secretary needed to be one step ahead of her boss and to do all his thinking for him, his organizing for him, and of course make the coffee for him. She told us to look at it as a marriage between a boss and a secretary. As I sat there and listened, I realized this could never be me. I didn't want to do all the thinking for a boss and I didn't want any type of marriage situation with one. When I asked whether all work situations had to be this way, the teacher answered, "If you want a good secretarial job and would like to keep it, you will have to treat it in your mind as if it were a marriage." I decided being a secretary wasn't for me, and I didn't take any more classes, but nevertheless college was an experience I'm not sorry for.

Right around this time, Jack's brother, Robert, called from jail. He had been arrested for robbery, and he said it was a bogus arrest on an old warrant that would be cleared up in no time. He added that he needed my help, as he didn't want to leave his landlady in the lurch. He asked if Carl and I would go get his suitcase from his apartment. He emphasized how heavy it was and told me Carl would have to help carry it. After some convincing, I finally agreed.

He was right about the suitcase. It was so heavy it felt like there were rocks in it, and it took both of us to carry it to my car. The suitcase was locked, of course, and we were curious as to what could possibly be making it so heavy. We lugged it into my apartment and decided to look inside, since we couldn't stand the suspense any longer. We jimmied the locks, got it opened, and removed the top layer of clothes. Underneath, it was completely full of quarters. I had never in my life seen so many quarters!

When Robert called that evening, I asked him what in the world was going on. He told me they were quarters from the bar he'd broken into. He then told me I was now involved in his crime because I had them in my possession. What a creep! I was simply terrified, and Jackie, Carl, and I talked about it and decided to get rid of them, but there were so many this was impossible. We tried to count them, and there were over nine hundred eighty dollars there. I knew the police would be looking for somebody trying to get rid of quarters at all the banks, and I also knew that because I had gone to Robert's apartment and picked up his suitcase, I would somehow be implicated.

Sure enough, the police soon started cruising up and down the alley we lived in. I knew they were looking at me. Then they started standing outside our house during the daytime. Soon after this development, Jack phoned and said he needed me to pick him up and take him to see his brother at the jail. I told him I didn't want to do that, but he convinced me to take him. I had an ulterior motive in mind. I would do that for Jack if afterward he would take the quarters out of my house. He agreed, so I picked him up at a location on the other side of town and took him to see his brother.

On the way back to town, I was pulled over by five unmarked police cars. They jumped out of their cars with their guns drawn and ordered Jack out of my car. He got out with his hands up, and they threw him against one of their cars, kicked his legs apart, pulled his arms behind his back, cuffed him, and took him to jail. I was not questioned at all; they told me to go home. I was now petrified. I wanted to get those quarters out of my house before I was brought in for something that wasn't my doing.

That night, a plain-clothed detective knocked on the door to my apartment. He wanted to talk to Jackie, Carl, and me. He told us they'd been watching Robert and Jack for some time now. He said that when they'd come to Kalamazoo the first time, the pick-up truck and motorcycle had been stolen. Robert had broken out of jail in the upper peninsula of Michigan and had stolen the motorcycle there and driven it to Traverse City to meet up with his brother. In Traverse City, they'd stolen the truck, loaded the motorcycle in the back of it, and driven to Kalamazoo, where they'd stayed with us those few days until they'd sold the motorcycle and the cap to the truck.

During this stay, the officer told us, the apartment above us had been broken into, and many items had been stolen. He said, "Like, for instance, that television set over there. Even though these people said it was a nineteen-inch color television set, it could have been this small thirteen-inch black and white TV. If they reported that they had a really expensive high chair for their baby stolen also, it could have been as simple as this one you have at your kitchen table." Then he told us Jack and Robert had gone to Texas and stolen their mother's boyfriend's credit cards and had flown to New York, where they'd had a good time.

The detective continued, talking about the latest robbery involving the quarters, but I was mortified. The whole picture flashed through my mind, and I knew Robert and Jack had done everything this man had said. The detective gave me his card and told me to call him if I could think of any information that would be helpful in retrieving the stolen articles and the quarters.

After he left, I looked at Jackie and Carl and said, "Oh, my God, this television and high chair were stolen from those nice people in the apartment above us who were on *The Price Is Right*! What am I going to do now? I don't want to go to jail!"

None of us wanted to go to jail. I knew the officer knew I had those quarters in my possession, as well as the stolen television set and high chair. I felt stupid for ever believing Jack and Robert, and I was angry at myself for fearing Jack as I did. I hated them both equally for getting me involved in their massive crime spree. I was also embarrassed about getting my sister and Carl involved, but most of all I was embarrassed for myself.

Soon after this, Jack called and ordered me to cash in those quarters and come and pay his bail to get him out of jail. We'd already tried cashing in some of the quarters to get rid of them, but it had been slow going. There really was only one thing I could do, and that was call the detective and tell him the truth. He met me at a Burger King parking lot a few blocks from my apartment, and I told him the whole story. I told him I'd had no idea Robert and Jack were on a crime spree and I'd had no idea Robert had broken out of jail. I told him I was fearful of Jack and that I was at the tail end of my divorce from him and that he was mean and beat me up all the time. I told him Jack had threatened me from jail to cash in those quarters. I told him Robert had called and asked whether Carl and I would go and get his suitcase for him and we'd both agreed to do that. It was so heavy we'd decided to look in it, which was when we'd discovered it was full of quarters. I told him that when Robert had called me back, he'd told me we were all involved in his crime now.

I told the detective we'd cashed in some of the quarters for fear of getting caught with them. I told him the people who'd lived above us were very nice and I was embarrassed about Jack and Robert ripping them off and sorry I was so ignorant that I couldn't figure this all out before he'd come to my home. I told him to come and get the quarters and to please leave me out of this mess, as I was just trying to survive without getting hurt by Jack.

The officer assured me I wouldn't get into any trouble, and he came and got the quarters, as well as the television and high chair, and that was the last I heard from him. He kept his word with me, and I know he believed every word I said. I was just grateful I didn't have to go to jail for being stupid.

Jack called one more time, threatening me as usual, but I told him I'd told the police everything. Then I went to see Robert at the jail and told him the same thing. He told me I was an idiot for giving them back those quarters, and now he would be sent to prison over it. I was amazed this criminal thought that because he'd stolen the quarters, they now belonged to him!

Though I felt a lot better after all this was over, I couldn't get over the feeling that somebody was watching me at night. I was sure someone was lurking outside my house in the dark. I didn't know who it could be, but I could feel it, and it was evil. I felt even more vulnerable because of the physical location of my apartment. It was a downstairs apartment and would have been easy to access. It didn't have the best locks in the world, and if someone had really wanted to come in, he or she could have come through the back, through my bedroom window. The whole backside of the house was bushes and leafy trees, and it would have been easy for someone to hide there and peek in the sides of my shades. I started to stay awake at night for fear that if I fell asleep, I would not hear someone break in. I wondered whether I was just being paranoid because of the negative activity caused by Jack and Robert, but I really didn't think so, as I'd never had this feeling before.

During this period, our little sister, Tay, came to live with Jackie and help her out. Jackie's baby was several months old now, and Tay was seventeen or eighteen. In retrospect, I think Jackie was trying to help her. When Tay got mad at Jackie, which was often, she came downstairs to stay with me. I always welcomed her because I was afraid to be alone, but Tay was a strange girl, and I wasn't sure just how to take her. She had an unpredictable, explosive personality, and I think she had some sort of mental disorder that had been overlooked all her life. She was fun loving most of the time, but she could switch instantly to a raving lunatic. You never knew whether she was in a good or bad mood. She was the type who could be very dangerous under the right circumstances, and she had a lot of deep-seated anger.

Just like with Jackie and me, Mom had made Tay's life miserable. She'd never treated the boys as miserably as she'd treated us girls, and I think she was probably resentful of Tay's beauty and felt competitive with her, which was probably the case with all of us to some degree. Tay had even gone to court to try to have herself removed from Mom's custody, but though Mom hadn't wanted her, she'd gone out of her way to thwart Tay's efforts to get away from her legally and had likewise gone out of her way to cause Tay to fail, just as she had with Jackie and me. Mom never cared a bit about any of us graduating from high school, and she did everything within her power to keep all three of us from moving ahead in life, so Tay, too, suffered greatly at the hands of Mom. Only when she was quite a bit older did Tay discover the skull fracture in her head that was a remnant of her childhood of abuse. I learned about this only recently as well and at that point could only speculate about what had happened to Tay, as when we were growing up, I'd thought Mom doted on her.

Jackie and I both tried to accommodate Tay while she was in Kalamazoo, but there was no expression of gratitude or appreciation for the favor of living someplace for free. That was typical of the little kids, though. They always had us to pick up after them, wash their clothes, and cook and clean for them. Tay really needed help, but the likelihood of it coming from Jackie or me was unlikely.

Once when I needed to go grocery shopping, she agreed to watch Andy for me. That was very helpful, since Andy was at the age where he grabbed everything in sight. I was gone a half-hour longer than I said I would be, and when I got back to the apartment, Tay and Andy were gone. I went upstairs to look for them, and I found Tay sleeping in Jackie and Carl's bed with all the shades pulled down. Andy, age one and a half, was running around alone getting into everything.

I asked Tay what was going on, and she flew up out of the bed and slugged me in the jaw so hard she nearly knocked me out. She said, "You know what's going on." She then grabbed her already packed backpack and flew out the door. That was the end of her, and neither Jackie nor I heard from her for three years. We didn't know where she was, and we were terribly worried.

Even though I knew Tay's behavior was out of line, I felt guilty. She was my sister by birth, but I didn't really know her. Even when she was little, she had acted quite strangely and had been exceedingly quiet and shy and had usually kept to herself. That was too bad, as she was so beautiful, the prettiest of us three girls in my opinion. When we were young, Jackie and I used to compete with each other to be her favorite sister. We fell all over ourselves trying to get her to like us the best. She doesn't remember it that way. She says we were always mean and vicious to her, but I know that wasn't true, as I have a clear memory of how much we adored her.

In the end, we found out she'd hitchhiked to Florida after leaving Jackie's. I was stunned, as I knew better than most how perilous hitchhiking could be. Sometimes you just have to accept things the way they are, but that is tough to do when you love somebody so much. I don't even know whether it was love I felt for Tay or just the leftover residual from when we were kids and I was responsible for her, but I always hoped she would make it in life and get some help to manage her unstable disposition.

Shortly after Tay left, I met a married couple named Fred and Cindy. Fred was Jack's boss at one point. They seemed like a nice couple, but I had reservations about anyone who was connected with Jack. They were Christians, and while it would have been unusual for Jack to make friends with such people, they felt a connection with Jack and seemed concerned about his soul.

They came to my apartment to meet me and talked a lot about Jesus, which normally would have turned me off, but there was something about what they said that made me want to listen. I wanted to hear something new and positive. Up until now, nothing but the birth of my son had hinted to me that there was something in life besides drama and confusion. They invited me to their home to talk to them further, and I accepted their invitation. They cooked a fabulous dinner and afterward talked for hours about the goodness of Jesus Christ. I had never talked about Jesus before this and didn't know much about him, just that he was God's son and I had seen him on the ceiling of my bedroom when I was three years old and that I had felt grateful to God both when my life was spared while hitchhiking and when Michael had been adopted.

I was surprised to find myself listening carefully, and I was amazed at how I hung on every word as they explained how Jesus had changed their hearts and lives. They told me that to have Jesus come into your heart, all you had to do was ask him in, and he would be there. There was no ritual involved; you just had to ask. I asked what Jesus would want in return, and the answer was even simpler: he wanted me to know he was the son of God and had come to earth as a man so he could be crucified and die for our sins.

I was simply amazed! I knew I was missing something in life, as I had no peace in my heart, and I could readily see that these people were happy. They had joy in their lives and in their hearts, and I wanted that for myself, so I kept on listening and not just with my ears but with my heart.

When it was time for me to go, I asked whether I could come back and talk to them more about Jesus. They were delighted and assured me they would welcome me anytime. They told me to call them day or night if I had a question. Somehow, I believed they meant it! I thought this just might be the direction I needed to go in life. I was miserable, and I wanted to love life, too, but most of all I wanted to love myself. My heart was being called, and I just needed to follow it.

I didn't want to seem like a pest, so I didn't call them right away. I needed to think about all they'd said. Within a day or two, they'd called me and invited me over again! I was more than happy and even excited to go back to their house, so I got ready, packed up Andy, and we went. This was a treat to both Andy and me. I didn't socialize much, and these were the first people I'd met in Kalamazoo who held my interest. I guess you could say I hungered for their knowledge.

While Andy played, we talked. That night they explained in detail how Jesus had transformed their lives and thoughts from negative to positive ones. I wanted to know Jesus even more than I had before. I asked again what I had to do to have Jesus come into my heart, and they once again said all I had to do was ask him in.

It all seemed too simple to me; I felt there must be some sort of catch. In all my years, I had never read one word of the Bible. How could Jesus know who I was? I didn't really even understand why he'd died for us, but I was willing to learn. I knew I hated my life as it was, and I wanted a meaningful change. Though I'd had no concept of love and caring until the birth of my son, I knew there must be more out there. I just needed to find the key, and Jesus was the key! I don't know how I knew this for certain, but I did know. I was being called by Christ to come to him.

I was a naked soul, desperate and ready, but I was still afraid living at home. I told them I always felt like somebody was watching me. When I left that night, they gave me a Bible as a gift. It wasn't the King James version; it was simplified, so it would be easy for me to read. They told me to open it anywhere and just start reading. They also told me to take the special oil they were giving me and after I asked Jesus to come into my heart, to anoint all the rooms in my house and ask Jesus to bless and protect my home.

When I arrived home that night, I did exactly that. I got down on my knees and asked Jesus to come into my heart and be part of my life. I went from room to room with the oil they'd given me and asked Jesus to bless my house and keep us safe. I started to read a little bit of the New Testament and then sat and meditated on all I'd learned that night. But I didn't feel a bit different inside, and I was a little perplexed and saddened at this. I wondered why I didn't feel a miraculous change. I was a bit disappointed, but I nevertheless believed Jesus was in my heart, regardless of what I was feeling. I watched a little bit of television, hoping Andy would fall asleep, but he didn't, so finally I laid him down in my bed and lay down beside him. I rubbed his little brow and kissed his little forehead and said a little prayer. I didn't know how to pray, so I simply thanked God and Jesus for the things I had in my life that were good, most of all my son. With that I fluffed my pillow and positioned myself face up where I felt comfortable.

I was just ready to doze off when all of a sudden I felt a bolt of electricity come into my big toe and shoot all the way to my forehead. The force of this shock was so powerful it forced me into a sitting position. Just as suddenly, I felt hands on my chest pushing me back into a lying position, and I found myself unable to breathe. The voice inside my head was wickedly savage, saying, "You're gonna die. *You're gonna die!*" It was loud yet not audible. These were the voices of all hell's demons combined into one.

Then, as I was catching my breath and feeling the impact of this horrendous event happening in the safety of my own bed, I felt another, inaudible, internal presence that soothed and calmed me. I had instant wisdom of this tranquil presence and knew intuitively who it was. It was an intimate friend, and I knew not to be deceived by the evil force. I knew I would not die. I felt so much comfort that the evil presence was overpowered. I closed my eyes, knowing I was not alone and that I was completely safe.

As I lay savoring this love and comfort, it happened again. The bolt of electricity from my big toe to my forehead jolted me into a sitting position. I gasped for air as if the wind had been knocked out of me. The powerful hands pushed me back into my bed, crushing my chest, depleting my oxygen supply once again. The horrifying voice screamed again inside my head, "You're gonna die. *You're gonna die!*" Frightened anew and desperate to breathe, I found that my comforter came once again with his calming presence. It was like being washed with love. I could actually feel it flush through my veins with indescribable warmth. In the comforting arms of Jesus, I was once again told to lie back down and not be fooled by the great deceiver and that Jesus himself was with me. I knew it was true, and I relaxed once again in his comfort.

Three more times this same sequence of events occurred, and not once was my sleeping son awakened, for this was a personal battle in my innermost being. Unequivocally, this was a spiritual battle for my soul between heaven and hell. I began to understand just how powerful the devil really was and just how hard he would fight to keep each and every one of us with him. I finally fell asleep, and when I awoke the next day, I remembered the spiritual battle of the night before. All that day I wondered why this had happened.

As I looked around my home, I wondered if the Bible I'd been given had been cursed somehow. Since I had no previous knowledge about the written word, this seemed plausible. I also wondered whether the oil I'd been given was cursed. I knew then that I had to move. I went to my sister and told her I was going back to Traverse City, that I was afraid to live in my apartment any longer, and I started to pack that day. I didn't really want to move in with my mother, but she'd been bugging me to come back to Traverse City anyway. Mom seemed to enjoy the game of love me/hate me and in fact seemed to thrive on it. She seemed to intentionally lure me into her good graces just so she could pull the rug out from under me. I knew that, but she was very convincing when she pretended to be concerned about Andy's and my welfare. Besides, I still wanted to believe my mother really did love me, and maybe this time it would be for real. I had been gone so long I felt she would be delighted to be around me, and never in my wildest dreams did I imagine she would throw me out with my little boy who was now talking. In addition, I was simply terrified to be alone in my apartment.

I called her, and she told me I could stay with her. I then called my dad and asked whether I could have my old job back. He told me I could and that I needed to pay him back the few hundred dollars I still owed him on my car. Once again, I didn't have any furniture to take except my baby bed, so moving would be easy. I knew I had to finish out my month for rent, and though I was trying to convince myself I was not being hasty in my decision, the fact was I was just plain scared to be a single woman with a child in that neighborhood. I couldn't shake the overwhelming feeling that somebody was watching me.

One morning shortly after my decision to move, I was changing Andy's diaper when my front door was kicked open, and there stood Jack. He looked at me and said, "I came to exercise my visitation rights." Suddenly, I knew he was the one who had been watching me. It was his evil presence I'd felt at night. He reached down and picked up the wet diaper I'd laid on the floor and whipped me in the face with it. I got up quickly and ran from him into the kitchen, where he ran after me and pushed me into the stove.

I was scared, but I'd also had enough. How dare he come into my house thinking he could once again frighten me into submission? He wanted to destroy me and my life. He didn't want me; he just didn't want me to have a life without him. Our divorce had been finalized a month earlier, and I was angry that he wouldn't leave me alone, angry that he had lied to me and used me in his crime spree, angry that he had embarrassed me with those nice neighbors, angry that he had involved my sweet little boy in his senselessness, and most of all, I was angry because I was so afraid of him.

When I looked in his eyes, I knew I was looking at evil. When I realized that, I lost control of myself, and just like that, the tables turned. My fear turned to rage, and I knew I was invincible. I began hitting him, and I fought as though I were a man. He tried getting away from me and making his exit out the now broken door he'd destroyed by kicking it in, but I jumped on him and fought him all the way to the alley. He tried to get away from me there, but I wouldn't let him. We fought up the alley and down the next street. He made his way back toward my home, and I was right there, still fighting. I fought that man with no fear in my heart at all. I looked at him as the devil, and I knew I was going to win this battle, regardless of my being a woman.

He pulled my head down between his legs by my hair, and I bit him so hard in his balls I made him scream. By then we'd made our way back to my apartment. He tried running up the stairs toward my sister's apartment with me pulling his legs off the steps every inch of the way. He finally made his way to the top of the steps, and when Jackie and Carl opened the door, he begged them to make me leave him alone. I was so frenzied that when my brother-in-law grabbed me and told me that was enough, I slugged him, too. Jack left, and Jackie and Carl ran to get Andy while I calmed down. Carl later told me I was foaming at the mouth as if I were a rabid dog. I told him, "I was a rabid dog!"

After I'd had time to collect my thoughts, I realized I'd had another independence day. Sure enough, Jack left me alone from that day forward, never to bother me again. In retrospect, I don't know why I'd never fought back before. Probably because I was never able to fight when I was little, as my oppressor was my father. Thus, odd as it may sound, this very unpleasant chapter of my life and my fear of Jack came to an abrupt end that day.

Although the next couple of weeks were better now that Jack was finally out of my life, I still had sleepless nights. In fact, I started having terrifying dreams of being murdered. I just couldn't wait to move from that house and that neighborhood. It had nothing to do with prejudice, but a white girl living alone in an all-black neighborhood just doesn't fit in. I am embarrassed to say that I had pushed Jesus to the back of my mind at this point. I was still frightened by the incident in my bedroom, and I was afraid to take that giant step toward Christ alone. The only Christians I knew were Fred and Cindy, and as nice as they were, I didn't want to go back to them because of their connection with Jack. I wasn't sure whether their Bible was cursed or even whether a Bible could be cursed, but I knew I didn't want to read it just in case.

I was definitely confused right then, but I believe that Jesus knew this and that he never left me. I likewise believe he has been with me my entire lifetime. Jesus was always non intrusive with me, but his showing himself to me on my ceiling when I was a child burned itself into my memory at a very early age. He knew I would suffer in life, and he also knew I would find him when I eventually sought peace. For that reason and many others, Jesus will always be my hero. He gave me a gentle kind of love I'd never had before, and he was ready and waiting when I was ready.

With the month finally up, it was time to move back to Traverse City. I left with something of a broken heart, as I knew I wouldn't be seeing my sister and little nephew much in the future, but this was a chapter I needed to close. I needed to move on as a whole, independent person and not lean on Jackie as I had as a child. I would always love her, but I needed to establish my own identity, and I needed to live in an environment that felt comfortable to me.

Chapter 7

✦

*Coming to Terms with Myself
and My Drinking*

I t was good to be back in Traverse City. This was where I was most comfortable; this was my home. You might think the spiritual epiphany I'd had that one scary night in Kalamazoo would have moved with me to Traverse City and given me a whole new perspective on life, but that didn't happen. Somehow, I lost sight of that and did what I did best. Of course, that would be sabotage my life by my own actions, my own hands. Life could have been so much better now that the drama with Jack was over and I'd been sober for so long, but this just wasn't going to be, not when I was going back to work at the bar.

Mom was really nice to me at first and seemed to have missed Andy and me. I didn't like the idea that I was backtracking by going to her and my father, but I figured I would get over it. I felt as though I needed them at the moment, since all I'd been able to think about was leaving that apartment. With Dad, I knew I had an instant job that was familiar to me and where there was some comfort, as odd as that may sound, without having to see much of him. With Mom, even though our history was rocky, at least I had a place to stay until I had a few paychecks under my belt.

I started work right away and hired a baby-sitter to look after Andy while I was gone. All in all, things were moving right along. I'd just had my twenty-third birthday, and it was now summertime, and I was feeling fine. Then I met up with a fellow I'd known since I was thirteen years old. Nick used to be a bad boy, the kind you slapped in the face for being vulgar, which in fact I'd done many times.

Though he used to scare me, he somehow seemed different now. He'd had a motorcycle accident that had ripped off his leg, and he was much humbler and wearing a full-length cast on that leg, as the doctors were determined to save it come hell or high water.

I started to enjoy Nick's company very much. He had a boyish charm about him now, and I was impressed with his kindness to me and with the seemingly compassionate side to him that I hadn't before known existed. He used to come down to the bar and visit me all the time. When it was slow, we played cribbage. He asked me out on numerous dates, and finally I said I would go out with him. We started dating once or twice a week and I continued to see him every night at the bar as well. He really seemed to liked me a lot, too, and that was the beginning of my demise. He wasn't pushy with me about sex, though he made it clear he was extremely interested. He bided his time and lured me in. Being gullible, I fell for it.

When we first began dating, neither of us were drinking. It was nice to be with somebody sober and just have fun, but working at the bar gave me easy access to alcohol. Though I started out slowly, just one drink here and there, soon I was drinking to excess. Nick was an alcoholic, but he hadn't taken a drink in a year until he'd met me. Before long, he was drinking to excess also.

I started dating Nick regularly, and the gentleman he was at first soon disappeared. He was more or less a biker sort of guy, pretty rough around the edges, just the way I liked my men. He drove a motorcycle on our dates and rigged it up so he could ride it even with his full-length cast on. Mom liked him, so she was always willing to watch Andy when we went out. Nick could be very charming, and he most definitely charmed my mother. Most of the time we just went "T T" hopping, "tavern to tavern" hopping, though one time Mom offered to watch Andy for a whole weekend so Nick and I could ride over the Mackinac Bridge on a bike run. I had been so cooped up in Kalamazoo that I took full advantage of my freedom when it became available. I felt a sense of entitlement at being able to go out and have a good time. I was being selfish, not selfless. I should have kept my focus on my sweet little boy, but alcohol played a large part in my decision making and allowed me to make an excuse to keep on drinking.

My living situation hinged on Mom feeling friendly toward me, so being with Nick was good in that regard, but Nick and me together was not such a good thing. I guess for lack of a better explanation, we were a lot like gas and fire. We ignited each other, and we were mean to each other. Quite simply, we were bad for each other, but we couldn't come to grips with it.

In spite of dating Nick, I had been home only five or so weeks when Mom decided she'd had enough of me. Drinking had become my focus in that period, so I hadn't bothered to find a place of my own yet. I would like to say her kicking Andy and me out was out of the clear blue, but that was her nature, and I knew it when I came home. I had only myself to blame, as I was the one who'd changed my focus to dating Nick and drinking. I'd already forgotten how important life was and how precious my little boy was. Jesus had been pushed to the back of my mind, and drinking had taken over my life.

Mom's problem, as usual, was that she didn't like any of us kids talking to Dad, so my working for him was a continuing bone of contention. I told her this was a job that earned me fast money I needed to pay off the rest of my car, but she couldn't get over it. If she'd had her way, we all would have hated Dad for what he'd done to her. God forbid she ever had the presence of mind to realize what the two of them together had done to all of us.

Since I refused to quit my job, I was out of a place to stay once again, with only my car to sleep in. The cycle of my life was repeating itself, and I had come full circle: I was now back in Traverse City without a home, but now I was dragging my son along with me.

I decided to go to an older man I knew who'd told me numerous times that he had a spare bedroom in his home. I'd known Ray for several years, and he was a nice man who helped a lot of people when they were down on their luck. He said I most certainly could stay in his spare bedroom, and since he didn't drive, he felt I was a godsend to help him get around.

It felt a little odd living at his house. I knew in the back of my mind he was hoping this desperate young mother would be so grateful to him that she would sleep with him, and one day I was lying down in my room taking a nap with Andy when Ray walked by. The door was open a crack, and he looked in. He told me I looked just like the women who posed in *Playboy*, only he found me a lot sexier than any of them.

I was dressed but only in cutoff shorts and a summer top. After Ray made that comment, I knew I needed to get my life in high gear and get my own place. He was in his seventies, and the very idea that he'd compared me to the women in *Playboy* made me sick. I was still working at night and taking Andy to a sitter, and

I was still seeing Nick, though not as often. I hadn't slowed down any on my drinking. If anything, since I didn't have to go anyplace else to drink when I was at the bar working, it had gotten worse. I just started to work and drink at the same time. I drank gin and tonic, so I figured I could fool everyone, including myself, into thinking I was drinking water.

A biker friend of Nick's had a place to rent, and I moved in at the end of July. I did have to cut down on my partying to make sure I had enough money, but somehow I came up with the first and last month's rent. It was a relief to be on my own again. Even though Ray had helped me out of a bad spot, I realized that kindness isn't always what it appears to be. When somebody has an ulterior motive to kindness, it isn't kindness at all. Many people come to us as wolves in sheep's clothing, and this was just another example to me. I didn't want to admit that Nick himself was such a wolf. I liked him too much to face that at the time, but I was about to learn some hard lessons in the months to come.

I sometimes worked my shift with a gal named Peggy. I had known her for years and she was very loose with men. To her, they were toys put on earth for her to play with. When she became bored with one toy, she found another to play with. I personally didn't care that she was trashy, and I hung out with her off and on that whole summer. Little did I know that I was becoming just like her. We drank together every night after work and I was drunk pretty much all the time, except when I was sleeping it off. Since my sitter spent nights at the house, it was very convenient to just keep drinking, but it was getting so bad that I began delaying coming home at night so I could drink and party more. I don't know what I was thinking, and I guess that's the point—I wasn't thinking. I was so far gone I couldn't see what I was doing to my little boy, much less to myself. Hanging out with Peggy, like hanging out with Nick, wasn't good for me at all.

Now that I had moved into my own place, I desperately needed a roommate to help with the rent, which would also give me more money so I could continue to party and drink. There seemed to be many prospective renters, but when it came right down to it, they just wanted to hang out there and not be committed to paying any rent. That was nice for them, but it didn't help me. Peggy had a place with a boyfriend who knew nothing about her wild side, so I didn't even want to ask her.

Then my old buddy Susan told me she wanted to move in. I thought about it for a long time and decided I'd grown up enough to be able to handle her. I told her she would be responsible for her half of the rent and for half the utilities, regardless of whether she had a live-in boyfriend. If we wanted our boyfriends to pay us, that would be up to us, but the rent agreement was strictly between us. Susan agreed to my terms and moved into the spare bedroom. Since she still slept around a lot, there was quite a bit of traffic going in and out of her room. As long as I ignored that, things were fine, and it went pretty smoothly for a while. Her rent was always on time, and her half of the utilities was always paid. I couldn't ask for anything more than that. Andy and I had our own bedroom, so regardless of who was over, if you got tired of it, you could simply go to your room and shut your door. Since Susan, like me, partied all the time after work, our house quickly became the after-the-bar-closed party house as well as the flophouse for sleepovers.

Then, one night after the bar closed, Peggy came over to my house and crawled in bed with me and revealed she had a crush on me. I was shocked, as I'd known her for years. I was a wild girl, but not that wild. I now realized she'd alluded to having a crush on me when I'd lived at Ray's house, but I'd been too stupid to put it together. She understood that I wasn't interested, but she was embarrassed. It put a damper on our friendship and made us uncomfortable with each other, which at the time probably wasn't a bad thing. I didn't want her to think I couldn't be her friend any longer, but there was a noticeable strain between us from that point on. I knew I had to see her at work, and I didn't want it to be so uncomfortable that I would have to quit. Besides, I knew that if there were a problem job-wise, Dad would take her side.

Shortly after this, I began noticing that when I had to work with her, our cash register always came up short by twenty dollars or so. The deal at the bar was if the register was short more than five dollars, whoever was on the cash register had to pay it back. When it came up twenty dollars or so short on my shift with Peggy, she would pay back ten dollars, and I would pay back ten dollars. Ten dollars went a lot further then than it does now. This was a great deal for her, as she would take the money and pay only half back. It was no skin off her teeth, as she still made out in the end.

I didn't want to make any accusations about her, as I'd already seen Dad defend her once, so I just told him I wanted to work a different shift, days only, and be the only person on the cash register. That worked out a lot better for me in the long run, and Peggy and I drifted apart once we were no longer working together.

Around this time, a little girl about twelve years old was living with her aunt in one of Dad's rentals. I soon heard she'd been raped by the men living in the downstairs apartment. To my surprise, I found out it was Dad who'd turned the men in! It appeared he was obsessed with helping this poor little girl out of her horrible situation, and I knew something had to be going on, for he wasn't that nice. My dad wouldn't care about anyone raping a young girl, nor would he step in and be a hero unless there was something in it for him. Sure enough, one day the aunt who had custody of this child called my house and asked me to come and talk to her. I had not yet met this woman or the little girl, who was called Pumpkin, and this call came out of the blue. Nevertheless, I agreed to meet her. When I walked into their apartment, I felt sick as the picture unfolded for me.

The aunt was an older woman in a wheelchair while Pumpkin was mentally slow and, like the two sisters, easy for my predator father to manipulate. Here they were, living in a second-story apartment without wheelchair access. This made the picture very clear, and I knew right away what was going on. The ultimate "wolf in sheep's clothing," Dad had offered the aunt this place to live, knowing her inability to get around gave him full access to the little girl.

This old woman was on the ball about my dad. She looked at me and said, "I know you can help me; I know you know about your dad. He is manipulating my niece and taking advantage of her. Can you help me? Please tell me what you know about your dad."

I was stunned. I had never met this woman in all my life, yet somehow she had come to me for help. I looked at her and said, "Why did you call me? What made you think I could help you?" Now I know it was God who prompted her to call me through his son Jesus Christ, but at the time I was puzzled. I looked into her face and saw her eyes become bloodshot and teary, and I saw all the fear she felt for her helpless niece since she herself was helpless. She simply replied, "I don't know why I called you. I just know you know your dad, and I'm hoping you can help me. I'm desperate, and I want to know about your dad!"

I started out by telling her that I had an unhealthy fear of my father and that I was going to get into trouble for helping her. In spite of this, I knew that no matter how much I feared my dad, I could not ignore this situation. I had to tell this woman the truth. I knew she was desperate and that my dad basically had her captive in her apartment while he manipulated her young niece. In addition, if there was one thing I'd learned while living with Jo and her husband, it was that talking about Dad's abuse was healing. So, I told her how Dad had abused all of us. I told her how manipulative he was and how his abuse was not just sexual but also mental and physical. I told her my father was never nice unless he had something to gain from it and that she was justified in her fears.

She then asked whether I would talk to a woman sheriff about him, and I agreed to do so. I was worried, since I was still working for my father, but I knew he had to be stopped. He had no conscience; that I can say with certainty. He had no remorse for what he'd done to any of us. Quite the opposite, in fact, as he'd routinely spread horrible rumors that his kids were thieves and liars. This of course was to ensure that he would never be implicated for his sexual abuse of any of us, since no one would ever believe us. He'd started this along with Mom when we were small, and it had always worked beautifully.

I figured my father was the one having sex with Pumpkin and that when she'd begun hemorrhaging and had been taken to the hospital, he'd had to come up with something to tell the doctors. That was why those men had been arrested for raping her. It was Dad's testimony to the doctors that had caused their arrest.

I was afraid of my dad knowing I was aiding this woman. I knew he would go to extremes to protect himself and his reputation, and I was afraid I might end up dead if he knew what I was doing. I knew about the man who used to frequent Dad's bar who'd been murdered some years before by a hit and run driver, and I knew Dad had been questioned by the police about it. Laughing, he'd told me the police thought he might have somehow been involved. I can't say for sure whether he was or wasn't, but I can say with certainty that the police knew he was a slippery man who walked the edge of the law. The dead man was the type who would blackmail somebody if he had the goods on him, and I always thought that was probably the case in this situation.

For one thing, my dad had a lot of money, more than could really be accounted for, and nobody knew exactly what he did to obtain it. He along with the two sisters,owned the bar I worked at, and he also rented rooms at the various houses he'd bought with the sisters' money. That kept a constant flow of money coming in, and since he rented by the week, he never had to go through any eviction process. If he didn't like a renter, he simply didn't rent to that person the next week. But he didn't work, and though I can only speculate on the source of his abundant income, I've always figured it was something illegal and immoral. I was worried about this little girl, but I was also worried about myself. I made all this clear to Pumpkin's aunt, but I still agreed to talk to the lady sheriff.

Before this meeting, I went to my siblings and told them what was going on. I wanted their support to help put Dad in jail. I wanted them to tell what they knew and had lived through. I especially wanted my sister Jackie to help this little girl avoid the torment we'd lived through.

I was completely shocked and dismayed at their response. Jackie denied that Dad had ever sexually abused her, and the rest of the family did the same. They didn't want anything to do with helping me out. They said they didn't want their names dragged through the mud, that they'd been through enough and didn't want their reputations ruined. They didn't want to be on the front page of our small town newspaper, as they knew Dad would rise up against them and fight us all in court. They still feared him, and at their ages, they just wanted to move on with life.

I couldn't believe what I was hearing. Dad had such a grip over his kids even now that not one of them had what it took to stand up to him. Not one of them jumped at the opportunity to lock Dad up for his transgressions. I knew that if this went to court, I would need them to stand beside me or he would be acquitted, but it was beginning to look as if I would be standing alone.

At least I knew I could find solace with Nick. He would surely understand how important this was to me and stand firmly by my side. I thus got the shock of a life-time when instead he told me it would embarrass him to have his girlfriend's name on the front page of the paper. He was afraid his reputation would be destroyed, and he said he would break up with me if I went public with this.

I had only to check my conscience to know what I had to do. There was no way I could cower to my dad just to save my reputation. I didn't care about that. The way I looked at it was that if people thought my reputation was tarnished because of something done to me against my will as a child, I didn't need those people in my life.

I didn't give Nick the chance to break up with me, and instead I broke up with him. I just hoped that someday I would get over how my family dealt with this. I have since talked to most of them about this, and they say they didn't want to be revictimized by him and have him tell more lies about them. Right or wrong, those were their feelings, though I'm hopeful that now, as mature adults, they would go after him with full force if they had the opportunity.

The sheriff arrived at my home at our appointed time, and I asked whether my words would be kept confidential. She assured me they would and asked me whether a woman from Protective Services could come over while we talked. I agreed, as long as this too was kept confidential. I explained my fear of my father and that I was still working at his place of business. I didn't want Dad to find out it was me talking until he'd been arrested. They understood, so I began telling them about my life with Dad. I told the police officer that even though the rest of the family had all lived through this, they refused to get involved. Then I told them what I thought he was probably doing to Pumpkin.

They informed me they'd suspected my father of molesting this young girl all along. They figured he'd had the other men brought up on charges of rape to cover up what he was doing. Then they told me they would have him in custody before the night was over, and I was elated after all these years, he would be caught and brought to justice. I knew that after he was in jail, I would be able to testify against him and help this little girl out without being afraid anymore. When they left, I felt a great sense of relief. The family secret was now out in the open, and something would finally be done about Dad. What's more, telling on him and having him arrested would not only liberate my soul, but it would also save this innocent young girl.I got a call from Peggy at the bar within a few hours of the meeting. She said, "Rhonda, I don't know what you did today or what you said about your dad, but he is so angry you'd better go and hide." I was scared now. I knew what I'd said to the cop, and I knew Dad would kill me if that's what it took to keep himself from going to jail. I didn't know what to do. I kept somebody with me at all times that night, and then I learned Dad had disappeared and nobody knew where he was. He was gone for three days, and I was terrified the entire time. When he returned, he informed everybody that Pumpkin and my brother Roger were married and that Pumpkin was now living with him and was under his care.

I was stunned anew at Dad's conniving brilliance. When I finally talked to Roger, he told me that Dad had taken him and Pumpkin downstate to Grand Rapids, where he'd found Pumpkin's biological father and made a deal with him. He'd paid this man $1,000 to go with them to Mississippi to sign a marriage certificate so that Roger and Pumpkin could be married. Since they were both underage, they needed parental consent to marry. Dad also paid Roger $1,000 to marry Pumpkin until she turned of age. By doing that, he took the control away from her aunt, which broke this old woman's heart. I still feel horrible for her, God bless her soul. In addition, he would not go to jail for molesting her, as he could now keep her with him legally. They were never able to pin the initial bleeding on him because they'd never been allowed to question Pumpkin and had only questioned the aunt. Now, with Pumpkin a minor and in his legal custody, they would never be able to question her out of his presence.

When I talked to the sheriff again, she told me Dad had been just an hour or so ahead of them, but now they could not pursue this matter any further. It was over, and they hadn't gotten him. I'm sure Dad felt more powerful than God having outfoxed the cops, and I was incredibly disappointed that he hadn't been caught. I knew my life was safe again, but I also knew Pumpkin's life would never be the same. She was now legally in Dad's grasp and would be living with him to boot. My heart was so sad. I felt that I'd failed that poor old woman who'd come to me for help, but there are those in life who simply get away with murder, and my dad was one of them.

Though I went back to my life as though nothing had happened and my dad never said anything to me about it, I didn't get over this soon. Roger was only seventeen at the time, but I couldn't believe he'd sold out another human being for money. By the same token, I knew he, too, had been victimized by both our parents and had a drinking problem. At his age, he simply couldn't have appreciated the scope of what he was doing. I also believe that while Roger may have escaped the alleged sexual abuse from Dad, since he was a lot younger when Dad was around, he may well have been sexually abused by Rod. Roger won't talk about it, nor does he talk to Rod, and he hasn't for years.

Feeling sorry for myself and my failures, I used this incident as an excuse to drink even more, and I didn't care how bad my hangovers were. I was drinking again by noon or so the next day regardless of how rotten I felt. In spite of this, I managed to keep my job and pay my sitter and all my bills on time. To me, an alcoholic would not have been able to do that, so I convinced myself I wasn't an alcoholic. I was in terrible denial, but I didn't think the alcohol was destroying any part of my life. I spent time with my son every day, and I adored him, so I figured I was doing okay, even though more and more people were beginning to sleep on my couch and my floor. Pretty soon, I didn't know a lot of the people who were staying at my house, but I didn't want to seem uncool to my party friends, so I didn't say anything.

Five months after I returned to Traverse City, I ran into my good friend Delbert again. He told me he'd found the Lord and was a Christian now, and this was exciting to me, since I wanted to ask important questions of somebody I could trust. Jesus was brought to the forefront of my mind once again, and I told Delbert about my experience in Kalamazoo and asked him whether a Bible could be cursed. He told me he didn't think so and said that the word of God is never void. Like everything else I never shared with him, I didn't let on that I was drinking heavily. This at least made me realize there was something wrong, but I would have been embarrassed for him to know, especially since he was so excited that I'd, too, accepted the Lord into my life, at least on the surface.

He invited me over to the home he shared with his girlfriend, Sherrill, and her two little boys and I was immediately wary. I remembered Sherrill from school. She was one of those girls who would tell lies to any man who would listen just so she could sleep with him. Worse yet, she was the kind who would do anything to fit into the "cool" crowd. I used to avoid her at all costs, though I tolerated her when I had to. She made me sick, and I couldn't believe my friend Delbert was not only living with her, but he was also going to marry her. He was old enough to have seen through her, and I tried to tell him he was making a mistake, but he wouldn't listen. He said she may have had a "victim complex" in the past, but now she was a brand new person in Christ. He also told me she would be delighted to know that I, too, was a new person in Christ and would love to have me for dinner.

I knew better, but he made it hard to say no. After all, I was very happy to see him again, and I just couldn't hurt his feelings. I was hoping for the best, but it just wasn't to be. I knew the moment I walked into their home that this would not be a pleasant visit because of the thick, tense atmosphere. I tried to ignore the daggers Sherrill was throwing at me with her eyes, but soon she started yelling at her little boys. Dinner was being put on the table as I walked in the door, and there was no visiting with her, just her acting up with her kids and slamming the cupboards to intimidate them and to intimidate Delbert, though he didn't realize it. Those precious little boys were soon bawling their eyes out. They weren't doing anything wrong, but she was relentless in her rage, and there was nothing new there, and I could see now that she was definitely not a brand new person in Christ.

I knew she was just angry because of my presence in her home, and I was so upset at this scene that I excused Andy and myself. I told them I didn't feel well, and we left. Sherrill feared me and my presence because she knew I knew what she was. Exposure would have put an end to her plans for Delbert. Plus, she knew he really cared about me, and it was obvious she was jealous of Delbert's feelings for me.

Poor Delbert. He'd never learned to read this type of woman. He'd made stupid choices for wives in the past, but I could clearly see he was about to make the granddaddy mistake of them all with Sherrill. She was a conniving, selfish person and was much worse than his two previous wives, but his upbringing had been just as dysfunctional as mine, and, like me, he was muddling his way through the best he could.

Even so, I knew his life was going to be destroyed by Sherrill. She would bring him to his knees and would do it under the guise of Christianity and love. She already had those boys calling him "Dad." This really bugged me, as he wasn't their dad, and they weren't yet married. Christian or not, I knew she hadn't changed a bit. She was still looking for a free pass in life and was lying through her teeth all the way.

I knew Delbert didn't know why she'd behaved as she had at dinner and that he was embarrassed. I could clearly see it in his face, but whatever the explanation she gave him, he believed her. He thought he was being a hero and a good Christian by saving her from the world. She was truly a damsel in distress in his eyes. After all, she'd convinced him that the state of Michigan had taken her two little boys and wouldn't give them back, and all she'd done was place them with the state because she'd had to have a hysterectomy and there was no one else to take care of them.

Unfortunately, this wasn't true she'd just wanted her freedom and made the rest up to lure Delbert in by convincing him the "mean state of Michigan" was being unjust to her. At the time, no one could have told him the truth, but Sherrill hadn't wanted her kids, nor would she let either of the two fathers or their families have them. The state of Michigan was just being extra cautious, as she'd shown no interest in her little boys for six months until Delbert came on the scene and wondered where they were. Always softhearted with kids, Delbert had leaped to her rescue and helped her get them back. His feelings for children gave her the reason she needed to go and get them. She gambled that this new man she was after would be putty in her hands if she had her sons, and he was!

Though I knew better, this situation, too, became yet another excuse for me to justify my drinking. I felt sadder inside than I'd ever felt before, and I couldn't figure out why. I was refusing to look at myself deeply and to "fix" the problem. I had a number of male friends who regularly took me out drinking with them, men who went out of their way to come get me, and it wasn't long before the light switch was thrown on and I figured out why.

One night I was out drinking with these guys, and we ended up at the bar I worked at. Peggy was working that night, and she refused to serve me because I'd had too much to drink. The next day when I went to work, all my regular customers said, "Wow, what a show last night. Are you going to do that again?"

When Peggy came in at the end of my shift to begin hers, I asked her what everybody was talking about. She told me to sit down and then proceeded to tell me what I'd done the night before. I couldn't believe my ears. She said that after she'd refused to serve me, I'd stripped down to my waist and danced topless all night long. I thought I'd gone home, and though at first I didn't believe her, customer after customer came in and said the same thing.

I was mortified. I couldn't believe I'd done that, and then I realized I'd had a blackout episode and that I'd lost hours while I was drinking. I was slowly coming to grips with how serious a problem I had and was now beginning to peel through my "denial shield." This wasn't the first time I'd thought I'd gone home after a few drinks and people had told me differently, but I'd never believed them before. I started to wonder about the men who always made sure I went out with them. I wondered what the true motives were of my good old buddies. I obviously didn't always remember what an evening entailed, so God only knows what I did with them.

After this, I tried to quit drinking, but I didn't succeed. Then I tried to slow down my drinking, but that, too, was a fruitless effort. In the meantime, I was getting into a lot of fistfights in the bars. Some of the fights I remembered, and some I didn't. One night while I was out, I ran into my old boyfriend Nick. He instigated a fight between another woman and me, and I was banned from the bar we were in, which happened to be owned by my landlord. I was embarrassed, but still I didn't quit drinking. Finally, I faced the fact that I couldn't stop, not that I wouldn't stop.

I was well on my way to destroying myself, but God himself must have seen my weakness and intervened before the downward spiral spun me completely out of control. One morning I woke up with my usual hangover. My son was hungry, and when we walked out of the bedroom and into the living room, everything seemed different. My son was stepping over all the people who were crashed on the floor, asking me, "Mamma, who is this? Mamma, who is this?"

He ran into Susan's room to say hello to Steve, her latest boyfriend, and came running back saying, "Mamma, that's not Steve...Who is that, Mamma? Where's Steve?" Andy liked Steve because Steve played games with him. All of a sudden, it was as if God spoke to me. It wasn't audible, but he said very clearly, "Is this what you want for your life? Is what you want for your little boy? Is this what you want him to remember you as?"

I looked around and "saw" for the first time what was really going on. I saw strangers passed out from their drunken stupors the night before. I saw my slutty roommate with a different man every other week. I saw beer cans everywhere. I saw what I was exposing my little boy to. Most of all, for the first time, I truly saw what I had become and my possible future, as well as my son's. I even spoke my answer out loud and said "No!" It was at that moment that I quit partying and drinking and put an end to all the people flopping at my house as they pleased.

I woke everybody up and told them to get out. I didn't want this anymore, and I most certainly didn't want them to feel welcome to come back. As you might expect, these "friends" disappeared from my life when I quit partying with them, which was very sad to me and was also a sad realization about drunks. They were my friends only when I was like them.

I believe in divine intervention, and I believe that when I asked Jesus to come into my heart, he did just that. That was what that spiritual battle was all about that scary night in Kalamazoo. Jesus wasn't willing to let me to ruin my life, and he stepped in to correct my destructive behavior in the nick of time. To this day, I'm grateful for the new eyes he gave me that day.

My next lesson concerned my job. For a while, I continued working at the bar even though I'd finally stopped drinking, but it never felt the same again after I admitted my problem to myself and truly "saw" what alcoholism was. At first I couldn't quite put my finger on exactly what it was that seemed so awful. I'd always believed that if people wanted to hang out in bars, it was their choice to do so, but I finally realized it just didn't feel right to me to work there anymore. Still, it was an easy enough job, and right then I couldn't afford to go back to school and learn anything else.

One day, it was very slow, and I was bored out of my mind. I had washed all the glasses and cleaned everything in sight, but still there were no customers. Finally a man came in who'd been there before and sat down and ordered a beer. I hadn't liked him the first time I'd met him, since he'd been cocky and rude when I'd waited on him, but he seemed more pleasant this time around and asked whether I wanted to play pool. This would certainly help pass the time, so I said yes. When I played pool, I played for money. I was good enough to win, and since people at the bar seldom tipped well, this was a way to make extra money. I was afraid to ask this man's name, as the first time he'd been in he was rude when I'd asked him, but soon I won all his money, and he settled for sitting and making small talk with me.

I reminded him of his rude behavior, and he immediately apologized. I finally asked what his name was, and after we'd talked for several hours, Pat asked me out on a date. This was truly an odd day, as there were no other customers the whole time he was there. Only after we'd talked for some time did I accept the date, and I did so mostly because he was a professing Christian. He seemed so nice, and he spoke to me about the goodness of Jesus Christ, and as before, I was hungry to learn more. He also had a pocket Bible in his shirt pocket, and while it may seem stupid, I was impressed with that and knew he must be for real. He then asked me to go to church with him that weekend, and I told him I would, even though I'd never been to church before. I was truly ready to grow in the Lord.

I was hungering for a refreshing change in a man, and I thought maybe Pat would be different, since he was a Christian. He loved to talk about Jesus, and I was at that crossroads in life where I was ready to hear more. I was interested, so I told him I would make dinner for him that night, as I didn't want to go out to the bars anymore. He was gracious about my invitation and said that would be lovely.

I was more excited about dating him than any man I'd ever met. Finally, a good Christian. This was going to be quite a change for me, but I was ready for that kind of change. I wanted to live right for my son's sake as well as my own. I was also excited about getting to talk about Jesus again. I wanted to relive the same scenario I'd experienced with Fred and Cindy, a good dinner and a wonderful talk about Christ afterwards. Finally, it looked as if I was on the right track.

Chapter 8

Sober and in Earnest: Marriage Number Two, a New Baby, and a New Life

After meeting Pat, I felt my life might finally be on the right track. He was very handsome and polite, and he seemed to know just how to talk to me and hold my interest. Our dinner date at my home went well, and he seemed to like Andy just fine. This was very important to me, as I'd always kept my dating life separate from him. I hadn't even allowed Nick to build a relationship with Andy. It may sound stupid, but I thought it was best that way, since I knew I didn't have a great track record with men.

I took Pat home after dinner. He was beginning a new life, having just gotten out of prison, and he didn't have a car. He told me he'd been an awful human being until he'd gone to prison. That he admitted this on our first date represented honesty to me and was something I valued a great deal. In prison, he'd found Christ and had committed his life to serving him. He said he'd been sent up on a false charge, but he added that he'd deserved to go to prison, since he'd always gotten away with far more than he'd ever been caught at. He said that if not for the prison sentence, he wouldn't have come to know the Lord.

I was amazed and impressed by this, also. This man was not only honest, but he'd also taken his horrific circumstances and had found God and was grateful for that. I'd never met anybody like Pat, who was so willing to see the upside to the downside, and I couldn't help but sit up and take notice. I had known many rough characters, and Pat's attitude was different. I never would have dreamed I'd date an ex-con seriously, in spite of the fact that I'd dated many unsavory types, but the way Pat relayed his past to me convinced me to take a chance. He was very intelligent, which I found stimulating. Because I, too, had made so many bad decisions, I felt I could not judge his life before he'd met Christ.

I picked him up for church that Sunday, and he had on a pair of wrinkled dress pants. He didn't own an iron, so we promptly stopped at my house so I could iron them for him. He told me Jesus didn't care that his pants were wrinkled, but I told him, "I care!" We were a little late to church, but no one noticed. How could they have? This was a jumping Pentecostal church, and the people were simply wild, throwing themselves onto the floor and falling down for no visible reason. Though I hadn't been to a church since I was three years old for a mass spoken only in Latin, I'd never seen anything like it. I wasn't sure I approved, but I had nothing to compare it to, so I decided to ride out the storm and see whether it grew on me. Pat and I attended services there every Sunday for quite some time. To all outward appearances, it looked as if he'd made his peace with God and was committed to serving Christ, which once again impressed me about him. I was observing him closely, as I didn't ever again want to be fooled, and what I saw looked good.

One Sunday, I saw a woman in church I knew well. I know you're not supposed to judge people while you're in church, but I couldn't help it. I knew this woman, and she wasn't a nice person. I sat and watched her carry on, cry, throw herself onto the altar, and be slain in the spirit. She did what people would do in a building that was on fire, and I was completely disgusted by her antics. When we left that day, I told Pat I knew her and that she was a fake. He looked at me and simply said, "That is between God and her. It's not our job to judge what Christ is doing with any person."

At first I was a little peeved, but I knew he was right, and over the next few months, Pat and I learned about Christ together. He knew I'd read very little of the Bible, and he was patient with me and got me a new Bible to read. I was still afraid to read the one that had been given to me, even though Delbert had said it couldn't be cursed. I was just starting to understand how God worked in our lives, and it was a slow process for me. When Pat heard there was a big revival coming up, I agreed to attend with him. The preacher who was coming had a healing ministry, and I was interested in being healed of the migraines I'd suffered since I was a child. I wasn't sure what to expect, but I attended every night of the weeklong affair.

Each night, I prayed I would have a migraine so I could go up front and be delivered from them. While I waited, I sat back and watched everybody else run up to the prayer line to be healed from their various ailments. The last night of the revival came, and I still hadn't had a migraine all week, which was most unusual I hadn't gone an entire week without a migraine since I was a child. Finally, during the prayer line on this last night, the minister stopped everything and said, "God just told me there is a young woman out there needing deliverance from her migraines she has suffered for years. No, she hasn't had one migraine all week long, but he's calling you up here now for healing!"

I couldn't believe what I was hearing! God saw my heart and knew my thoughts as I was sitting there. I was amazed that he would pay that much attention to me, and this confirmed that God loved me and that I wasn't insignificant at all. For certain, I knew that God saw my anguish that week and understood that I needed to know he was real. I was equally impressed that this man of God with the healing ministry listened to God and heard his voice. This was a miracle for sure, and I was so excited I could hardly stand it. My heart literally leaped within me at this personal invitation from God, and I jumped up as though there were springs on my feet and ran up to the prayer line. When it was my turn, I told them I was the one God had spoken about. The preacher said, "Why didn't you say so?"

Soon he and several other men laid their hands on me and started praying. As they prayed, I felt warmth run through my veins throughout my entire body, and then I started to vibrate. This wasn't anything visible to the eye; it was something happening on the inside. I could actually feel something happening to me. This was only more confirmation as to how real God was. The night I'd asked Jesus into my heart, this was what I'd thought would happen, but instead I'd noticed nothing until the frightening moment I'd gone to bed. This was finally it, and when they finished, the good brother told me I was filled with the Holy Spirit and was healed. I truly felt filled with the Holy Spirit, and I knew there would never be any man or woman on this earth who would be able to tell me otherwise. I was finally healed of my migraines, and gaining victory over a dreadful condition that had plagued me since childhood made me so happy I felt as though I could have floated out of that building. Indeed, I felt like I was floating the rest of the week.

I felt different when I left church that night, as if I were a brand new person, and I wanted this feeling to last forever. I'd needed conformation that Jesus Christ was real and would never leave me, and here it was. I still didn't know much about the Holy Spirit, but I had certainly felt him enter my body and flush through my veins, and I was excited.

The next day was not life as usual. When I got up, Andy and I ate breakfast and played until I had to go to work. When I walked into the bar I'd worked at off and on for five years, I felt displaced. I didn't recognize what I was feeling, so I tried my best to shake it off. I checked in, put my purse behind the bar, and started my shift. It just so happened that the bar was very busy that night. I was working a split shift of both days and nights at that point, and though everything looked the same, the place seemed foreign to me. I visually scanned the bar and realized for the first time in my life that I was looking at sin. I not only saw sin, but I also felt sin, and I wanted to run. I felt tremendous discomfort, and I knew I couldn't work there any longer, so I put in my two weeks' notice that night. As soon as I did, a strong resolve came over me.

I must confess those were two hard weeks for me. I'd always overlooked how annoying drunks were. I'd always overlooked having to "baby-sit" certain individuals to keep them from getting out of control. I'd never minded before, but now I knew I'd never be able to work in a bar again. That was good, since as a recovering alcoholic I certainly didn't need the temptation of being around booze. Even though I now had a good grip on my drinking, I knew I'd been one of those disgusting drunks I was looking at, and I'm sure people had hated being around me when I was drunk. Such reflection helped me to know that my decision to quit drinking was the right one. I knew in my heart I would never be a drunk again, and that chapter of my life quietly closed on my final night of work.

Pat and I continued dating. He was working at a plumbing supply company, and I started a new job at a little family grocery not far from home. We had previously discussed getting married, and now we found ourselves making active plans to do so. Pat said he would be honored to be Andy's stepfather, and I believed him. Andy needed a dad with good moral standards, and I thought I had a good man who had learned his lessons and who had a deep commitment to Jesus. What could go wrong when Jesus was the center of my life? Unfortunately, I never thought about what might happen if my partner decided Jesus was no longer the center of his life. I just assumed that once you'd made that commitment, it was there for life because it was just that, a commitment.

Since I'd been married before, we decided to keep our wedding small and simple. It was time to meet Pat's family, so we made arrangements and drove downstate. To my surprise, Pat's family essentially ignored Andy and me our entire visit and instead smoked pot and drank. None of them seemed to understand how dangerous alcohol and drugs were, including the parents, in spite of the fact that Pat's oldest brother had died while driving drunk, an accident that had left behind a wife and small son and had also killed his best friend.

I was disgusted with all of them and soon decided it was a good thing we lived three hours away. It was apparent that Pat's siblings didn't care that he had struggled with drugs in the past and had even gone to jail because of his drug habit. Instead, they seemed to want to sabotage his efforts and make him feel as if he wasn't part of them if he didn't partake with them. Pat drank a beer from time to time, but I'd never seen him drunk and didn't feel he had a problem with alcohol. I simply hadn't yet made the correlation between drugs and alcohol. I thought they were different, and I didn't yet know that an addict was an addict and that drugs and alcohol were the same in that regard.

I was frankly astonished to see such a callous lack of compassion and respect for Pat and the positive changes he'd made. I knew I was one of his positive changes, and I was as determined as he was to stay straight. Our trip back to Traverse City was a quiet one. Though I wanted to expound on my true feelings about his family's drinking and drug use and their behavior, instead I somewhat guardedly told him I thought they'd treated me rather rudely. His reply was not what I expected. He told me this was my imagination and that they were just a little hard to get to know. This was pure denial on Pat's part and should have been a red flag for me, one of many that were to come, but I failed to see how serious this was.

In my heart, I knew he was making excuses for his family, but only later would I realize I never should have ignored his denial. It was my first warning sign that he was unable to discuss problems, and I certainly didn't realize what a snowball effect this would have on our lives. I thought that because our relationship was based on God, things would somehow magically fall into place. This was one of those theories that sounded great, but the reality was that individuals have free agency over their lives and their decisions. This was as true for Pat and me as it was for anyone.

On the positive side, Pat showed great interest in Andy, and this was a giant bonus for Andy, or so I thought. He even wanted to adopt him so he would officially be his son, and Andy seemed to like Pat, too. Though our relationship had a few riffs, including the visit to his family, nothing seemed that out of the ordinary to me. After all, I was just at that point in my life where I was sorting myself out and dealing with my own realities. I'd wanted a Christian man who didn't have children, and I also wanted someone who would treat my son as if he were his own. Andy was special, the finest child on earth in my opinion, and I wanted it to remain that way. A man with no children of his own would be able to love Andy without any favoritism toward his own children getting in the way.

I put my few reservations aside, since Pat seemed so perfect otherwise, and we chose a wedding date. We also took one more trip to see his family the week before the ceremony. I wasn't looking forward to that trip, and I suffered the same stomachache I'd had when I was a child when my father was around all week. I didn't realize this agony was another red flag. I just thought it was the devil trying to rob me of my happiness, so I decided to put up a good front for the sake of my future husband. I simply cannot exaggerate my surprise or horror when we arrived at his parent's house and a little boy about nine years old walked up to Pat and said, "Hi, Dad!"

I was so shocked I didn't know what to say. I didn't want to make a scene with Pat's whole family standing around, and by the looks on their faces, it would have given them great pleasure to see me react. They had the look of naughty kids who'd just pulled off the prank of the century. They didn't like me and had orchestrated this to be cruel to me, but never once did they think about how despicably they were behaving to that little boy by putting him into this position.

When Pat and I were by ourselves, I asked who this child was and, if he was his son, why he hadn't told me he had a child. Pat told me Tony was an old girl-friend's child. He admitted to a fling with Tony's mother right before she got married and told me that when the baby was born, the marriage broke up. Judy had told everybody the baby was Pat's, and his whole family had accepted this as fact. Pat said he'd gone along with it for Tony's sake, since Judy could be irrational, and that it wasn't a big deal. He said he'd been pushed into accepting this information without any medical confirmation that this was a fact and that he wasn't an active participant in the boy's life. Indeed, the only time he had any contact with the child was when the mother, who couldn't let go of Pat, would call him in an attempt to make him feel guilty about not being with her. This seemed horrible to me, but I nonetheless corrected Pat and told him I felt it was a big deal when a child called you "Dad."

A few minutes later, the phone rang. Surprise, it was Judy, this young boy's mother. She just happened to have Tony's things ready so he could come stay with us in Traverse City for a week. I should have taken notice right then that Pat didn't have the nerve to stand up to an ex-girlfriend or his family, but I couldn't say anything on the way home since Tony was with us. I knew none of this was his fault, but I was furious. This certainly wasn't something I wanted sprung on me the week before our wedding, and I spent that whole week thinking maybe I should call it off. In retrospect, I clearly should have, since this was the biggest red flag of all.

On the way back from taking Tony home, Pat and I had a long talk. He told me he hadn't had much of a relationship with Tony, but his family did. He explained this was something Judy did every time he became serious with anyone. She was still in love with him, of course, and Tony was the giant wedge she hoped would stop him from marrying me or any of the other women he'd been involved with in the past. When we got home, he took out every letter she'd ever written him from his box of personal belongings. The letters she'd written while he was in prison were few and far between, but when he got out and started to date me, they started coming at the rate of three per week. Every letter was written to try to motivate Pat to come back to her. In one letter she wrote, "All Tony does is sit and stare out the window waiting for you. What would he ever do, Pat, if you married anybody besides me?" She wrote this one while living with another man who'd been present in Tony's life for six years at this point! That poor kid—she was putting ideas in his head, and none of them was his fault.

I should have just walked away, but Pat explained things to me in his typical way: everything would be okay as long as God was the center of our lives. All I can say is I was gullible and believed him. He also told me he was aware of Judy's tactics and that she was a desperate woman, but he wasn't going to let her use her son to destroy our plans.

Our wedding day finally came, and it was to be just a small gathering of family members, a few from mine and a few from his. My mother had traded in her trailer two years earlier and had purchased a home in Traverse City, and our plans were to go to her house after the ceremony for champagne and wedding cake. We were about to leave for the church when I suddenly asked Pat whether he thought we should really get married. His answer was, "I don't know; what do you think?"

We went back and forth like that all the way to the church. I don't know what either of us were thinking. This was clearly an indication that something was seriously wrong, but neither of us had the guts to stop it at this point. In fact, I once again thought this must be the clever devil himself who was trying to ruin my life. I hadn't yet learned to distinguish the voice of God in my heart from what I thought was the devil. I'd been afraid to marry again and had promised myself I wouldn't unless I was sure, but now I wasn't sure, and it seemed like I was breaking my promise to myself. Though this caused me great internal anguish, we both decided that what we were feeling were pre-marriage jitters.

We pulled up to the church, and when we walked in, I couldn't believe my eyes. Pat's whole family was there and some friends to boot! I hadn't wanted a big wedding, and only a few people from my family had been invited. I looked around at my future in-laws and couldn't help but start laughing. Though my family had dressed for the occasion, some of his family didn't have enough respect to. Our ceremony wasn't formal, but it was held in the church. I would have thought this would have given them an idea of how to dress, but obviously it hadn't. Then I thought that maybe this was the best they knew how to do, which was an even funnier thought to me. This combined with the debate Pat and I'd had in the car on the way to the church suddenly gave me the overwhelming giggles. I was able to collect myself sufficiently to walk down the aisle, but then I looked around and once again thought about the car ride to the church, about my new in-laws-to-be, and about Tony, and all of a sudden I simply couldn't hold back my laughter. Even during our vows I couldn't stop laughing, and pretty soon the pastor started to laugh, then Pat started, and then everybody was laughing. Laughter is contagious, and no one was any the wiser as to why I couldn't stop laughing throughout the ceremony.

I certainly had a chance to say "I can't do this; I can't marry you," but I didn't. The frustrated pastor finally simplified it for me and decided to form everything into a question. All I had to say was "Yes" or "I do," and I was glad when it was over. The pastor told me this had never happened to him before, but he made light of it by saying this was a joyous occasion for me. He liked Pat a lot, of course. Everybody loved Pat, and the pastor thought I was one of the luckiest girls in the world to marry such a great guy.

After the ceremony, Pat's family charged right into Mom's house and made themselves at home, grabbing the champagne out of the tub where it had been kept on ice and uncorking it and slugging it down from the bottles. I guess they never noticed the beautiful glasses sitting on the table with the two special "bride and groom" glasses. I was embarrassed for them, but they had no shame. That was just how they were, and it was a grim realization for me, even though there had been plenty of hints before this. I just never in my life would have believed there were people who were so slovenly. It was as if this were their party, not ours! Of course, Pat never said a word to any of them or asked them to wait.

We managed to save one uncorked bottle of champagne for our toast. None of them cared; they just kept right on slugging their bottles like ghetto drunks. In the confusion, I lost Pat. Mom's house was small, and since he'd vanished into thin air along with his brothers and friends, I assumed he'd left the party. I stalled as long as I could, but everybody was waiting for me to open the presents. I told them I thought I should wait for Pat, but after an hour or so, I decided to open the gifts alone. This didn't seem right, but nothing else seemed right about the day, either.

When Pat finally returned, his tie was undone, his shirt was untucked, and he was so high he could hardly walk, much less talk. This was my new Christian husband. I took him out back and asked, "What do you think you're doing? I had to open all the presents myself. Why are you so wasted?"

He just looked at me smugly and said, "This is my wedding, and I'll celebrate the way I want to!" This was certainly true to form in terms of how the rest of his family behaved with no respect for the situation at hand, but to say I was upset would be a gross understatement. I felt like such a fool. I now knew for certain this was not the man he'd portrayed himself to be, but once again I'd ignored the red flags and had no one to blame but myself.

I was too upset to have a good time the rest of the day. We had prearranged for a large table at a very nice restaurant for our wedding dinner, and I thought most of his family, except his parents and a sister, wouldn't be able to afford to eat with us. Unfortunately, I wasn't that lucky. They all wanted to come to our dinner, and they were so disruptive at the restaurant I couldn't even visit with my sister. They continuously banged their plates to get us to kiss and hooted and hollered the rest of the time, never noticing or caring about the other patrons trying to dine in the restaurant. This was "their" party and "their" good time, and they didn't care about anything but that. It topped off the whole wedding day disaster, and I knew for years to come that I would never forget this day. I was grateful when everybody left and went home. I was exhausted and mentally drained, but there was still one more disaster left to go before the night was over.

Pat had been in charge of reserving a motel for our wedding night. This had been his only wedding-related task, but he hadn't done it. The problem was this was summertime in our resort community, and the motels were always full. To cover up for his mindlessness, he said we would drive to another, smaller resort town an hour away and that it would be more romantic to stay there anyway. After we drove all the way there, we discovered they had no vacancies either. It was four o'clock in the morning when we finally returned to our own home and went to bed. I was tired, angry, and fed up with Pat, and somehow I knew this was only a prelude of things to come.

The next day wasn't much better. We woke up late, and even with Andy staying at Mom's, the romantic breakfast I'd planned was out of the question. Even worse, I had no idea part of Pat's family was still in the area camping, the part who were the most inconsiderate of me and who didn't really like me, and Pat soon informed me they'd already made plans for us for the day.

I knew I didn't want to see Pat as he'd been the previous day, high and disoriented. High Christian moral standards and his family didn't go hand in hand, and I decided Pat was a chameleon. He was good around good people and bad around bad people. I stood my ground and told him I would not go to their campsite. I had no intention of spending one minute longer with them than I already had. I told him he seemed to have little or no self-control around his family, and then I asked him what kind of person lies about their moral standards and about Jesus. He just looked at me and said, "You met me in a bar; what did you think?"

You know, he had a point there, but he was failing to take responsibility for his own actions and his own deceit, not only to me but also to himself. I told him I'd never thought of that before, but I also told him I wasn't going to the campsite and that he wasn't taking my car. He didn't have a car, so he was stuck with me unless he wanted to hitchhike. He was angry all day long. I had to admit that the handwriting was on the wall as far as our marriage was concerned, and this was when I began to figure out the connection between alcohol and drugs and their addictive powers.

This was by far the grimmest reality check I'd had so far, and I talked at length to the pastor from our church and asked him what I should do. He said, "God can heal all things, and all things are possible in Christ." I knew this was true, so I thought I would try to make the best of it since we were already married. I knew it wouldn't be easy, but I was hoping beyond hope we could make it. I was prepared to try my hardest and pray for direction, but Pat was hard to deal with. He wasn't the type to yell and scream at me. In fact, when he was angry, he did the exact opposite. He went for days on end without speaking to me or acknowledging me at all. I was made a "Joe Smith" all over again, this time by my husband, and to my horror, I began to realize there was a strong resemblance between Pat and my father. Although Pat was not physically violent with me, he had many of the same attributes Dad did, as had Jack. I also began to realize that I was attracted to this type of personality, and with this realization, I was finally back in school, the school of life, but I still had a lot to learn.

We moved shortly after we married, and since Pat had sprained his ankle, a friend helped me move the heavy things to our new house, and then I went back and cleaned the house we were moving out of. I had to steam the carpets, wash the walls, clean the stove and refrigerator, and make minor repairs. I also did some touch-up painting. When I finished that, I mowed the lawn. It was almost nine o'clock in the evening by the time I was done, and I was dirty and sweaty, as it was in the nineties that August day. When I got to the new house, I made my way through the narrow path of stacked-up furniture to look for Pat. He was sitting with his ankle up and asked, "Did you pick up a six-pack of beer for me?"

I was shocked. Neither of us drank anymore, or so I thought, and I just looked at him and said, "Why would I have thought of doing that? Of course I didn't stop and grab a six-pack for you!" He was instantly angry and punished me by not talking to me for four weeks. Four weeks and not one word to me! Not a "Good morning," not a "Hello," and not a "Goodbye." Nothing, not a word. He talked to Andy during this period, but shut me out of his life as if I were not there.

His adoption of Andy was well underway, and I was worried when I saw this kind of behavior. He finally began talking to me again, but by now my concerns had extended beyond his "presto change-o" personality. This wasn't just about me anymore; it was also about the welfare of my son. I loved Andy with all my heart, and he was three and a half now and very impressionable, as all children are at that age. I didn't want the long-term effects I was afraid Pat would have on him.

I decided to leave Pat before things got any worse, but learning this turned him around, and he had a great explanation for everything. He told me he'd always had a problem with relationships and explained that he was working on it. He mustered all the sincerity he could, including tears, and implored me to hang in there. He actually made me feel sorry for him! In fact, I soon felt guilty for even thinking of leaving him.

Looking back, it's obvious that I was really in my element here. After all, as a child, I'd felt a lot sorrier for Bob than I had for myself. I'd lived my entire life with more pity for others than I'd had for myself. I'd mastered overriding my own feelings and had learned to disregard my conscience and to empathize with others. Maybe this was a defense mechanism from when I was a child so I wouldn't feel my own pain, but it wouldn't be until much later in my life, after much counseling, that I would realize how abused I was emotionally and spiritually by Pat. I just figured that since he didn't hit Andy or me, what was going on wasn't abuse. Plus, I believed that love could conquer all, even though I didn't really know what "love" was. I could understand Jesus' unconditional love, but I didn't feel "in love" with Pat. Even now, married for the second time, seeing and holding my brand new son after his birth was the only real love I'd ever felt. As much as I'd needed and worried about my siblings as a child, what I'd felt for them didn't seem like love, certainly not like the love I had for my little boy. It's hard to explain, but I knew even as a little girl that there was something between my siblings that wouldn't let us bond like a family should. Maybe I felt love for them, but it didn't feel like it. As far as Pat went, I just expected that love would grow as the marriage progressed, and I still hoped that because he remained a professing Christian, we would be able to work everything out in Christ.

One night Pat and I went to a movie our pastor had recommended at a neighboring church, and we ran into Delbert and Sherrill. I hadn't seen them since the night Delbert had invited me to their house for dinner. After that fiasco, since he knew Sherrill couldn't function in my presence, Delbert had disappeared from my life. Because Pat knew Sherrill's ex-husband, he instantly disliked Delbert, so he sat there hating Delbert while Sherrill sat hating me. It was sort of humorous even then, especially since we were sitting in a holy place with other Christians, and after the movie we all had time to chat. It had been at least a year since I'd seen Delbert. I was happy to run into him again, and I could tell the feeling was mutual.

After asking Pat whether he would mind, I invited Delbert and Sherrill to our home for dinner, and Delbert jumped at the invitation. After all, I was his dear friend, and he was genuinely pleased to see me again. I knew Pat wasn't too excited about having them over, but being a "good Christian," what could he say? I did ask him first, and he had the option of saying no if he didn't want them there. As I planned for the evening, I hoped it would go a little better than the dinner at their home.

When they arrived, Sherrill initially seemed cordial. She was apparently less threatened by me now that I was married, but it wasn't long before her true colors emerged. I had made Southern fried chicken for dinner, not knowing she hated chicken, and instead of being gracious about it, she made no bones about how she felt about the food I had spent the entire day preparing. She kept poking the chicken with her fork while she told a very long, windy story about working at a chicken processing plant and what they did to those chickens. Finally, I suggested she just eat what she could and ignore the chicken. I was getting very frustrated with her antics and decided she needed to be shut up, as she was monopolizing the conversation.

There was plenty of other food, but she continued to complain about the chicken. This really made me angry. I wanted this to be a nice occasion, and she was doing her best to sabotage it. I could see Delbert was becoming extremely embarrassed, so I tried to smooth everything over for his sake. I felt sorry for him, as he'd always been so gracious about others' efforts. Of course, he should have never been fooled by Sherrill, but who was I to talk? I certainly was living with my huge "Christian" mistake, and I'd already caught Pat in several lies. He supposedly didn't do drugs any more, yet I'd caught him smoking weed and God only knows what else. He wasn't cheating on me either, but I'd found lipstick on his undershorts and had seen numerous receipts from his business trips that listed two dinners instead of one. Most of all, he'd professed to being a Christian with high moral standards, and he clearly wasn't.

For his part, Delbert had no problem eating the chicken. In fact, he told me the meal was delicious and that chicken was his favorite food, and he ate several helpings. Pat didn't say much of anything at the table that night. He usually didn't when he was annoyed and annoyed he was. He was doing a slow burn over Sherrill's behavior and the fact that Sherrill's ex-husband, who was also a Christian, had told him Delbert had stolen his wife from him. Delbert tried several times to strike up a conversation with him, but Pat would not reciprocate and was in fact very curt with Delbert.

It all made for an interesting evening, and once I got past the insults slung at me by Sherrill and the fact that Pat was acting out, I had a great time. Delbert and I did most of the talking, and we talked all evening long. I had made a cake for dessert, and when it was served, Sherrill didn't have anything insulting to say. She must have realized it was a fruitless effort at this point. During the course of the night, Delbert mentioned he'd joined a group of Christians that met every Wednesday evening, and he encouraged us to come. Pat had heard of the group and some of his Christian friends attended, so we agreed to check it out.

We went the next Wednesday night and liked what we saw. The group was not affiliated with any church; it was the brainchild of a self-proclaimed minister of God, an older man, who had started this ministry to help young Christians in Christ find their way. Though I still didn't know a whole lot about being a Christian and living a Christian life, I was willing to give it my all. It was nice to be part of a group of young people for fellowship, and in this group we read and discussed the scriptures and also prayed for each others' needs. Soon, I looked forward to Wednesday nights. Though I'm not a huggy kind of person, everybody seemed to hug each other hello and goodbye. I felt the love of Jesus in my life, and the bonus was that we could bring our kids to these meetings, too.

Pat was still working for the plumbing supply company, and his job sometimes took him out of town overnight for deliveries. Having people around who had the same interests as I did made these trips more bearable. It wasn't that I missed Pat when he was gone; it was that I was afraid of the dark, a residual effect of my childhood, and I was afraid to be alone at night. More often than not these days, I was walking on eggshells to keep the peace, and having Pat gone was in many ways a relief.

Soon, we heard that a speaker was coming to town I wanted to hear. At first Pat wasn't sure he could go with me, and finally he told me he wasn't interested in going. He said to find someone else who was interested and that he had to go out of town that week for a delivery. Just like clockwork, we'd gotten into one of those silent fights he was so good at and I knew this was why he didn't want to go. After all, he was going to be gone only one night on his delivery, and the revival was going to last more than one night.

Then Delbert happened to call and asked whether we were planning to go. I said Pat didn't want to, and he said Sherrill didn't, either, and I jumped at the chance to go with him. I never gave a second's thought to the fact that I was going with someone else's husband or that he would be going with someone else's wife. I just never looked at Delbert that way back then. I was just excited that despite Pat and his hatefulness, I got to go. I'd found the first revival I'd attended exhilarating, and I just knew I'd have the same experience this time. Plus, I needed to be with people who liked me. I needed to feel wanted in this world, and it was getting increasingly hard to sit at home with Pat while he pretended I wasn't there.

On the last night of the revival, Delbert and I stopped at a restaurant for coffee. Pat had just left on his trip, and Andy was with a sitter. I didn't think there was anything wrong with going for coffee with Delbert after the revival. We'd always been friends, nothing more. Pat knew I was going with Delbert, and he didn't ask me not to, and Sherrill likewise knew Delbert was with me. Of course, saying no would have required that Pat break his silence to me, and his pride wouldn't allow him to do that.

We'd been chatting at the restaurant some time when the leader of our Wednesday night group came in and said, "This doesn't look good, you two!" The insinuation was offensive to me. Delbert was my friend, and it was none of this man's business to make such a comment. Maybe it was selfish to sit there with a good friend who happened to be married instead of staying home, but I guess I just didn't care what this looked like to someone else. Now I think it probably wasn't such a good idea, but I didn't give it a second's thought back then, and I was insulted that someone would think I had an ulterior motive in being with Delbert.

When Delbert took me home, we talked out in the car for a while. Finally, I felt as though we'd talked ourselves out. I thanked him for a wonderful time and then leaned over to give him a kiss goodbye. Frankly, that kiss devastated me. I knew right then I had more feelings for Delbert than I'd ever admitted to myself, and I was stunned that those feelings existed. It's hard to explain how I failed to recognize them. I just thought I liked Delbert because he'd been so kind and caring to me all these years. I don't know how to explain it myself, except to say that at the moment I kissed him, the lights turned on, and I knew. I also knew Delbert realized the same thing at the same moment, and I quickly got out of his car and ran into my house. I couldn't face the reality of what I'd just felt, and I knew that had I paid attention to my feelings before, I wouldn't be in a marriage that was such a disaster and neither would he. He'd been married to Sherrill less than a year and had already caught her having an affair with his own brother.

In my devastation, I slammed the door shut behind me and got down on my knees and prayed. I knew this revelation about my true feelings for Delbert would get in the way of my marriage, and I knew that only Jesus could help me with this dilemma. I knew I'd better trust Jesus and not myself to do the right thing. In my mind, my marriage was already miserable, and my pattern would be to try to justify leaving Pat and seeking out Delbert. I was afraid Delbert would do the same thing with his marriage. I felt that would be wrong, but I was afraid our attraction to one another would overpower us. I needed God's strength to help me do the right thing, regardless of what my heart felt, and this was a big moment for me. I knew I had to give up the friend I'd had for so many years, and I was incredibly sad, but I thanked God that I had been praying and learning to put my trust in Jesus and his word. I was going to need all the help I could get.

I was obligated to attend one more event that would involve seeing Delbert again, a birthday party for one of Sherrill's sons, and I knew in my heart this was the last time I could see Delbert. As a Christian, I needed to focus on my marriage, and I could never do that with him in the picture, even as my friend. This was an unspoken truth between us.

Pat refused to go with me, so I went to the birthday party alone. I could hardly sit there without thinking about our marriages and what a joke they were, nor could I look at Sherrill with anything but total disdain. I knew Delbert and I each had a hard road ahead of us with the bad choices we'd made, but if Christ could forgive our spouses, we could, too. I prayed for the success of Sherrill and Delbert's marriage as well as mine and for the incredible strength it would take to sustain two such rocky unions.

It goes without saying that Delbert and I never saw each other again throughout the years we were married, and shortly after the birthday party, Delbert and Sherrill moved away. I wondered how he was doing now and then, but I knew as well as he did that we could not be around each other if our marriages were to work. It was God who helped us both understand it had to be this way. I prayed that God would help me to forget the feelings I had for Delbert and to please just let me remember him as the friend he'd always been. Over time, that happened, and though I continued to struggle with my marriage, with Jesus in the picture, it didn't seem as bad as it would have otherwise. I was grateful for my faith, and I knew that even though things were rough at times, at least I had Jesus to lean on.

Since Pat and I had so many struggles, we started going to counseling with our pastor. He believed finalizing Andy's adoption would make our family complete and would stabilize us. It was so far underway that we decided to go ahead with it, and Pat was as smooth with the lady from probate court as he was with everybody. She was so impressed with Pat that she told us she would push the adoption through quickly, for she felt he was going to be a great influence on my son. It made me feel better to know I wasn't the only person who fell for Pat's charm. In addition, since Andy had already begun using Pat's middle name as his own, she said she would add that change to the adoption. At the time, Pat seemed to love Andy, so that at least made me happy even if nothing else did.

Then I found out I was pregnant. I wasn't sure I was ready for a new baby, nor did I know how Pat was going to feel about this "good news." We'd been married only three months, and so far it had been a major adjustment for both of us. Frankly, I was scared to tell him. With the adoption barely completed, I was afraid this would change his mind about being Andy's dad.

His reaction was what I thought it would be. He wasn't all that thrilled, but he seemed okay initially. He'd always known I couldn't take birth control pills, which made me sick, but I guess the shock of finding out about the baby made him want to put the responsibility of prevention on me. When he tried that, I told him he knew the risks as well as I did and that a baby was the result of sex. I figured he'd eventually get over the shock of becoming a father, and he did ultimately seem delighted with the news at times, even calling his family and sharing it with them. I, of course, wasn't fooled by any of this. Actions speak louder than words, and the more life went on, the wiser I was getting to his ways.

Unfortunately, I was as ill with this pregnancy as I was with Andy, and Pat soon became tired of my all-day sickness. I knew that babies didn't improve unstable marriages, but I put my trust in Jesus and just kept praying. We continued to go to our prayer group on Wednesday nights, and we also began receiving guidance in our marriage from this leader, and the others were happy to hear we were expecting.

As my pregnancy progressed, our Wednesday night prayer leader started coming over to our house on a regular basis to share the word with us. He told me the Lord had told him I was a strong woman and was going to use me in his ministry in miraculous ways. He told me it didn't matter how new any of us were in Christ; it was our hearts and minds that mattered to Jesus. This was good news to me, and I prayed nightly and thanked the Lord for the wonderful blessings he had given me, despite the negative things in my life. I wholeheartedly believed I needed to be thankful for what I had.

In spite of this, to my dismay, life went on with Pat as usual. Instead of thinking of my ever-larger belly as a growing baby, he told me I was putting on weight, and he didn't appreciate that any more than he enjoyed me being sick. Pat personalized everything as if it were part of a master plot to somehow make his life more miserable, and while I used to think my hurt feelings were just a result of being pregnant and feeling extra sensitive, in retrospect I can say he had a mean streak and loved to hurt me. He was still running around on me and getting high, so he needed to find reasons to justify his behavior. I couldn't prove what he was doing, as he was sneaky, but his response whenever I asked him about his behavior was, "Do you have pictures?" When I'd say "No," he'd respond, "Then shut up, unless you have pictures and proof."

It was now wintertime, and I figured he'd evaded the issue of his "son" Tony and what should be done about him long enough. I told him he might have avoided doing the right thing so far in life, but now that I was pregnant, I wanted to know the truth. I asked him to undergo a paternity test, and then I told him that if Tony was his biological son, it would be only right to change the birth certificate and let Judy's ex-husband, who'd been paying Tony's support all along, off the hook. I felt they were playing a nasty game, one way or the other. If Tony really was Pat's son, he needed to become part of our family and Pat needed to step up to the plate.

When Pat finally called Judy, she came unglued. He handed the phone to me, and she told me they didn't need a paternity test. She was a good "Christian" girl, she told me, and she and Jim had decided not to sleep with each other for the six weeks before they were married. However, she and Pat had had a one-night stand on July 4, one month before she married Jim, so she knew her baby was Pat's.

Some nice Christian girl! I saw through her from the very beginning. I told her it wasn't that I didn't believe her; it was just that some things didn't add up. She and Jim didn't sleep together, but she'd decided it was okay to sleep with Pat? And if Jim was paying child support and was listed as the father on the birth certificate, why did he call Pat "Dad"? I told her I was pregnant and that the truth needed to be known. I needed my kids to know for sure whether this was indeed their brother. I reminded her that she'd involved me the day she'd sent her son home with Pat and me, and I told her it was downright dishonest to charge a man for support for a child who wasn't his own.

You would have thought I'd asked her to cut off her arms! The bigger surprise was that Pat said he understood how she felt. He told me he'd told her when they were going together that if she ever had a child, she'd better not list him on the birth certificate, as he would never pay support for any kid. I told him I didn't care what he'd said in the past; he needed to be put on the birth certificate and take responsibility for that boy if he was his. He agreed and added that was how he felt before he knew the Lord. Pat knew just what to say and how to say it when he was in a pinch.

An hour later, Pat's mother called. She asked to talk to me, and he handed me the phone. I knew his family didn't like me much, and I was pleased she'd called. I got on the phone, ready for a nice visit, and instead I was verbally attacked. She yelled at me up one side and down the other. Judy had called to cry on her shoulder about my request, and she said, "Why don't you leave what isn't your business alone? Since my son married you, he hasn't come down here at all to see us. You don't have the right to try and change the way things have been in our family for years!"

She was wrong about that, and I knew it, and I firmly stood my ground. Pat wasn't married to Judy, and to allow her complete dishonesty to continue was simply not right. There are times when you have to do the right thing, and I knew this would be the right thing for Tony, for the ex-husband, and for Pat, regardless of any other outcome. Pat's mother didn't like it one bit, however, and continued to berate me until I started to cry and handed the phone back to Pat. I refused to give her the pleasure of knowing I was upset, but I expected Pat to take up for me. Instead of chewing her out for making me cry, they had a very pleasant conversation. When he hung up, I asked why he hadn't said anything about how she'd treated me. He told me, "That's between you two. She never said she was angry with me!"

I felt betrayed. Pat was supposed to stand up for me, even to his mother. She was accusing me of sticking my nose into business that wasn't mine, yet she stuck her nose into the same business! I was so upset that after he left for work the next day, I packed up some clothes, dressed Andy warmly, put him on his sled, and walked to my friend's house to stay with her. I knew it was now or never in this marriage. All I wanted was for the right thing to be done with Tony so my children wouldn't be pulled into this mess that everybody seemed to think was okay.

I called my sister after three days, since I was thinking of moving back to Kalamazoo, and she told me Pat was looking for me, quite frantically to my surprise. I called him a few days later and told him he needed to let his mother know this was our marriage and the request we were seeking from Judy was not unreasonable. He told me to come home. He agreed to call his mother and let her know he would not tolerate anyone treating me as she had.

In spite of his efforts, not only did his mother continue to hate me, but also Judy never agreed to the paternity test, though she did slink out of sight for some time. The loser in all this was Tony. I think the real reason Judy didn't want a paternity test was she feared it would show Pat wasn't Tony's biological father. I think she herself wasn't sure who the father was. In any event, this was the first and last time Pat stood up to his mother. He told me that even if it was the right thing to do, it wasn't how his family handled things.

I was at least enjoying Wednesday night fellowship. I liked our discussions and readings, and it gave me great pleasure to pray over people. Then one night as we were in the middle of a prayer, the leader stopped us and said directly to me, "I never heard you pray in tongues!"

I looked at him and said, "I don't pray in tongues." He replied, "You're not filled with the Holy Spirit if you don't pray in tongues." I told him I was filled with the Holy Spirit, and he told me to prove it by speaking in tongues.

I didn't know what he was talking about. All I knew was that I was saved and filled with the Holy Spirit. I stood my ground and stood on my faith, as I was sure that when I was prayed over by those men, I had indeed been filled with the Holy Spirit. Even so, he was putting me on the spot, so I told him, "I am saved. I know that I'm saved and that I'm filled with the Holy Spirit."

His face was now very red, and he yelled, "You say you're saved and are filled with the Holy Spirit; prove it by speaking in tongues!" He was starting to scare me. Everyone was looking at me, and I didn't know what to do, so I answered, "I am saved, and I am filled with the Holy Spirit, and you have no right to ask me to prove that to you!"

He then walked toward me and stood over me and yelled, "Prove it, then! Prove it to me! I see no evidence that you are filled with the Holy Spirit; you prove it!" I started backing away from him, and he moved with me until my back was literally against the wall. I was now in tears. I hadn't read far enough in the Bible to know what he was talking about, but I said, "I don't have to prove my faith to you or any man. I am saved, and there is no man on earth who can tell me I'm not, and I don't have to show you or anybody else by speaking in tongues!"

At that point I started crying so hard I couldn't speak a word, and I left immediately. I didn't understand what had triggered this. Why would this man pick on a pregnant woman and bring her to tears? This didn't seem God-like to me, and this was the same man who'd come to our house and told me the Lord himself had said I was strong and was going to be used in miraculous ways. Even worse, why hadn't Pat or any of the other Christians sitting there stopped him?

When I got home, I got on my knees and begged Jesus to give me the gift of tongues so I could prove to the leader that I was filled with the Holy Spirit. I prayed until I fell asleep, and when I woke in the morning, I had utter clarity about tongues. Christ simply said, "No." I was not going to receive that gift, and the Lord was quite specific in telling me this was something I desired for the wrong reason. I told Pat this, and amazingly enough he said this was fine, but I refused to go back on Wednesday nights.

It just so happened that I didn't have to make the decision not to return to our group. That very morning, the group leader and three other men knocked on our door. The leader asked if Pat was home, and I told them he was and invited them in. The leader said, "We'll wait here on the porch." I got Pat, and we both went out on the porch. I was then informed this talk was private and would include only Pat. I told the leader that as long as he was at my home, what they needed to say to Pat they could say to me.

The leader then asked Pat to meet him at a restaurant, and Pat agreed. When he returned home, he told me we were still welcome on Wednesday nights but that when it came time to pray, I would not be allowed to pray with them or to lay hands on anybody. When I heard this, I became upset all over again. I asked Pat what he'd said, and he replied, "What I'm understanding is that we're still welcome to be a part of the group, but you want my wife to leave her Bible at home!"

I was astounded he'd had the nerve to say this! He usually liked to remain the "nice guy" who didn't make waves, but he agreed that what they'd done was wrong and out of line with what Jesus would have any of us do. He didn't want to go back on Wednesday nights either, but they were not about to give us up that easily.

A few weeks later, there came another knock on my door. It was the same men, and once again the leader said to me, "We're here to see Pat." Again they wouldn't come in, so I sent Pat to the door. This time I stayed back. When Pat came back in the house, he told me they'd said I was filled with evil spirits and so was our house.

This was so absurd I was completely stunned. How the leader had convinced the other men of this was beyond me, but from then on, I was essentially shunned from that group. It hurt for some time, mostly since I didn't understand what had happened or why, but I knew I had strength in the Lord, and I stood on my faith alone. However, the leader was right about one thing: I was the strong person in that group. I was strong enough to stand up to them and let them go.

I did remain friends with one of the wives in that group, and I'm glad to be able to say the leader never amounted to much. As it turns out, this self-proclaimed preacher who was never ordained had some strange ideas about what God wanted from him. I later found out that he was upset because some members of the church he attended wouldn't acknowledge him as a minister ordained by God and wouldn't let him preach. He was what I like to call "a legend in his own mind" with visions of grandeur, and all he did was destroy his group, which fell apart a few months later.

For our part, Pat and I decided to find a new church. Though our present church was okay, it was just too much at times with people falling down in the aisles and at the pulpit. We decided to try out the church we'd seen the movie at, and we immediately liked the minister. He was a very kind, compassionate man, and he not only talked the talk, but he also walked the walk. I could feel his love just standing next to him, and this seemed like a good place for us to grow as a family. Soon I loved getting up and going to church on Sundays, which was an enormous step for me. Though I'd enjoyed aspects of our other church, I'd gone more out of obligation than anything else. The other church had preached fire and brimstone and had used scare tactics. For example, we were constantly told that if we didn't tithe ten percent of our income to the church and lightning struck us dead, we just might not go to heaven.

I never did buy into that. When I gave my ten percent, I subsequently went without food. I believe we all should give but give what we have, not what we have not. My duties as a loving mother came first, and I firmly believe that was the way Jesus would have it.

I was getting bigger every day when we made the transition to our new church, and Pat still acted like I was getting fatter just to aggravate him. We didn't see eye to eye on most things, and though I knew he was frequently dishonest with me, I was still hoping beyond hope that things would work out for us. I felt I owed that not only to myself but also to my family. We seemed to gel a little better once we started attending the new church, which gave me hope. To be fair, I think Pat also wanted our marriage to work, but only on his terms and without giving up those parts of himself that he didn't want to change.

One of the things Pat and I were struggling with was whether to begin breeding and showing dogs. Pat wanted to, and he told me this had been one of his dreams since he was a little boy. It's always nice to chase your dreams, but I wasn't sure how I felt about giving up mine so he could have his. My dream was still to raise horses and I really struggled with this, so much that it proved to be a battle within my heart and soul. There were several reasons I was hesitant to get into dogs. First, I had a problem spending the kind of money it would take to acquire a show puppy at this time. We had a baby coming, and our finances weren't that good. God forbid that I had a conscience regarding our bills and needs, but it didn't seem right to allow our household to go into debt to chase his dreams right at this time.

Second, I was afraid I'd get stuck holding the ball with the dogs. Pat seemed to have a habit of initially liking things but then becoming bored and leaving them behind. I simply didn't trust him to follow this through to the end.

Third and most important, I hadn't liked what he'd done to my old dog Tuffy. When we'd moved into our new house, we'd understood that we could have no dogs. Well, I had Tuffy. I hadn't raised him from a puppy; he'd come from friends who'd had to move. He was a very sweet old dog and was never a bother. When we'd moved, I'd decided to take him anyway, and I'd figured we could get a kennel for him to stay in outside. He was not a barker, and this was acceptable to the landlords. However, Pat didn't want to spend any money on Tuffy. I really believe he didn't like that dog for his own selfish reasons.

One warm fall day shortly after we'd moved, Pat, Andy, Tuffy, and I had taken a ride along the bay, and Pat had pulled off to the side of the road and let Tuffy out. At first I'd thought he was letting him out to go to the bathroom, but suddenly I had a sick feeling in my stomach. I'd never dreamed he would do such a thing as abandon an old dog, yet I knew in my heart this was his plan, and I couldn't imagine anyone doing something so horrible except my dad. Without any warning, he jumped back in the car and drove away. Andy began screaming and crying, and I yelled at Pat to stop the car. Tuffy was chasing us as fast as his old bones could carry him, but Pat maintained a fixed stare on the road as if we weren't even there. He didn't seem at all bothered by what he had done, nor could we get him to stop the car and turn around. This was horrifying to me, a person who had always loved animals and who couldn't even kill a mouse.

Andy and I watched out the back window until Tuffy disappeared from sight, tears streaming down our faces as we lost our friend. The image will always be burned into my mind of that poor old dog trying his best to catch up to us, and I knew it would stay in my son's mind forever as well. We hated Pat for it, both Andy and I, and Andy cried all night long. He asked Pat whether we could go back and get him, and in a matter-of-fact tone, Pat said, "No, Tuffy is better off this way. He's a nice dog, and somebody will give him a home, and we can't have dogs here."

Two weeks later, Pat brought home two Doberman pinchers. So much for not being able to have dogs. He'd always wanted a Doberman, and this was his chance.

He gave one away and decided to keep the female. I firmly believe he got rid of my dog just so he could have this one, and I was furious about her being in my house after he'd dropped my Tuffy off on the side of the road like he was trash. I couldn't forgive Pat for that, but he told me, "You didn't raise him as a puppy, so I don't know why you're so upset about this." He never had remorse, but I refused to take care of this new dog and after a great deal of nagging and persistence on my part, she finally ended up going to my brother.

I just didn't feel Pat deserved any dogs after his cruel act. I knew that if I gave in, my own lifelong dreams would never come to pass. The problem was everybody we knew loved and adored "Mr. Nice Guy" Pat. When things went wrong, it was automatically my fault. Pat was just too smart to let anybody else see his mean streak.

I decided I needed to talk to someone who had no bias one way or the other, so I went to the pastor from our church. I told him the story of Tuffy and explained that giving in would mean giving up my lifelong dream of raising horses. We prayed together, and he told me to go home and pray to the Lord and await his answer. He told me to earnestly ask God to give me the desires of my husband's heart.

Even though I didn't like this advice, the pastor was so full of love that I knew he was speaking the truth. I prayed this prayer nightly for some time. I can't tell you at what point my desires changed, but eventually I forgot about the horses, and my dream did become raising dogs alongside my husband. I know many women would be aggravated at this, but my focus was not just on my husband; my focus was on Jesus. That is as plain and simple as I can explain it. I still felt like a liberated woman, but I was liberated in Christ. He had seen all my pain, and he certainly would never do anything to cause me further pain. My desires simply were changed to something else.

Together, Pat and I purchased the American Kennel Club's breed standard book and started reading. I knew Pat wanted Dobermans, but I didn't. I had always wanted collies, since my childhood dog had been a collie mix. Pat absolutely didn't want collies, so we kept reading and finally narrowed our choices down to German shepherds or Akitas. We both liked the fierce loyalty of the Akita and how they protected their families, so we decided that was the breed for us. We started reading *Dog World* magazine, since it had a breeder's directory, and we were surprised to find a breeder only thirty minutes from us. We looked at their dogs and liked them from the very beginning.

Then we wrote a breeder in Ohio and requested pictures of his dogs. It just so happened that their top stud and bitch were due to whelp at any moment. The price was five hundred dollars, as much money as I'd spent on any of my horses, and we sent in a deposit of fifty dollars. We wanted a brown pup with black overlay, and once the pups were born, we learned they had a male that fit that description exactly. As soon as we sent them the remainder of the money and the pup turned eight weeks old, they would ship him to us. That would be in July, right after our baby was born. Life was getting exciting now. Our family was about to change drastically, from a mom and dad with one little boy to parents with two children and a family dog.

Summer progressed, and I started feeling afraid of having another baby. I was so in love with my Andy that I didn't think it was possible to love another child as much as I loved him. I was embarrassed to think that, but my fear was real. I knew deep down that I would love my new baby as much as I loved Andy, but I just couldn't imagine it. I couldn't discuss this with Pat, as he couldn't have cared less about my feelings. He was still acting like I was getting fatter to annoy him, so Andy and I discussed the baby more than Pat and I did. He was excited about having a new baby sister, and he was insistent that it be a girl. One day my almost four-year-old little boy took an old rag, packed a clean shirt and pants in it, and tied it to a stick. He looked at me and said, "Mamma, I'm going to run away from home if I have a baby brother!"

I told him we get what we're supposed to get and that babies are a gift from God, but I felt sorry for him with his little stick and change of clothes. I finally asked why he didn't want a baby brother, and he looked at me and said, "I want to be the only brother in this family. I want to be the only boy." I was hoping it was a girl myself, but now I really wanted it to be for Andy's sake. I hadn't realized my son felt so threatened by this baby, and I assured him that if our baby was a little boy, he would still be special to me forever, but I don't think he bought it. I knew he'd been affected by the incident with Tuffy and that it had changed how he related to Pat. Though I never in my life would have done anything to deliberately hurt my little boy, here we were.

On July 4, we went on a picnic with friends. I climbed up and down a hill most of the day, hoping to induce labor but to no avail. I was already overdue, and that night, disappointed, I got ready for bed and climbed in, but I was restless and wide awake, so I got up and cleaned the house. I felt a little twinge of pain, but I ignored it as it didn't feel like a labor pain. Ten minutes later, it happened again. I took a bath just in case it was labor, and like clockwork, my pains started coming ten minutes apart. It was now three in the morning, and I was energized, so I woke Pat and told him I was probably in labor. Maybe all those climbs up the hill had helped after all.

I made him get the camera and take a picture of me in my bra and panties so I could look back someday and see the full effect of my pregnancy. Still full of energy but knowing I needed rest, I lay back down, hoping I could fall asleep. As soon as I stopped moving, my labor pains stopped. As restless as I was, I finally fell asleep. I woke to sunlight shining on my face and got up to make breakfast for my son and Pat.

The longer I walked around, the harder my labor pains became, so after Pat and Andy ate, we drove Andy to my mother's and called my doctor. When we arrived at the hospital, he had me lie down, and of course my labor pains quit. After an hour or so without any pains, he told us to go for a walk to try to start them up again. It worked. As we were heading back to my room, we passed the nursery with all the new babies in it. One baby in particular caught Pat's eye. She had long, dark hair that almost curled.

Just then a nurse wrapped that baby in a blanket and brought her out. Pat walked over to see her and told the woman she was handed to, "Your baby girl is so beautiful; you must be so happy." This lady looked at Pat and said, "I'm from the adoption agency. This baby is being put up for adoption." Pat was mortified and actually started crying. I think it was at that moment he realized he was about to have a baby, too. I was whisked into the delivery room, as my pains were tremendous, and Pat started chanting, "We're having a baby; we're having a baby!" I guess it finally dawned on him that I wasn't just getting fat to make him mad.

Then our baby girl was born. She was so beautiful, so perfect Andy's wishes were answered! I was exhausted and needed to sleep, but Pat sat in the room with me and our new daughter, Danielle, and held her all the time I slept. He was amazed at this birth; it was probably the first real event in his life, like Andy's birth had been for me. He was simply in love with his daughter. His big arms were so gentle holding that tiny baby. She had the most beautiful face I'd ever seen, with perfect features. It was round as could be, and her hair was dark and long. She brought out a softness in her dad I'd never seen before. He held her for hours, admiring her. She smiled at him as he talked to her, and he was so surprised. The nurse came in and told him it was just gas, but he knew better, and so did I. That baby did smile at him when he talked to her, not once but many times. I recognized what Pat was going through right then, as I had gone through it when Andy was born. He couldn't believe it himself. He was in love, and this was partly his creation, and the lights turned on for him, at least momentarily. When I finally woke up, Pat was still holding his daughter in his arms, smiling and talking to her. It was a brief but precious time.

Coming home with a new baby was exciting, too. Andy was delighted to see his baby sister and wanted to hold her right away. We sat him on the couch and put pillows around him and laid his baby sister in his lap. He beamed with pride holding her all by himself; he really was her big brother!

My fear of not loving this baby as much as I loved Andy passed at the moment of birth. There was something special about Danielle. She was so sweet, and she rarely cried. I thought that maybe something was wrong with her, since I didn't know babies could be this good. I could put her on a blanket on the floor, and she would lie there for hours and look around. She had the ability to self-entertain and seemed to have no insecurities. She started out right away being good and remained that way throughout her life. In fact, she slept through the night the first night I brought her home. I was impressed and a little nervous. Andy hadn't slept through a whole night until he was two and a half years old. Needless to say, I was completely delighted with my little boy and little girl. To me, we were a complete family.

Now that Danielle was here, it was just a matter of time before our new puppy was shipped to us. The day he came, I packed up the kids and drove to the airport to pick him up. Then I put his crate in the car and drove to my husband's workplace so we could all open it together. He came outside and cut the tape, and here was the most beautiful puppy I'd ever seen. We all ogled and fussed over him, and he instantly became a part of our family. We named him Jabo, and when he turned six months old, Pat entered him in his first show. The show was downstate, and he went by himself. I stayed home with the kids, anxiously waiting to see how Jabo did. He was the only Akita entered, so of course he won, but thereafter we found it hard to gain the points he needed to achieve a championship title. We thought he was so beautiful he would just go out there and win, win, win, but we were about to have a rude awakening. Neither of us really knew what we were doing, and though I tried to read as much about dog shows and Akitas as I could, I couldn't quite grasp how the point system for achieving championship status worked.

Pat trained Jabo at least once a day for fifteen minutes, and we kept in close touch with our breeders, but we weren't winning like we thought we should be, and Pat decided the problem was probably him. He suggested I do the showing myself, and though I was afraid, I practiced at home with Jabo and entered him in an upcoming show. I was so scared I couldn't sleep for the entire week before the show, but when it was my turn to go into the ring, I somehow mustered the confidence to do so.

We still didn't win, but we continued trying. At the thirteenth show, three other Akitas were in the ring with him, and we took fourth place. I started to realize that when there were two Akitas in the ring, he would place second. If there were three Akitas in the ring, he would place third, and so on. I looked at the dog we loved so much and couldn't see his flaws. After we left the show that day, we pulled over to the side of the road and both Pat and I cried. We had spent so much money on this dog, on the kennel, and on all the shows, and he hadn't beaten one single animal.

I looked at Pat and said, "How are we ever going to advertise him? What would we say? At stud, the dog who hasn't beaten any dog in the whole state of Michigan? Pat suggested we take him to a former breeder who was now a judge for a critique.

As soon as we got Jabo out of the car, she started to laugh. She looked at us and said, "I can see the problem right now. You need to take this baby home and let him grow up!" We thanked her for her help, feeling a little foolish that we'd never noticed that our puppy who was gangly and all legs needed maturing. This was a true-to-life example of the old saying "Love is blind."

Summer was right around the corner once again, and my mother wanted us to buy her house from her. We'd been looking for a new house, but I wasn't sure I wanted that one. It was a lot older than what I was looking for, and Pat had proven to be very lazy about fixing things. What's more, it was only an acre lot, which meant I would still be unable to have horses. We'd already applied for a loan for low-income families, and we could have built a new home. I tried to convince Pat that was the best thing to do, since a new home would need little maintenance, but he didn't agree. Finally I conceded, even though I didn't want to do business with my mother.

Before we could close, the house had to be brought up to code, and I knew that would take a good amount of work. We finally agreed on terms, and in the midst of the remodeling, I applied to a local dog grooming business for a job. The owner, Susie, told me she wasn't interested in training anybody just then, but I bugged her until she agreed to hire and train me. If we were to survive in dogs, I needed to make more money than I was making at the little corner store.

The closing turned into a nightmare. Through no fault of our own, the closing date was moved up, and we barely had enough time to meet our end of the deal, which included painting, rewiring, redoing the bathroom to bring it up to code, and wallpapering the entire house. I panicked. Pat was too lazy to help me, and there was just too much to do in just two weeks. Then Mom told me she wanted the washer, dryer, refrigerator, and stove from the house. I told her they'd come with the house when she'd bought it, and I'd assumed they were coming with this purchase. All the other houses we'd looked at had included these items. When she said they weren't coming with the house, I told her I'd changed my mind and I didn't want to purchase the house anymore.

Mom's response was to go to the minister of my church to plead for help dealing with her unreasonable daughter. She portrayed herself as a victim once again and told them I was backing out of our already agreed-upon deal, and I couldn't believe it when the pastor I so admired and his wife and some of the elders intervened on her behalf. I told them all it wasn't just about the stove, refrigerator, washer, and dryer. I just didn't want to purchase the house anymore. I couldn't get the work done on time, and I couldn't afford to buy the appliances she was going to take. The pastor told Mom she should reconsider and leave that stuff, since it was there when she bought the house.

Then I told the pastor I couldn't believe she'd gone to them to tattle on me. I had made a sound decision not to purchase the house. We hadn't signed any papers yet, and now I was the bad guy for changing my mind. Ultimately, the pastor felt terrible about getting involved. He said that mom had come to him in tears, and I have no doubt that she did. She was always a good victim, and she had a way of convincing people of her tales of woe. Nonetheless, before everybody left that day and against my better judgment, I had agreed to purchase the house after all, but now I had to hustle to get everything done. I worked at my job in the daytime and at the house at night. True to form, I didn't get much help from Pat. His time in the evening after work was his time to do nothing, and that is exactly what he did the majority of the time.

By the day of the closing, I was exhausted. I barely finished steaming the carpets before the inspection. Buying my first home should have been a joyous moment, but I was too tired to enjoy the fruits of my labor. I still can't believe all I accomplished in that two-week period. I wallpapered the kitchen, Andy's bedroom, and the hallway; painted the living room walls and all the ceilings; painted the cupboards; scraped the old paint off the basement floor and repainted that; and steamed the carpets. I did the whole house, except the bathroom, in my "spare" time. My spare time was when I wasn't working and taking care of the kids. Of course, I was allowed to come home and cook for Pat and the kids during this period.

By this time, our second anniversary was right around the corner. To celebrate, we planned to attend a big Akita show in Ohio. Several days before we were to leave, Pat unexpectedly took the first of what I soon came to call his "mini-vacations" from home. He took our car and left the kids and me stranded. He came back about noon on the day we were to leave on our ten-hour trip, and when I asked where he'd been, he gave me the silent treatment. Finally he told me he'd been downstate with his sister and her best friend. I knew this unscrupulous sister well. She was a drunk who did drugs all the time. Her baby had been born severely mentally and physically handicapped as a result, but not even that had slowed her down.

He portrayed the best friend by saying, "She's just like a sister to all of us." I knew he was lying, and I told him he had no right to run off and spend time with another woman. He acted offended I'd made such an assumption, and that was the only excuse he needed to say he didn't want to go anywhere with me.

I decided I wasn't going to let him ruin our plans, and since I had Jabo ready to go, I jumped in the car and left Pat at home with the kids. I deserved the break, and if I'd stayed home, he'd just have ignored me anyway.

It was an exciting weekend. I saw many Akitas, and I was learning to understand the different types, as well as the different stages they go through in maturing. The trip was not only educational, but it also was fun. I wanted to be a great breeder, and I was beginning to realize that most of the other breeders had huge egos. That was not for me; I wanted to be able to recognize problems and to excel with my breeding program. I didn't ever again want to be in the position we'd been in with Jabo and not be able to see the faults in my dogs.

I have to admit I hardly thought of Pat the entire weekend. By the time I got home, I'd decided to pretend nothing was wrong, and of course I was happy to see the kids. They had missed me, too, and I knew when I saw their faces that I would do everything in my power to keep them in smiles. Indeed, that became my ultimate mission in life and dictated my decision to try again and again to work things out with Pat.

Chapter 9

⟩✦⟨

A Marriage Disintegrates, but Life Goes On

I was now entering a new phase in life, one that consisted of many twists and turns in the dog show world and many twists and turns with Pat. When Jabo turned a year old, I bought Pat a two-year-old bitch he'd had his eye on from the breeders who lived only thirty miles away. Aubrey took to all of us, including the kids. I was hoping beyond hope the dogs would fill the void in his soul. This was also the year Pat had told me he would get a vasectomy if he felt our family was large enough. When I brought this up, he informed me our family was indeed large enough, but he was not going to do that to himself. I couldn't afford to take time off for surgery, much less afford a tubal ligation, so we both dropped the subject.

Pat was still periodically disappearing on his mini-vacations, but he spent a lot of time with the kids when he was home and seemed to enjoy them. I loved being with the kids, too. They were fun loving, and they missed me when I was gone. By all appearances, we had a perfect family, and even though I worked, I was committed to family life when I came home. I cooked dinner every night, and after dinner, I cleaned up the house, did the dishes, got the kids their baths, and put them to bed. It was all fairly routine, as in most homes, and it was usually 10:30 or so before I had any time to myself. Of course, Pat's relaxation started from the moment he walked in the door after work until he went to bed. I often wondered whether Velcro were stuck to our Lazy Boy recliner that wouldn't permit him to get out of it to help. He typically sat and watched TV while dictating to me what needed to be done. As far as he was concerned, my job was "recreational fun," so I didn't need to relax when I got home.

For these reasons and more, I began to harbor a great deal of hostility toward him. I asked him daily what he would like for dinner, and his reply always was, "I don't care. Surprise me!" The truth was he did care, and he would invariably complain about what I'd made. It was one of his famous set-ups, and this way he could justify being angry at me. I knew the scoop I knew what men did when they were looking for an excuse to walk out, and sure enough, Pat's brief disappearing acts continued.

Then I began to get sick often, and I wondered what was going on. We went to several shows downstate with Jabo, and I barely made it through the ring. I didn't even want to think about being pregnant again. Even though Pat had refused to get a vasectomy, I knew he would consider a pregnancy my fault. I delayed going to the doctor for fear he would give me the news I dreaded, and since Pat didn't pay much attention to me, I got away with this for some time.

When I was about four and a half months along, I made a doctor's appointment, and soon learned I needed an ultrasound. Not only was I pregnant, but the doctor also thought I might be pregnant with twins. I decided to keep that part of the news to myself. That night I made dinner as usual, cleaned up the dishes, and got the kids to bed. Then I took my chances and told Pat I was pregnant. As I'd expected, he was furious, but I reminded him he'd refused to get the vasectomy he'd promised me and that it wasn't merely my responsibility to practice safe sex.

The next day, I told the kids they were going to have a new baby brother or sister, and they were thrilled. Andy was five and a half now, and Danielle was just more than one and a half. This time, Andy wasn't insistent that it had to be a baby sister, and I was pleased with his progress on the boy/girl issue. I kept reminding myself that it didn't matter what Pat thought; this was the greatest blessing God could give any woman. Other than my fear of going through labor again, I now felt completely at peace about having this baby. I didn't care anymore what Pat thought; this was my baby, just like the others.

Though I was even sicker with this pregnancy than I'd been with the first two, I refused to complain and continued to work every day. I had no choice, since we now had two dogs and two kids and Pat's income alone wasn't sufficient to pay the bills. I was hugely relieved when the ultrasound showed only one baby. At that point, I felt like the luckiest girl in the world, even though I had many problems with this pregnancy. Shortly after it was confirmed I was pregnant, an unknown pain began, one I'd had for a couple of days when I was pregnant with Danielle that had dissipated on its own. Now, the pain in my side was so severe I was doubled over and couldn't walk. After a blood test, the doctor told me I needed to spend a couple of days in the hospital. I had an infection, and he needed to do more testing.

Pat was still so angry with me that he refused to discuss my condition. I called my mother as a backup to watch the kids in case he took off on one of his mini-vacations, and the next morning he silently dropped me off at the hospital. I was put in a room right away, and an IV containing strong antibiotics considered safe to use during pregnancy was begun. I was there all day, and when evening came, I called home to see how things were going. When Pat heard my voice, he said, "So, what do you want?" I told him, "I thought I would call and see whether you and the kids are okay."

He said, "They're fine, and I'm fine. Is that all you want?" His voice was monotone, with a meanness I'd never heard before. I told him I wanted to talk to the kids, so he put them on. They were full of questions that I answered the best I could. After we'd chatted, I asked them to put their dad back on the phone. He got back on and said, "What do you want?" I told him I didn't want anything and that I was sorry I'd bothered him. With that, he hung up on me.

I had my own unanswered questions. My doctor was checking me for sexually transmitted diseases and asked over and over whether I'd been with anybody else. I knew for certain I hadn't been with anybody else, and I told him so. Then he asked whether Pat had been faithful to me. I told him I wished I could say with some certainty that he'd been faithful, but I couldn't. I knew Pat hadn't been faithful, but the doctor would have to talk to him to get any answers. Just getting him to come to the hospital was going to be a trick.

I ended up staying in the hospital an entire week rather than the couple of days the doctor had anticipated. On top of that, I had no visitors the entire time. Pat never once came to see me, nor did he bring the children. Far worse, I was diagnosed with pelvic inflammatory disease, a sexually transmitted condition. I wasn't at all happy with Pat, but when I went home, he continued to give me the silent treatment.

I don't know how I got through this period except by changing my center of awareness and focusing on the kids. Of course, I felt nothing but revulsion for Pat from that point on. We didn't have a lot going for us before I went to the hospital, but after this, I had no feelings left for him. The furthest thing from my mind was ever being intimate with him again. I felt I needed to keep him around for the kids' sake, but I could barely carry on a conversation with him, much less let him touch me. He made my skin crawl, but I went on with life as best I could.

Soon after I came home from the hospital, Aubrey came into season, and we bred her to Jabo. We placed an ad in *Dog World* magazine and received many calls, but we lost three puppies in that litter, two that died at birth and one that lingered for three days. It was incredibly traumatic to watch that pup slowly die while I stood helplessly by. No matter how many times I kept putting the puppy with Aubrey, she would remove it from the rest of the litter, and it would be off by itself crying.

We were taking turns with other families having a once-a-week prayer group at each other's houses, and it just so happened it was our turn the evening the third puppy died. I sat through the whole meeting and parayed for her life. When the last person finally left, I sat down and bawled my eyes out. I knew this was part of breeding, but nonetheless it was a painful experience. I thought I even saw a tear in Pat's eye.

The surviving pups grew into fat, fluffy puppies, and we kept three, two girls and a boy. The boy, Bigg's, was turning out to be gorgeous. He was massive and stunning, everything a breeder strives to get in a lifetime of breeding, and here he was in our first litter. Unfortunately, we still had a lot to learn about dogs. Nobody had ever told us we couldn't keep males with males and females with females. I knew Akitas were fighting dogs and aggressive toward animals of the same sex, but I didn't realize they would fight if they were from the same family and had grown up together. It never dawned on me that in a dog's world, sires, dams, littermates, sons, and daughters mean nothing.

Unlike Jabo, who grew fast but took a long time to mature, Bigg's grew slow-ly and stayed massive. At six months old one, of the bitches came into season, and Jabo decided to eliminate his competition. Pat had been kenneling the two males together, and after a great deal of nagging from me when I saw how they were fighting, he finally agreed to put them in separate kennels, but he put them side by side. They not only continued to fight, but also Jabo ultimately tried to pull Bigg's through the cyclone fencing by his tail, and broke it in the process.

It took three more dogfights and one very bitchy wife for it to sink into Pat's head that these two dogs could not be side by side. Even so, because he'd put them in such a position for so long, they couldn't even look at each other anymore with-out having an altercation. I was simply furious that such a stupid situation had developed. Pat had since been told by other Akita people that he couldn't kennel two males together, but he was so obstinate he had to push the limits. It was a high cost to pay for an otherwise perfect Akita who was now sporting a bad attitude toward other males as well as a broken tail.

The breed standard is specific that Akita tails must curl up and over their backs and dip to or below the back. An uncurled tail is a disqualification. I worked on Bigg's tail every night and stretched it by hand so the ligaments wouldn't heal tightly and uncurl it worse than it already was. I did this for several months, but his tail remained so-so. However, when I walked him and another male tried to approach, his tail went way down onto and past his back, just as it should. I knew I needed to try to finish his championship as soon as he was ready to show, as his tail would worsen in time. It was hard to devote that much time to him, and I prayed I could hold on until he completed his championship.

Summertime was approaching, and I was looking more and more pregnant every day. I asked Pat to show Jabo for me in an upcoming show, and not only did he do so, but he also won with him. Jabo showed his heart out for Pat that day, and I was thrilled, as I didn't want Pat's interest to wane. On top of this, Rick and Rita, the original breeders we'd gotten Jabo from, were bringing our pick of their litter, a black and white pinto female, to the show. They'd taken the pick from our first litter, and now it was our turn. We were on top of the world.

When we went to get our puppy, we were surprised to see that she was fawn and white, not black and white. I'd been specific about the color we wanted, and I exclaimed, "This puppy isn't black and white!"

Rita replied, "She was black and white yesterday before we left for here!" I looked at her in total dismay, but that didn't phase her. I put the puppy on the ground to see her walk and look at her conformation, but all she did was cower. She certainly hadn't been socialized properly. I was more than a little upset, but she was pretty, and I figured I could look past the color issue.

Rick and Rita were also delivering two other males that day who supposedly were littermates. All I can say is these males were like night and day. One was at least eight inches taller than the other. Rick and Rita were supposed to be reputable breeders, and I was getting my first glimpse at what appeared to be dishonesty.

The next day, I discovered our new puppy was as cowhocked as could be. This is a serious conformation fault, and if she didn't grow out of it, she could never be shown. I called Rita, and she said, "That's funny; she was straight as a ruler when she left yesterday!" I responded that she was also black and white two days ago and left it at that. The pup was obviously a leftover they couldn't sell, but we decided to keep her anyway.

In spite of his win with Jabo, Pat's interest in the dogs and showing was declining at a rapid pace. It seemed the more I became involved, the less he liked being involved himself. I couldn't understand this. Our first litter of puppies was stunningly beautiful, just what we'd prayed for. They weren't even a year old yet, and here he was already dropping the ball. On top of this, he'd taken several of his mini-vacations since I'd gotten pregnant and had also begun to embarrass me in public. Other people thought he was just being funny, but comments in front of my peers such as "Ron, you're sharp as a marble!" let me know better.

He also refused to help out at home. The yard hadn't been mowed in months, and one June day a few weeks before the baby was due, I came home from work, and it looked as if our house were sitting in a field. I'd asked Pat repeatedly to mow the lawn, and he kept saying he would, but day after day, it continued to look worse. I was very embarrassed, and I begged him to please mow it now. It was a Friday night, a beautiful evening to work outside, and he looked at me and said, "If you want the lawn mowed, do it yourself."

I was so angry I did just that. I went outside and started our push lawn mower and started mowing. I was hoping he'd feel guilty that his hugely pregnant wife was out mowing the lawn while he was inside relaxing in his Velcro chair, but I finally realized he simply didn't care. In fact, when I walked into the house after two solid hours of mowing, he was in bed asleep. I was angry, and I mean good and angry. It's very sad to be shaken into reality like this. There simply was nothing in the world that could make him feel any guilt.

I continued to work until a week before my due date, as we needed the money. I had a doctor's appointment on June 30, and as the doctor examined me, I told him I was in labor right then. He told me I was feeling false labor pains. I told him I knew the difference and that I was in labor, and for the first time I began second-guessing my choice of doctors. I'd decided to go to him since he was supposed to be an excellent obstetrician as well as family doctor, and though he'd seen me throughout this entire pregnancy, he now took Pat off to the side and told him I needed to make an appointment for a week from today. As we left, I told him, "You won't make it to the hospital to deliver my baby later on today because you've convinced yourself you're right."

I was quite upset, but Pat just gave me a dirty look. When we got home, he went to work. I had pains all day long exactly ten minutes apart. They weren't that strong at first, but as the day wore on, they did, too. I cooked dinner while stooping every ten minutes, doubled over with pain. They were getting very intense, but since they were still ten minutes apart, I knew I had plenty of time to get to the hospital. I managed to make dinner but just barely. I wanted to keep it simple, so I decided on spaghetti. Pat came home from work right on schedule and complained about having spaghetti again. Then he ignored me, except for giving me those condemning sideways glances he was so good at.

The pains were so intense, though still only ten minutes apart, that I decided to get the kids ready for bed early just in case I had to go to the hospital. Then I did the dishes and went to bed, but I was in so much agony I kept Pat awake. This was the first pregnancy in which my pains didn't stop when I laid down. My very annoyed husband finally decided to take his pillow and sleep in the kids' room with them since my moaning and groaning was keeping him awake. I eventually got up and called my mother to come stay with the kids. It was now three in the morning, and my pains were so severe I wanted somebody to kill me, but they were still ten minutes apart, just like clockwork.

It finally occurred to me that I might be in trouble with this baby, so I woke Pat up and told him I needed to go to the hospital immediately. He slowly got up and went into the bathroom, and soon I heard the shower running.

I couldn't believe it! As I sat there waiting for him to come out, I noticed that my pains seemed to be coming quite a bit faster than ten minutes apart. I started to time them and realized they were now less than one minute apart. Though they hadn't stopped, they'd slowed down while I was in bed. Now that I was up and moving, they were right on top of each other. I went to the bathroom door and yelled, "Hurry, my pains are less than one minute apart!" He said, "Hold on; I'm almost done." I told him, "I can't hang on; you're going to have to deliver this baby yourself if you don't hurry!"

He came out walking at the pace of a turtle. The more I pushed him, the slower he moved. He refused to help me to the car, though by now I could hardly walk. When we arrived at the hospital, I was in so much pain I could barely talk to the nurses at registration. I was happy when they grabbed a wheelchair to take me to maternity. Somebody had finally seen the urgency of the situation, and when I was wheeled away, Pat was left in the dust filling out admission papers.

The doctor on call came in and, as I'd predicted earlier that day, told me my doctor would not be able to make it on time because my labor was too advanced. My water hadn't broken yet, and he asked, "What's going to happen when I break your water?" I told him, "I will have this baby by the third contraction!" He looked at the nurse and said, "Let her have one contraction here, and have her to me in the delivery room by the second contraction." Finally, somebody was listening to me. He knew I knew more about my body than he did. He broke my water just as Pat came in the room, and sure enough, by the third contraction, my third baby was born.

They handed me my beautiful baby girl and laid her on my stomach, and I was amazed to see she looked just like Danielle! I even said, "Hey, this is the same baby I had last time!" She had a soft, round little face, with the same sweetness as her sister. The only difference was that this little baby had blue eyes and, at first, red blotches. She didn't cry at all. She just lay on my stomach and stared up at me. She was beautiful, as all my babies were, and once again I knew I had received a very precious gift. I asked Pat to hold her when they began to stitch me up, and he just looked at me and said, "No, I don't want to."

Soon, we were moved to a room with curtains and low lighting, and I asked him again whether he would like to hold his new daughter. Unlike after Andy's and Danielle's births, where I'd still had energy, I felt extremely weak after having this baby. My arms felt like rubber bands, and I was afraid my newborn was going to fall off me to the floor. Pat told me he was too tired, and when I tried to tell him how much I wanted to sleep, he replied, "Don't we all." I don't know why he even bothered to come to the hospital. I'd been in labor twenty-eight hours by then, and I was exhausted. I finally told him to just leave, and I decided to name my baby without his help. I chose Elizabeth Anne, a beautiful name for a beautiful baby, and with Pat gone, my tension diminished to nothing.

Later that morning when my doctor came in, I gave him a hard time about not delivering my baby and asked whether he remembered that I wanted my tubes tied. He told me I was scheduled for surgery just then, so off I went. I was relieved, as I refused to have any more kids with Pat and I didn't want to seem irresponsible.

As usual, he didn't visit me in the hospital, but I called home later that day to talk to the kids. They were excited about their new baby sister and wanted me to come home right away so they could see her. I told them I would be home tomorrow and they could fuss over Elizabeth as much as they wanted then. I was so happy to hear their excited voices. This was their baby sister, and they shared my joy. Then Pat got on the phone and told me Danielle had fallen out of bed the night before and hurt her arm. He said she could hardly move it. He'd taken her to emergency, and they'd said it was just bruised and didn't need an X-ray, but he told me if he even touched it, she started to cry.

I felt terrible. Danielle had just moved to her "big girl" bed and wasn't used to it yet. I really wanted to go home now. I talked to her again so I could ask about her arm and told her I would be home the next day and would kiss it and make it better.

My homecoming was full of excitement. The kids were so excited they could hardly contain themselves. I walked into the house and sat the baby carrier right smack in the middle of the table, and they both got up on the table and just oooed and aaaahhed over Elizabeth. This was a precious moment in time. They gently touched her soft skin with their little hands and made their introductions to their sister themselves, just as excited over Liz as Andy had been the day Danielle had come home. They both talked to her in tiny soft voices, and she responded to them. I was amazed at this, but even infants can tell when they are with other children, and she knew who they were even then.

When I reached out to help Danielle off the table, she cried and said I'd hurt her sore arm. I took her shirt off and immediately saw her collarbone protruding from her skin. It looked like it was broken in half. I told Pat I needed to take her to the doctor immediately. When we got there, he told me he didn't have to do an X-ray to see that it was broken. He also said they didn't cast collarbones, that they healed on their own.

I took Danielle home and knew there was nothing I could do, but she was a real trooper. Unless you forgot and touched her chest or arm, you never would have known she had a broken collarbone. She didn't complain or whine about it; she just wanted to play with the new baby.

Though I didn't want to, I went back to work when Elizabeth was three weeks old. The bills were stacking up, and I had no choice. I was breastfeeding her, which made working even more difficult, but nothing was as difficult as Pat's passive-aggressive behavior toward me. I would call home just as I was ready to leave and tell him not to feed Elizabeth. My breasts would be so full and sore that just moving my arms caused excruciating pain. I would walk into the house with my arms out from my sides, saying, "Where's my baby? Where is she?" I must have looked like some kind of zombie monster from the movies.

Pat in all his cruelty would say, "I just fed her and put her in bed. She's sleeping." He'd fed her on purpose. He knew it took me only ten minutes to get home from work, but his excuse was that she was crying, so he'd fed her to quiet her down. I knew better, since he did this every day, and it wasn't long before he went on another mini-vacation.

When Elizabeth was six weeks old, I began showing Bigg's. He was beautiful but a handful, since he was determined to beat up every male in the ring with him. He was too much dog for me to handle, but he won almost every time I showed him. Though our success was gratifying, Pat became even more hateful. When we had our next litter and I was paying a lot of money for my ad in *Dog World*, he told prospective buyers who called that we didn't have any puppies for sale at the time. At least he was still cleaning the kennels every day, but I had to be careful about my behavior around the dogs. If I said I liked a particular puppy, he went out of his way to be cruel to it. If I said the sky was blue, he said it was black, and so our marriage went.

Although he appeared to be the nicest guy in the world to everyone else, he became more condescending and cruel to me as time went on, and I began to be able to predict when he was about to take another mini-vacation. Quite simply, he would work extra hard to make me mad just before he left so he could storm out of the house. The kids loved their dad immensely, and this was where my quandary lay. There was nothing I wouldn't do for them, and he knew it. This gave him the freedom to come and go as he pleased, because he knew I wouldn't hurt the kids by throwing him out.

One night, I had a dream about our dogs. I woke up and told Pat that by the end of the year, we would have the top-producing bitch in the country. He laughed at me, but I stood on my faith and wrote the breeders Aubrey had come from and told them this was going to happen. We truly were blessed with these beautiful dogs, and I felt this vision had come from God himself.

Sure enough, Aubrey did indeed become the number one producing Akita bitch in the whole country that year, which essentially meant that more pups out of her achieved championship status than from any other dog. Jabo was also ranked as one of the top five producing stud dogs that year. I was so thankful to the Lord for this vision and this confirmation of his presence in my life. I was ecstatic, to say the least. I knew people thought I was crazy for sharing my vision from God, but I'd always hoped I could be a good example for Christ.

To my surprise, our success did not have the effect I'd anticipated. Though a few people in the dog world seemed happy for us, most were mean, bitter, and hateful. We had gone from raw newcomers to the top very quickly, but I believe it was part of God's plan, and we certainly did work hard for it. Unbelievable as it sounds, Pat did not in the least appreciate that we were one of the top breeders of Akitas in the country. He continued to refuse to go to the shows with me, but at least I was often able to take the kids. My plans were to continue breeding and showing, even without Pat's support. I prayed about this and felt led to keep going. We had the hottest breeding pair in the country right then, and it didn't seem right to stop just because he'd decided he wasn't interested. In fact, I felt I would be doing a disservice to the breed by failing to produce puppies. My pups were not only beautiful, but also their conformation was correct. It was the conformation this breed needed so badly. There were lots of pretty Akitas out there who were a disaster when they moved, with their legs going every way but the way they were supposed to.

At one of the shows, I met a woman named Barb who owned the younger brother to Jabo, and we became friends. I knew there was something a bit odd about her, but I needed somebody to travel with, and she did also, and soon we were going to all the shows together. Shortly after we began traveling together, I came home from a show, and Pat left, just like that. We hadn't had a fight; he just left. He was gone for eight weeks, by far the longest period he'd stayed away, and the kids missed him like crazy. Elizabeth cried every single night for her daddy, Danielle suffered in silence, and Andy was angry.

Their sadness broke my heart. Andy was nearly seven, Danielle nearly four, and Liz almost two. I could certainly live without Pat, but could they? They were awfully little, much too young to see anything other than the daddy they loved. I was sad for them and sad for myself, as I knew I would have to continue to sacrifice my own feelings for them.

When Pat came back, he told me he'd been staying with a friend who liked "sport fucking," a euphemism for recreational sex. No doubt Pat, too, had become a "sports" fan. The kids were thrilled to see him, and though I would have nothing to do with him physically, I continued to put up a good front for their sake. He had been home a little over a month, driving me crazy since he'd been fired after his last mini-vacation and wasn't working, when he decided we'd all go to an upcoming dog show downstate that would also allow him to visit the family that meant so much to him. We were only going to stay for only a day, so

I figured I could handle it. As expected, he took off and got drunk and came back with empty beer cans all over the inside of my car. I was infuriated and told him we had to go home right then. We were barely out of the driveway when he had me pull over and he got out. He told me he wasn't going anyplace with me, that he was leaving me and the kids.

They were visibly shaken and started to cry and begged him not to go. I said to him, "Don't you have any compassion for these kids?" He looked into the car, first at me and then at the kids, and said, "I don't want you, and I don't want these fucking kids. You don't mean anything to me, any of you!"

This devastated the children, and they started crying hard. They'd never seen this side of their father. I was shocked he'd said this, but he was drunk, and like most drunks, he didn't care about anything. Still, it was all I could do not to jump out of the car and try to kill him. He might as well have put an ice pick through my heart, hurting the kids like this, and we cried most of the way home. I knew they would never forget this, and though this wasn't the first time Pat had left us, it was the first time he'd spewed his anger at them. I'd never wanted them to see this part of him, and I'd protected them from a lot. They hadn't seen the time he'd held me down in the back yard and spat in my face over and over, saying, "I hate you, I hate you, I hate you!" They hadn't heard him say on another occasion when he was leaving, "If you're finding it hard to figure out what to do with the kids, line them up and shoot them!"

They didn't know about the day off I spent cleaning the house, steaming the carpets, cleaning the refrigerator and stove, doing the laundry, washing the curtains and bedding, washing the windows and walls, and scouring the bathroom only to have him walk in, open the cupboard doors, and say, "My mother's cupboards would never be this disorganized."

They didn't know he jumped to help fix plumbing fixtures for other people while our own bathroom sink hadn't worked for years. They didn't understand his belittling remarks in front of my peers. They didn't know about the time he sat in his "Velcro chair" and looked at me with total distaste and said, "You're a fat pig; you're only fat because you want to be." They didn't know he bounced checks until he'd destroyed our credit with his irresponsibility.

Counseling surely hadn't helped us. We'd changed churches again when Danielle was about a year old when the pastor we'd liked so much had been replaced by a dull preacher, and we'd been going to counseling on a weekly basis at this church for a solid year. As always, Pat had managed to convince everyone he was Mr. Nice Guy putting up with a bitchy, nagging wife, and as much as I liked our new church, the view of the elder who counseled us was that I'd taken over the man's position in the household and hadn't allowed Pat to be sufficiently in charge. I was the problem in our marriage, not Pat, because I was assertive. He also thought I was "emasculating" Pat by "wearing the pants in the family," and I was told my heart wasn't as forgiving as it should be. We'd even had marriage counseling at the adult mental health center in town. There, Pat always sat silently, never saying a word, and nothing whatsoever had ever come from any of these sessions.

With Pat apparently gone for good, I needed to make more money to support my family and pay the bills, so I resigned from my job for another, more promising, position. This turned out to be a disaster. I was never paid what I was promised, and when I turned the company in, I was fired. This wasn't my fault, but in the meantime, my old grooming position was taken. Soon, I didn't have a penny to my name, and I had to apply for food stamps just to feed my children. I didn't dare ask my mother for help. She'd told me long ago that if I ever took Pat back, she wouldn't help me out, and I'd let him come home too many times for her liking.

We had twelve dogs by then, and before long, I could barely feed them. I didn't want to give any of my dogs away, but I didn't have a choice. I called my friend Barb and had her take two of my bitches. She was already keeping two others that we owned together, and if she had these additional dogs, I could at least breed them and make some money off the pups. Essentially, I took Barb on as a partner. I even put her name in my ad with her phone number, since I was so broke I had to have my phone disconnected. Being handed two of the top dogs in the country on a silver platter was the deal of the century for her, but for me, this year that had started out so well with four champions already credited to Jabo, and Aubrey was coming to a screeching halt.

These would be my most trying times, and my troubles were only just beginning. Soon my car broke down, and I couldn't afford to fix it. Luckily, I got a job at a plant down the road that I could walk to and from every day, and baby-sitters took care of the kids while I worked. I hated my life right then and knew we'd all be better off if I went on welfare, but my pride wouldn't let me. These were lean times to be sure, and looking back, it's all one giant blur. I couldn't even make my house payments during this period, so I went on moratorium for six months. I was so stressed out that one day I just sat on the couch and cried. I couldn't see any light at the end of the tunnel, and I hated Pat for not caring about the kids or how we were going to make it financially. As far as I was concerned, I never wanted to see him again.

The only thing that kept me going was the knowledge that the four bitches at Barb's were due to whelp soon. Selling the pups would help me dig out of the hole I was in, and though time seemed to drag, finally my litters were on the ground and ready to sell. My only contact with Barb was a collect phone call here and there from the pay-phone at work, but she said she'd gotten a lot of calls on the fourteen pups, and I was encouraged.

Then one day I called and received devastating news: the puppies had gotten distemper, an infectious virus common in young dogs, and were dying one right after the other. I was beside myself. I needed this money to bail myself out of debt, and I couldn't figure out how they'd gotten sick, since Barb worked at a veterinarian's office and had the shots they needed at her disposal. Then she told me a bad batch of shots was to blame but that one puppy was left out of fourteen. I had that puppy's papers in my possession, but she offered to temporarily keep her for me so I wouldn't have the burden of feeding and looking after her.

Though I was relieved at this, I was devastated the others had died. Barb sounded traumatized herself, and I felt sorry for her. I knew what it felt like when one puppy died; I couldn't imagine what it had felt like to watch thirteen of them die one right after the other. This was just an all-around bad situation. I trusted her explicitly with my reputation and to handle my affairs. Now, I just had to figure out a new plan.

The first step was to find homes for my remaining dogs other than those in my core breeding program. This I was able to do, but even now, with the majority of my dogs taken care of, I was struggling to keep my head above water. I also had to come up with enough money to file for divorce, purely a self-preservation gesture. Pat was racking up bills, and as they were turned into collection, they became my debt. To my dismay, I was already responsible for several thousand dollars of his bills medical bills can be collected from the other spouse, and he'd been treated for gout off and on. What's more, before he'd left, Pat had written a check large enough and without my knowledge from one of the stacks of unused checks still in the box. All my checks that month had bounced, and I was still struggling to catch up from that. I had one year from the date I filed to come up with the rest of the money for the divorce, and my goal was to catch up by then. Plain and simple, I needed to set the wheels in motion to protect myself against any more new debt, and just knowing I had a plan made me feel like a huge burden had been lifted from my shoulders.

I also filed for divorce for another reason. After leaving us as he had, Pat had showed up drunk out of the blue one day with a car full of his drunk friends, including his sister and her girlfriend, and he and a couple of his male friends had walked around the yard and then urinated outside in front of the children. Pat was smug that day and very threatening, and when I'd called the police, I was informed I couldn't force him to leave without a restraining order, but that wasn't true for his friends. Afraid of being arrested, they'd left before the police arrived. The policeman who came over informed Pat that if they returned, they would be arrested. After the police left, Pat's friends had picked him up in front of the house and he'd left.

I never wanted that to happen again, and thankfully, that was all we'd seen or heard from Pat for nine full months. The kids and I were functioning well in his absence when he showed up sober, with no warning, with all his things in tow. The children were ecstatic to see him. I equated their reaction to the little kid who'd found a puppy and who begged, "Can we keep him, Mom; can we keep him?" He walked in like he'd never been gone, and I found myself in a very tough position.

I told Pat exactly how I felt about his not having any contact with the kids during that whole nine-month period. If I were to let him stay, he needed to understand it was for their sake only. I told him he should thank his lucky stars he had kids or he wouldn't be here, but I don't think he believed me. Believe it or not, he thought he was a real catch and that I was just saying these things to hurt him. I took a deep breath and said a silent prayer to strengthen myself for one more go-round with him.

Of course, Pat immediately began going to church regularly, though I'd quit attending. During my nine months of struggle when my car wasn't running, only one person from church had come to see how I was. This was a lady who'd dropped off a bag of groceries at my home one night. She'd come while I was at work and wouldn't leave her name with the baby-sitter, and I've always assumed she was from our church. I had no car and no food in the house with which to feed my family, and the experience of having her bring groceries to us would bear witness to me forever. Whoever she was, I knew this woman listened to God, but as far as the others were concerned, I'd ceased to exist. They could talk about all the love they had in Christ, but they surely fell short of showing it.

I began attending church again, hypocrites though they were, for the sake of my children and saving my marriage. It may sound incredible, but I still believed that having a father in my kids' lives was more important than not having Pat in mine, and I was still willing to put my feelings aside for the sake of the children. Oddly enough, no one seemed to have noticed that we hadn't been there for so many months! Pat and I also began counseling again through the church, but this time it was marriage counseling, with a man appointed specifically to this position. Before we'd just counseled with an elder, and mostly he'd counseled me on being a better wife.

During one of our sessions, Pat confessed he sometimes wished I were dead. He elaborated by saying, "I'm miserable with you, but when I'm gone, I'm miserable not being with you!" Then he added to the counselor, "I've thought about killing her!"

I'd always felt that some part of him hated me enough to kill me, as his temperament was so much like Dad's, but hearing it from his own lips was truly frightening. Pat must have realized he'd said too much, for he started back paddling and said he wouldn't act on his feelings; that was just how he felt sometimes.

The marriage counselor was extremely concerned. He said that in general it was best that couples stay together for the sake of the children, but in our case he was no longer sure this was best. I replied that it was no longer even in the kids' best interest to have Pat around. If I were killed, they wouldn't have a mother.

I was literally walking on eggshells when another situation came up. I came home from work one night to find a business card from a state trooper sitting on the table. Pat told me his sister's close friend Alma was living in fear of her estranged husband, Robby, who used to be Pat's good friend. He told me this man, Robby, had been involved thirteen years before in killing a shoe store manager for the deposit he was taking to the bank.

Pat went on to say that Robby was a cold-blooded criminal who hadn't missed a beat since he'd gotten away with this murder. Because Alma was afraid for her life and was just like part of Pat's family and this man didn't have any conscience, Pat said God wouldn't let him rest until he'd told the police Robby had killed that young man without any sense of conscience for doing so. He added, "No woman should have to live in fear!"

Like my dad, Pat wasn't a nice guy, nor did he have any conscience of his own, so I said, "Pat, you've been sleeping with Alma all along, and you couldn't care less about any woman living in fear!" I also accused him of being more involved in this murder than he was telling me. I added, "You've now involved us in this horrible murder with a crazy man like Robby on the loose. You just want him out of the way so you can carry on with his wife!"

What could Pat say? He admitted he wanted Robby out of the picture so he and Alma could carry on without fear of being killed, and I was simply dumbfounded that he'd jeopardized us for his own safety. Though his urges to kill me terrified me, I was livid that he'd used me to get out of town until things cooled off. He was afraid the police wouldn't be able to do anything to Robby and that he'd find out who'd told on him. I was also furious that he'd been cheating on me with Alma, who'd been one of his steady affairs over the past thirteen years, not to mention the whole four years he'd been married to me. Pat defended himself by saying, "I've never cheated on you. Every time I've been with another woman, we were separated." In his mind, whenever he was gone, even when he went on a mini-vacation, we were broken up, so that wasn't cheating!

By this time, I was beginning to suspect there was much I didn't know about Pat's past criminal activities. I already knew that when we were dating, I was part of his master plan to get off parole. By hanging out with me and getting married and playing Mr. Nice Guy, he looked terrific to the parole board. On top of that, he had adopted my son and had received nothing but rave reviews from the head of probate court. I put all this together after I saw how our marriage was unfolding and how fast he got off parole because of his involvement with Andy and me. In retrospect, I think that not only was I conned by Pat but also so was the state of Michigan parole board, and today I very much doubt he ever had any intention of trying to make our marriage work.

After confessing all this to me, he was extra nice to the kids, and he also made sure the church was on his side. It had always played its role effectively for him in the past, and he needed it now more than ever to keep me in line. Sure enough, soon he'd managed to get a job working for one of the deacons and offices after they'd closed for the night. Because our car didn't work, this man purchased a car for Pat to use. It was just a beater, but it was a car nonetheless. LeRoy trusted Pat explicitly and bought into his Nice Guy act, but he was about to get his first taste of "Mr. Nice Guy" firsthand.

I'd planned to go to an out-of-state dog show for Mother's Day weekend with a friend. Without showing and winning with your dogs, you can't sell them, and I badly needed to begin recouping my losses. Pat agreed to take care of the kids while I was gone. Since we were showing early Sunday morning, I knew I would be back early enough to celebrate Mother's Day with them, and I just plain needed to get away to digest my circumstances.

We had a good weekend and did some serious winning, which I sorely needed. On the way back home, I called to check in. Mom answered, which surprised me. She immediately began ranting and raving, but I couldn't understand what she was talking about. Finally, she managed to tell me that Pat had asked her to come over, and when she'd lain down to take a nap, he'd left. He'd taken his clothes and was gone, having "borrowed" LeRoy's car without permission and taken off with it. I could hear the kids crying in the background, and I knew Pat must have planned all along to leave this weekend, with me out of the way.

I finally made it home to my heartbroken children after one of the longest drives I have ever endured, and the next morning LeRoy was at my house and was pointing his finger at me and saying over and over, "What did you do to make him do this?" LeRoy's teenage son was with him and he yelled at his dad to leave me alone. Leroy then said, "If you can make so much money on those dogs, why don't you quit your job and live off them?"

I'd heard many times through church scuttlebutt that I "put the dogs in front of" my family. I'd also heard our marriage was "wonderful" until I got into dogs. Pat himself had undoubtedly helped perpetuate that myth. Now I'd somehow forced Pat to steal LeRoy's car. I was stunned not only at this accusation but also at this grown man's behavior.

Shortly after this, I went to counseling one last time with the express purpose of announcing that I wouldn't be coming anymore. When I got to the church, I was surprised to hear the elders and the pastor telling LeRoy what a horrible person Pat was for stealing his car after all LeRoy had done for him. They talked about him like he was dirt, and at that moment I guess you could say I had an epiphany. I realized what really mattered to that church, and I said to the men standing there, "Don't you think it's funny how all of a sudden Pat is this horrible man for taking LeRoy's car? Time and time again, you all stood by and watched him desert his children, take our money, commit adultery, drink, and do drugs and all of you said it was I who was not as bendable as I should be! It was my heart that wasn't as forgiving as it should be! Now I see you're all angry at him for a stupid beater car that cost $250.00! I think you have your priorities mixed up. I won't need counseling from this church any longer; I can't respect it!"

With that I left. I meant what I'd said, and I knew I was right. Every time Pat had ever left me, he'd partied like there was no tomorrow. He'd had a drug addiction before being sent to prison and now obviously had an alcohol problem as well. He'd never wanted the "good Christian life"; he liked his old life too much for that and went back to it as often as he could. As the biblical verse from Proverbs says, "As a dog returneth to his vomit, so a fool returneth to his folly."

When I got home, I contacted my home fellowship leader and asked her to fast and pray with me. I needed an answer about divorcing Pat to come directly from Jesus, and fasting was the way to seek that answer. I felt I could trust her to fast with me, and hopefully we would get the same answer. She promised to share this with the rest of the home fellowship, so any and all who wanted to fast and pray with me could do so.

I fasted for twenty-seven days, with the exception of two salads I ate in that time period, and finally I attended our next home fellowship meeting. Much to my surprise, not one person knew anything about my fasting and praying. My home fellowship leader hadn't bothered to tell anybody, nor was she in attendance at the meeting.

I was disgusted, and I walked out of the meeting and went home. I felt I had my answer, for I knew in my heart what had to be done. Though I was confident divorcing Pat was the right thing to do, I still had to deal with the kids. In the end, I decided I needed to ask Pat what his plans were. All the times he'd left us, I'd never once lowered myself to ask him to come back. I knew I would have to swallow a lot of pride even to go downstate, much less ask him if he was ever coming home. I didn't even know where he was staying, but I prayed about it and asked for the Lord's guidance. I got somebody to watch the kids overnight and then drove downstate to his brother's house. John and Bev were both home when I arrived, and when I asked whether they knew where Pat was, I was amazed at how willing they were to help.

They told me he was living with a girl named Terry on the other side of town. I was surprised he wasn't with Alma, but I guess that wasn't a safe avenue for him at the time. John gave me directions to Terry's house, so I got in my car and drove there. I parked a block away and walked down the street to the address I'd been given. Right away, I saw Pat on the upstairs apartment balcony sitting in the sun with his dirty feet on the railing. I called out "Pat!" and his jaw dropped. I must confess, the moment was priceless.

He hurried down the steps to thwart my entering his new home, and I talked to him on the front porch for some time before Terry came bouncing down the steps on her way to work. I wasn't jealous, but I was angry that she felt it was fine to take another woman's husband and a father from his kids. We kept talking as she drove away, and I presented Pat with letters and pictures from the kids and told him how much they missed him.

We went for a long walk and talked about what was going to happen now. He told me he was "in love" with Terry and that he and I were a mistake. He informed me they'd already exchanged vows with each other and he felt that they were "married in the eyes of God" and that God had found him "the perfect woman in all ways." I looked at him and asked, "What about the fact that you are still married to me? What are you going to do about that? What about the kids? Don't you think your revelation from God about us being a mistake could have come before you decided to have these kids?"

He said to me in a calm voice, "I figured you would get around to the divorce yourself; we're getting ready to move to Florida." That was it. Even if I'd been able to talk him into coming home, it would have been only another Band-Aid, and I wasn't willing to live like that anymore. This was just something the kids would have to understand.

When I arrived home, they ran out to my car and were hoping for good news. Instead, I had to let them know their father was not coming home. We all held on to each other and they cried for the dad they loved so much. I cried for their tender broken hearts and knew there was nothing I could do to ease their pain. Inside, I knew this was a direct result of my choosing the wrong man, not only to be my husband but also to be the father of my children, and I was ashamed. I felt solely responsible for their broken hearts and could only ride out the storm and keep seeking the face of God to show me the right thing to do. I thought about this all night long. I knew how much I loved my children, and without Pat I wouldn't have had them. On one hand, the whole thing was wrong, but on the other hand, the whole thing was right. I just wished it had turned out differently.

Our lives grew after this. Pat and Terry did indeed move from Michigan, but not before he'd spent some time in jail for not paying child support. He'd told me all along he would never pay child support, and when he was true to his word, I reported him. I also finished paying my attorney so the divorce could move ahead and I could wash my hands of him forever.

My mother stopped by periodically to express her opinion of Pat in front of the kids. All she could focus on was how he'd ruined her Mother's Day and made her miss a big bingo game. I was so sick of hearing about it that I finally grabbed her by the shoulders and said, "What's wrong with you? Do you really think your bingo game is of any significance to anybody in this house? I'm sick of you acting like you are the only person who was affected by Pat leaving!" With that, I pushed her out the door. I knew I needed all the strength I could manage, for if I crumbled, so would my whole family.

One Sunday afternoon, my old boss Susie stopped over to my house to see whether I would like my job back. I wasn't making ends meet working at the factory for minimum wage, so I jumped at the chance. I started the next day, and by noon, I'd earned what I'd earned in a whole week at the factory. Now it was time to play catch up on the bills. I didn't yet have Pat's bad checks taken care of, I was still on moratorium with the house payment, and I was behind on the land taxes as well. I'd always hated this house, but I didn't want to lose it.

I still couldn't afford to have my phone hooked up, so I used the phone at work when I needed to reach Barb. I called her when a match was coming up only fifty miles away, and she said she would probably come, bringing the puppy who'd survived the distemper. That Saturday, I went to the show. She didn't show up, but I saw a couple with a young bitch about a year old that looked suspiciously like one of my breeding. I approached them and asked where they'd gotten their puppy.

They named my breeding business, and since I knew they hadn't gotten the pup from me, I asked whether they had papers on her. They did and said that when they'd purchased her, she was supposed to be five months old. It was strange, but the papers they'd just received said she was just now five months old, and they'd had her over four months. I asked whether Barb had sold her to them, and they replied "Yes!"

I told them who I was and that Barb was a friend who'd helped me out while I was going through a divorce. In turn, they told me Barb had told them she'd come into the business because I'd had a mental breakdown and was so crazy they shouldn't even try to talk to me.

I went straight to a pay-phone and called Barb. She answered the phone, and I asked what she was doing. She told me she was sitting there doing nothing, so I asked how the puppy was. She said, "Doing fine. She's sitting here right now next to me. She's such a good little girl."

I told her, "You're lying. She's not there with you because she's standing here with me!" Barb burst into tears and said, "Oh, God, I'm so sorry I lied. I was broke, and I needed the money, but the other dogs really did die!"

I was so angry I hung up on her in mid-sentence and approached the people once again. I told them the papers in their possession were from an entirely different litter, one four months younger than the dog they had. I informed them I had the papers for their dog. I asked how much they'd paid for her, and they told me $1,000.00! I told them this was not their fault in any way and I would be happy to give them the rightful papers. They were very gracious, and I gave them my address and went home.

Then I wrote the American Kennel Club and asked them to send me copies of all the paperwork concerning the other litters Barb had co-bred with me and indicated were dead from distemper. I finally received the package containing all the information on my bitches and their litters, and there it was in black and white. Barb had lied about everything. She'd not only forged my name but she'd also stolen my money. Not one puppy had died; she'd sold every single one of them and had kept the money, $14,000 in all. I'd intended to split the money with her, right down the middle, but she'd gone ahead and stolen every penny in spite of knowing that my small children were going without.

Barb soon contacted me and gave me a weak explanation that I didn't buy, but it was better than nothing. She tried to convince me she'd had a mental breakdown and had almost lost her house. She begged me not to turn her in to the American Kennel Club, since they would have revoked her breeding privileges, and she agreed to pay back every penny she'd stolen.

It may sound unbelievable, but I agreed. I felt this was the best I could do. I didn't feel like paying an attorney tons of money to go after her in court, and I didn't want to ruin her life. I just wanted my money. I retrieved my bitches from her, but the situation bothered me so much I began breaking out in hives. I couldn't believe a trusted friend had taken such advantage of me when my life was in crisis.

After I received one payment in the mail, I thought maybe she'd gotten the idea of honesty and integrity, but then I learned she'd taken all her dogs to a vet and had put them to sleep and left town. When I heard this, I knew there would be no compensation for the dogs she'd stolen from me.

I had to do some real soul searching after this about whether I wanted to stay in dogs. I really didn't like dog show people in general. In the dog world, people seemed to regularly twist the truth to their advantage, which in turn made it easier for them to justify lying and stealing. Frankly, I never saw so many liars and thieves in my whole lifetime as when I was showing and breeding dogs, and this goes for many of the judges as well. The business was supposed to be about judging good dogs, but it simply wasn't.

The only good news was that my divorce was soon finalized. Since Pat was living somewhere in Florida, I mailed the papers to his parents' winter home, also in Florida, knowing they would give them to him. I hoped this would make his day and that he would marry his girlfriend and stay away from usforever. For once and for all, I wanted Pat out of my life.

Chapter 10

Raising My Kids, Pat Comes and Goes, and Meeting Delbert Again

As it turned out, Pat was out of our lives this time for nearly four years. I tried to be both a mom and dad to the kids in those years, all the while holding down a six-day-a-week job. It wasn't always easy, but the kids and I had always been close, and I think that's what sustained us. I made sure we had regular family nights out, and in the summers, I managed to take them to the beach at least once a week. Things generally went smoothly, and in spite of their father's absence, the girls excelled in school and were busy with many after-school activities.

Andy, however, didn't do as well. His grades started to fall, and I was fearful he was not going to make it, but the school showed little concern and chalked it up to his immaturity. By the time he was thirteen, he was floundering, and I soon realized it was more than just poor grades. Frankly, he had regressed, and the tricks he was pulling at home and school made me recall when he was in the first grade and got caught stealing from the lockers and desks when the other kids were at recess. I'd taken him to counseling then, and we resumed counseling now. Saving him from himself as he made the transition from little boy to young teen became a major focus, but I was rendered helpless. I knew I was a good mother, but this boy needed a father, and I could clearly see that he was struggling with growing up. He was afraid to let go of his childhood, and he was traumatized by becoming a young man. He also started liking girls, and even that seemed to scare him at this age. He would go out and try to be "cool" around girls, but then would come straight home and play army. I agonized for him, but soon he was rebelling against anything that required responsibility, from doing chores around the house to letting me know where he was.

It didn't help that he was the oldest boy in his class. Though I'd enrolled him in kindergarten at age five, almost immediately I'd been asked to delay his schooling for a year because he was so immature. I'd obliged and kept him home that extra year, and now he was looked up to by all the other younger boys in his class, which gave him the power to pretty much control things as he wanted. This was not a good thing for my son, who was already a master manipulator of people, even of teachers. Like my dad in that regard as well as Pat, Andy had a special charm about him from the time he was very small, and it was easy to see we were headed for serious trouble.

I can honestly say that the biggest part of Andy never wanted to grow up. Even when he was a toddler, he wanted my undivided attention, to the point that he would invent things for me to do to keep me focused on him. That little boy would bring me his diaper bag and powder, take off his diaper, and lie down on the floor for me. Needless to say, it was hard to potty train him.

To my great surprise, while I was struggling to keep Andy on the right path, a demon from the past reared its ugly head when the authorities picked Pat up for felony nonsupport and desertion and abandonment. He was sentenced for the nonsupport and for joy riding in the car he'd "borrowed" from LeRoy all those years before, and I was glad, even though the wheels of justice sometimes turned too slowly. The bad part was he was in jail locally and began writing to the kids. He was trapped, and as always, the kids were his good old standbys. Though I was concerned, I never suspected he'd re-appear at my house. However, I was worried the kids would be let down by any promises he might make and then break.

Sure enough, he promised Danielle he would come to her cello concert the night he was getting out of jail after his year-long sentence. She was now in the sixth grade and was elated. After all, it had been four years since any of the kids had seen their dad, and their excitement and anticipation were tremendous. Since Pat hadn't lost any of his ability to charm people, his old boss was happy to bring him some clothes and had dropped them off at my workplace. When Pat arrived, he immediately changed into them and then told me he was going downstate. I was furious. I told him, "You can't do that to Danielle; you're going to break her heart! Please Pat, don't do this!"

That didn't matter to him, and when Danielle found out her dad wasn't coming to her concert, she cried her eyes out. All three kids felt the impact of this lie, and they were devastated. Two weeks later, Pat phoned, just before Christmas. I answered, and he asked to talk to the kids. For the first time ever I told him, "You're not going to talk to the kids anymore. I'm tired of you toying with their feelings. Do not ever call this house again." With that, I hung up.

Christmas morning came, and of course we were up early. Like kids everywhere, mine were too excited to sleep. Pretty soon, there was a knock on the door. It had to be only 7:00 a.m., but there was Pat, lugging three huge garbage bags full of presents, one for each of the kids. He waltzed in like he owned the place and knew he was an instant hero and the greatest dad on earth to surprise them like this after not seeing them for four whole years. Mr. Nice Guy was at it again, and of course all was forgiven on the part of the kids at the mere sight of him.

Not even five minutes after his arrival, the phone rang. It was Terry, telling him he'd been there long enough and it was time to get back home. I laughed as he tried to convince me she wanted to be part of the kids' lives. I told him, "Oh, I can tell she does. You've been with her four years, and she hasn't met them yet!"

He left, but the kids were so happy they'd gotten to see their dad they didn't care. Even Andy was happy that day, and he'd been the angriest at Pat these past few years. All that mattered now was their dad had cared enough to show up.

It was six months before we heard from him again. Then out of the blue he called and told the kids he and Terry would like to have them visit. I told Pat I needed to meet Terry first. He assured me that would be no problem, since she really wanted to be part of their lives. He called back a few days later and told me Terry had no desire to meet me, that she didn't want to be part of my life, just the kid's. I told Pat, "Sorry, but if she's part of my kids' lives, she will automatically be part of my life. That's just how it goes, and I do need to meet her before my kids go anywhere with her."

He thought I was being totally unreasonable and hung up on me. The kids' hearts were broken, but a week or so later, he called again and promised he would come see them Memorial Day weekend. They were so excited they could hardly stand it. I was leery, as I had a feeling this was just another one of his lies. Sure enough, two days before he was supposed to come, he called very early in the morning and told them he had the flu and would not be able to make it. They hung up the phone and just cried. Even though they were older now, it seemed this was an open wound he just kept pouring salt in.

After I dried their tears and got them on the school bus, I called Pat's house. Terry answered, and I asked why Pat had decided not to see the kids this weekend. She replied that she didn't know. I asked whether he was home, and she told me he was at work. I said, "Work! I thought he had the flu and couldn't work today; that was his excuse to the kids!"

She told me, "Well, the flu is going around down here." I cut her off and said, "I see, Pat has getting the flu this weekend on his schedule. You know, I don't have a problem with you and Pat, but every time he lies to these kids, they get very upset and cry. I'm tired of him lying to them and hurting them!"

I wasn't surprised when she retorted, "I don't care how you or your kids feel! Don't expect me to feel badly about any of this!" I knew she didn't care about the kids, or she would have made sure she and Pat had a relationship with them.

Shortly after this, I ran into Barb at a dog show, and we sat and talked about what she'd done. It had now been three or four years since I'd seen her, and she told me many times how sorry she was. You can call me a sucker, and I probably am, but I believe that when people apologize to you and ask for your forgiveness from their heart, you should forgive them. I needed to let go of the personal pain her betrayal had caused me, and I felt like a tremendous burden had been lifted from my shoulders when I did.

Her life was in flux, and she asked whether she could stay with me for a while until she found a place to live. I thought about this at length and came to the conclusion that sometimes you have to sleep with the devil to rid yourself of other unnecessary evils. I was still afraid of the dark and of being alone, though I'd kept this fact from the kids while they were small, and I'd also briefly dated a man after Pat had left who, like Pat and Jack before him, had violent tendencies and a problem with alcohol and who wasn't too pleased when I broke it off with him. He was still stalking me, and since Barb wasn't the type to be intimidated by a man, I knew I'd feel safer with her around.

I was steadily gaining progress financially, but it was hard to find a balance between my job and the kids. Andy was continuing to act out and began missing a lot of school, and soon I discovered he was using the school bus as his personal taxi to town and back. I found myself at wit's end trying to do the right thing with him. I'd also heard Pat had been picked up again and was back in jail for not paying child support. It wasn't like I was demanding an unreasonable amount. He only had to pay $25.00 per child weekly, and he could have had all the freedom he wanted if he'd paid his child support. Since I was left to raise the kids by myself, I felt this was a small price to pay for his complete freedom of responsibility.

Of course, when he was locked up, he regularly communicated with the kids. This made them feel good, even though I knew it was just another Band-Aid. They would take whatever crumbs were thrown their way, but crumbs were all he ever gave them and ever would. This time, he saw them briefly when he got out of jail before going downstate, and they just beamed. Talk about unconditional love—Pat would never know or understand how lucky he was.

A few months later, he popped up again. He called to talk to the kids and wanted them to spend Thanksgiving weekend with him, and I got on the phone before they got too carried away. I could plainly see they wanted to go, but I told Pat I felt funny about this since Terry had told me she didn't care about them or their feelings. He didn't believe me and tried to convince me otherwise, but I knew better. I told him so but added that I would let them come. There was a dog show downstate that weekend, and I knew they could stay in touch with me. If there were any problems, I could get to them quickly. I hung up the phone and felt uneasy, but I felt I had to give this a try since they wanted to see their dad so badly.

I was hoping beyond hope he wouldn't let them down this time, since he and Terry were getting their own way on how the visitation went, but sure enough, the call I dreaded came, and Pat told me it wouldn't be possible for the kids to come after all. He offered no explanation and made his call very short. Even though I'd expected this, it was still upsetting. To think I'd been prepared to break my own personal rule just so my kids could see their dad. As it turned out, their hearts were broken anyway.

It was now nearly Thanksgiving, and this was a very special holiday for us, one we loved as much as Christmas. In the past, I'd tried to have some of my family celebrate with us, but I'd stopped that as quickly as I'd started it. All my family ever wanted to do was argue. I wanted this holiday to be forever special to my kids instead of a time for family members to fight with each other.

The evening before Thanksgiving, I baked all the pies for our upcoming dinner. Each of my kids had a favorite pie, so I always made one pie that was theirs and theirs alone. We also baked the token apple and pumpkin pies, which filled the house with their wonderful aromas. By the time I finished, at least seven pies were cooling on the table. As I was standing in the kitchen and was finishing up my cooking, there came a knock on the door. The kids ran over and answered, and by their squeals, I knew it was their dad. I went to the door, and there he was, standing in the cold on the porch with his duffel bag and several other bags of clothes.

Just what do you do when you find yourself in this situation? I told him to come in. When I asked why he was here, he said, "I'll tell you later; I don't want to talk about it right now." Barb, sitting in the kitchen with me, was flabbergasted. I continued my work while the kids hung all over him in the living room. I tried not to show my disappointment, as I didn't want to ruin the kids' moment, but I found it extremely hard to contain myself. This man had been out of our lives more than four years now, give or take a few letters and phone calls in the recent months. Why would he show up at this point with all his clothes? There was something different in his demeanor, but I didn't want to be so foolish as to think he'd humbled himself over the years. There was something else going on; I just didn't know what it was. The kids were anxious to know if he was here to stay, but this was something I needed to think about, and I couldn't answer them. Even though they were older now, they loved this man to pieces, as awful as he was. At the very least, it was apparent Pat was going to be a never-ending dilemma in my life, a fact that made my heart sad. I'd made a bad choice in him, and I knew I'd bear that burden until I died.

I busied myself in the kitchen and stayed as far away from him as I could in my small humble home. The kids finally went to bed, and I kept cooking just to stay busy, as I didn't know what else to do. As I was washing pans, Pat came up behind me and tried to kiss me. I was startled and said, "What are you doing?" He said, "Well, I thought now that I'm here we could start where we left off."

How he possibly could have thought I would be interested in him is beyond me, but thank God I'd entered those dog shows in anticipation of the kids staying downstate with him. Though I'd decided to stay home after he'd canceled out on the kids, now I changed my mind. He could stay and visit with them, and I could get away by myself and digest what was happening.

Then Pat confessed I'd been right all along. When he'd told Terry his kids were coming to spend the weekend, she'd blown up. She told him he'd never asked her permission to have his kids visit. He said every time he was supposed to come see them she'd start a fight, but he'd always thought it was because they would have to drive so far. When he'd found out she was angry that he hadn't asked her permission to have them come to the home they shared, he knew she'd been lying to him all along.

Pat sort of tiptoed around me all Thanksgiving Day and was particularly nice and mannerly. Even though my mind was racing, I maintained my composure. When it was time to eat, I looked across my table and saw what my kids were most thankful for today. Even though they'd always loved this dinner, I knew it wouldn't have mattered today if I'd made hot dogs. My memory of sitting there is this: as I looked across the table at my children whose cheeks were so rosy from laughing and smiling, I thought, "Who am I to take their smiles from them?" I just couldn't do it. I hadn't seen their faces so bright in such a long time, and my heart melted for them and for their love for their father. I was sad for myself, as I knew what it would take to keep them in smiles, but I couldn't get past how incredibly wonderful it was to see their joy.

The next day went smoothly. Pat raked some leaves and brushed out old Aubrey and made himself generally handy. I ignored his efforts, as I'd seen his "nice guy" routine too many times in the past. He was being very passive with me, but I figured this was because he felt he had to be. He wanted to keep his foot in the door here, and on top of that he was homeless now. I was not impressed with his efforts, and in the middle of the night, I heard him get up and call Terry. He was talking softly, but I heard him beg her to let him come home. Soon, it was time for me to get up and head downstate for the dog show. I jumped in the shower, and when I got out, I went outside and loaded the dogs in the truck and then made a pot of coffee. Pat came in the kitchen and told me that when I returned on Sunday, he would be going back downstate. I replied, "Okay!"

He replied, "Well, what are we doing here? I'm on the couch, and you're in the bedroom. What do you expect me to do?" I laughed and said, "You need to do what you want to do. You're not going to push me into a situation I'm not sure I want. If all you want is a woman to sleep with, you need to go back to Flint!" After I'd made sure he wouldn't desert the kids while I was gone, I left.

I was at peace with Pat going home on Sunday, but I knew this would be hard on the kids. They certainly did love that worthless man, and I worried the whole weekend about what they were going to do when they found out he was leaving again. When I returned home, I found that he'd cleaned the entire garage and hosed it. The house was also spotless. I thanked him and told him he'd better get going while there was still daylight left, since he was planning to hitchhike.

He then informed me he'd changed his mind and that I was right. He shouldn't base his whole life on having a woman to sleep with, and he'd made up his mind that he didn't want to be with Terry. He wanted to stay here with the kids and me. He promised he wouldn't push me, and if I didn't want him to stay with us, he wondered whether he could stay until he found a place to live.

I told him I would think about it, and then I went into the house. Think about it I did. My former boyfriend was in jail at the moment, but he would soon get out. Even though Barb's presence helped tremendously, I was still afraid. It wasn't this man's physical presence I feared; it was what I couldn't see him do that scared me. He had threatened to burn my house down with the kids and me in it. If Pat was here, his activities regarding me would come to a screeching halt because he'd told me once he was afraid of Pat.

The kids would certainly be more than happy to have their dad here, and maybe this would even help Andy. I had to admit Pat was more than pathetic as a role model, but as far as I could see, he was generally fair to the kids, except for that time in the car when he'd been drinking. I was the one Pat had problems with, not them.

My problem was I didn't like Pat, nor did I respect him. The thought of living with him again made me sick, but there was no question my kids' demeanor had changed as soon as he'd shown up. The sparkle was back in their eyes, and I simply could not overlook the impact he had on them. There were a lot of things in life I didn't understand, but the one thing I knew was that I loved my kids with all my heart. Their happiness meant the world to me.

I spent the next few days and thought very hard about what to do. I reflected on things I'd done in the past because they were the right thing to do, even when I really hadn't wanted to do them. For instance, a few years earlier, I'd returned to adult high school. I couldn't very well tell my children how important school was if I hadn't graduated. The graduation ceremony was a cap and gown affair, and when they'd called my name, I'd heard my kids yell out, "That's my mom!" I was proud of myself for finishing after all those years, and having my kids in the audience was a wonderful bonus. It made going back to school worth it to me.

Another accomplishment was getting through those first couple of years after Pat had left. I'd worked hard, fought tooth and nail to keep this house I'd never wanted in the first place, gotten out of debt, and raised three kids by myself. This was my children's home, and they wouldn't have wanted to move. It had seemed to me that if I'd uprooted my kids, they wouldn't feel any stability. I knew kids who were moved around a lot, like military kids, and they never had a home base to ground them even as adults. I wanted my kids to always feel they had a home base. I'd never had one, and I knew what a difference it would have made.

I hadn't wanted to breed and show dogs, either, but I'd prayed about it and gone on to become more successful than in my wildest dreams. I'd even grown to enjoy it, and giving God a chance to work in my life had increased my faith not only in Christ but also in life in general.

Most important of all, I'd become comfortable with who I was. I never thought I'd be the person I was coming from the kind of childhood I'd had. I never thought I'd get past the parts of me I didn't like. I certainly never dreamed I could love myself, but with God's help, I'd learned to. This was my own personal triumph in life, that I loved myself in spite of all my mistakes and errors in judgment, and I knew that if I could do all those other things that had seemed impossible, I could do this.

It boiled down to this: a mother gets only one chance to raise her kids. She never gets a chance to go back and redo it. This was my only chance to try and make their lives meaningful and happy. If this was what made them complete, I could do it. My conclusion was Pat could stay. I could plainly see there were more pros than cons to having him home with the kids.

As far as his child support went, I dropped it. All I wanted was for him to be a good father and to show love to his kids. Every time someone told me I was crazy, my kids' faces flashed in my mind. Living with Pat was a small price to pay for their happiness. Once I'd made my decision, I put my mind on automatic pilot when it came to my personal feelings. If I caught myself thinking about how much I hated Pat, I simply pushed those thoughts out of my head and focused on the positives. This wasn't always easy, as Pat believed I'd realized I just couldn't live without him. I was brutally honest about my feelings, but I don't think he heard a word of it. Fortunately, I had a million and one excuses for not having sex with him. Since he was the one who had given me herpes, that seemed to be the best excuse. Whenever he tried coming on to me, I simply told him I was having an outbreak.

Despite Pat's presence, all hell broke loose with Andy, and he couldn't get in enough trouble. In his mid-teens now, he was the leader of the neighborhood pack and, oddly enough, was liked by the neighborhood parents as well as all his teachers. Andy was always a charming boy, and he would present himself as a polite, innocent young man when he thought there was something to gain. On the other hand, he was often controlling and demanding and the same schemer he'd been as a little boy, and before long, he'd decided I was his mortal enemy. Soon, I began to notice that I was regularly missing money from my purse. I used to cash my checks after I was paid, and I always knew exactly how much money I had. After living on the edge for so long, knowing my exact financial situation at any moment was a way of life for me. At first, I thought I was just losing my memory, but one night, I sold a puppy for a friend for $500.00. The buyers paid me in cash, and I put the money in my purse. I was going to take it downstate to my friend the next morning, and when I reached into my purse for the money, I found only $420.00. I'd begun to suspect Andy, but now I knew.

Things steadily declined from there. Andy began drinking, and he received his first minor in possession arrest when I smelled beer on his breath one night and called the police. He also continued stealing, even taking money out of my mom's purse at her home on one occasion. I told her she needed to call the police and file charges against him, and though she didn't want to do that, she did it all the same with my insistence. This was his second offense, and as much as I didn't want to have him arrested, I am a firm believer in "tough love," and I knew I couldn't remain in denial any longer about how much trouble he was getting into. It was a "do or die" situation as far as I was concerned. I wanted him to hate being on probation, and I wanted him to hate the price he would pay for his actions by having his freedom taken away.

Meanwhile, his grades were pathetic. I had been fighting with the junior high school since his seventh grade year to hold him back, but he kept passing with I's, E's, and an occasional D-. I was very upset, and I felt the school just wanted to pass him so they could get him out of their hair. His teachers liked him, but he never turned in any of his homework, and I simply don't believe the school wanted to make the effort to help problem kids. A quote from the principal at one point was, "I don't think Andy is one of those kids who's falling through the cracks."

At my last meeting with him after Andy's final report card in the ninth grade, he said, "Andy is just one of those kids who fell through the cracks." My son not only fell through the cracks, but he also fell into a crevasse, and I hold the principal at least partially responsible. This individual never told me I could have my son tested for learning disabilities, but when he was in the ninth grade, my boss told me about the testing that was readily available for students who were failing. I immediately requested that Andy be tested before he was passed into high school, and when I asked why no one had ever mentioned such testing before, the principal replied that he didn't think Andy needed it. Needless to say, he wasn't happy about having Andy tested. Again, I believe this was because he knew there was a good possibility Andy would end up in his school one more year.

During the testing, Andy was found to have significant learning disabilities as well as the attention span of an ant, and it was indeed recommended that he be held back. When he got off the bus the first day of school to repeat his ninth grade year, the principal promptly sent him home, and told him he belonged in the tenth grade, and I was aghast. His grades were not good enough to go to high school, and his paperwork said he needed to redo his ninth grade year, but somehow the principal won out, and he ended up in high school that year after all. I was livid at the entire school system, and in the end, predictably, my son dropped out. He just couldn't keep up with the rest of the class. I will never get over how unfair I felt this situation was. I knew more than anybody that Andy was a handful, but I knew he wasn't stupid, either.

Andy and I were still going to counseling together, but I couldn't see that it was helping. On the contrary, I could clearly see that he was manipulating the counselor. I couldn't sleep at night with all the worry. I didn't know my son anymore, and he treated me as if I were his enemy. I loved him so much, but there was constant conflict in our home. I even found it hard to concentrate at work, since I worried constantly about what he was doing when I wasn't watching him.

Soon after dropping out of school, Andy broke into the neighbor's house and stole six guns. We knew he'd done it, and so did the police, but no one could find any evidence. Then Pat found the keys to the neighbor's house hidden in a slit Andy had made in his mattress. I would never have found them there; I guess you could say it takes a criminal to catch a criminal. Pat immediately called the police, and they came and took the keys to see whether they fit. Sure enough, they did. They created a plan to come back later to ask whether they could search our house once again for evidence. When we gave them permission, they would search and find the keys tucked neatly in the slit. This way, they could arrest Andy and retrieve those guns before they got into the wrong hands and hurt somebody.

The plan worked beautifully, and Andy ended up being arrested and going to jail. He was now sixteen years old, and I fervently hoped that being in jail would be so distasteful he would never want to go there again. He was appointed a new probation officer and a psychiatrist and would be taken to a detention house to live when he was released. I was pleased with this, as I could finally sleep at night knowing exactly where he was.

When we met with the psychiatrist, he asked me what I thought Andy's problem was. I was brutally honest and replied, "He is a young man so full of anger toward me that I believe at this point in his life he could come into my bedroom and kill me, and by simply walking out of my room and closing the door, he could make himself a sandwich and eat it and watch TV. My son is a sociopath and feels only for himself."

The psychiatrist looked at me and said, "Whoa, wait a minute. That's a really strong statement to make!" As strong as it was, I knew in my heart it was true. Andy was the kind of person who could steal from anyone, even those he loved, but if somebody stole from him, he was outraged. He hurt only when it was personal; he seemed to lack all the normal feelings of compassion toward anybody else. My father, although never diagnosed or arrested, was a sociopath also. I was well aware of what a sociopath was, and frankly, Pat was one, too.

Waiting for the court date for my son, I enjoyed a normal life at home with the girls. With Andy gone, I could concentrate on them without the distraction of his trouble and anger. They appreciated the extra attention, since they'd been slighted since Andy had started his rampage years before. They'd always excelled in school and had tried their best to be good kids, and they were. I knew they felt like they always got the short end of the stick.

When Andy's court date came up, I was confident the judge would realize Andy needed to be kept under lock and key and would refuse to let him come home until his sentence at reform camp began. Nonetheless, the night before his court date, Andy called to tell me he would be home tomorrow. I told him I loved him but that I didn't want him home just yet and that I was going to try to see to it that he stayed where he was, at the detention house.

In court the next day, the psychiatrist told the judge about his conversation with me in which I'd said I felt Andy had some severe problems and seemed to have no conscience, and he recommended that Andy stay where he was for now. Then Andy got up and talked to the judge himself. He told her he thought the psychiatrist hadn't any cause to come to that conclusion without talking to him first. He masterfully handled the judge, and she was mesmerized by him.

I knew my son fell short in many areas, but one thing he was superb at was manipulating people and situations. He was at his very best right now, and in a strange way, even knowing the outcome wouldn't be what I wanted, I was proud of him. Sure enough, the judge ordered him to be returned to our home immediately.

At that, I stood up and asked to speak. She gave me permission, and I told her, "Your honor, I have no control over Andy right now, and I don't want him to come home. This is the first time in years I've been able to sleep at night and my daughters are not feeling overshadowed by his antics. Please, reconsider this and keep him where he's watched one hundred percent of the time, safe from himself."

She looked across her bench at me, denied my request, and said, "You will just have to try a little harder!" I was no match for my son that day. As he walked past me, he grinned and said, "I told you I'd be home today!"

He was home an entire month, until the day his sentence at reform camp for juveniles began, and it was a trying month to say the least. He felt unstoppable, having beaten me in court, and he acted like he was king. He knew he was looking at six months at reform camp, and before it started, he wanted to hang out with his friends.

When reform camp finally began, I put my heart and soul into the family participation weekend that was required once a month, even though I knew it would be pointless for Andy. Pat and the girls also attended with me for the six months of Andy's sentence. Though the counselors at this camp were extremely passive, at least they assigned extra schoolwork for misbehavior. That was the one good thing about this program: it included schoolwork that was individualized for each kid. Andy got through his tenth grade year this way, but nonetheless this state-funded program didn't have a high success rate. It seemed to me more a place where criminals exchanged ideas, and I think my son used it as an opportunity to hone his skills. The changes I was seeing in Andy over this period weren't the positive ones I'd hoped to see, and I could tell he was going to come out a little wiser than when he'd gone in.

During the period when Andy was at reform camp, Pat had begun to come and go again just like in the past, and it just so happened that he was gone when Andy finished his sentence and came home. In no time, without Pat to help me, that boy was controlling the house once again. He overpowered the girls, and made them feel responsible for him, and he put them in situations that compelled them to lie for him, since they didn't want to see him get in any more trouble. He did nothing I told him to do and generally gave me a very hard time. When classes started that fall, I was unable to keep him in school. Though he'd dropped out the year before, attending classes was part of his probation, and the school couldn't refuse him since he was still a minor. The only thing I could have done was go to school with him, and if I'd done this, I would have lost my job and my home. Andy had just turned seventeen, and I could see he felt invincible. I told him I would not sign for a driver's license if he didn't get C's or better in school, and needless to say, I never had to sign for his license.

Shortly after school began, Andy wanted to go to the homecoming football game and borrowed money from me to do so. To repay me, he promised to clean up a small area of the backyard on Saturday. Of course, Saturday came, and he didn't clean it. He told me he had the flu and didn't feel well. On Sunday, he likewise didn't clean it. On Monday, I told him he was not going to school until he'd cleaned the backyard as promised.

He was certainly angry that I'd called him on keeping his word with me. He argued that he needed to go to school and learn and that I was standing in his way of doing that. I told him to knock off the lies, that he wasn't going to catch the "bus taxi" into town today; he was going to stay and do what he'd promised he'd do.

By the end of the day, his court-appointed psychiatrist had called me at work and told me Andy had informed him I'd packed my bags and moved out of the house. He then told me that, by law, he had to report me for child neglect. In disbelief, I said, "How can you of all people be sucked into Andy's lies? Have you even been to my home? Have you even talked to my daughters? Have you even looked in my room to see whether my clothes are there?"

He responded, "I'm sorry; I'm going to have to file a report." I told him I was calling Andy's probation officer and telling her what was going on. I was so angry I was in tears. I had never abused or neglected my kids or my responsibilities as their mother, though if any kid had the power to bring a parent to abuse, it was Andy.

Luckily, Andy's probation officer knew the truth. Although she liked Andy very much, she knew he was a narcissist and didn't fall for his manipulation. He was breaking his probation by not going to school, and nothing ever came of the phone call from his psychiatrist.

Andy wasn't about to give up yet, though. When I got home from work that night, he and the girls were sitting at the kitchen table. Andy immediately informed me they'd taken a vote and didn't want me to live in the house with them anymore. I asked the girls whether they went along with this, and when they tried to speak, they were abruptly cut off by Andy who said, "Knock it off, girls; we discussed all this. We took a vote on it and don't want her here!"

I was simply devastated. Every bit of wind was taken out of my sails in one swift blow, and I didn't know what to do. Pat was again downstate, but I went right over to the phone and called him. For once, I knew where he was, for this time he'd left at my suggestion, as the situation with Andy was just too tense and Andy was trying his best to push Pat's buttons, too. I was crying so hard I don't think he understood what I was saying, but I finally explained what had happened and asked him to come up and stay with the kids. I told him I would still pay the bills, but I just couldn't stay here right now. He told me he would be there in three hours, and then I called Barb to come get me. I was so frustrated and so crushed I knew I couldn't be around my obnoxious son any longer. I couldn't handle his meanness anymore. I was even afraid of myself, for the one nerve I had left, he was on, and it would have given him even more pleasure and power to see me act on that frustration.

Barb now lived across town, so at least if the girls needed anything, I wouldn't be far away. I knew the girls were just going along with Andy, but I was devastated they hadn't stood up for me. As before, he had overpowered them, and when Pat arrived, I told him I needed him only for a little while, maybe six months. After telling him I would sign custody of the kids over to him until I returned home, I removed myself from the whole picture, and hoped it would help heal Andy's anger and my broken heart. I needed some time to regroup and regain my strength. Andy was one of those people who sucked all the energy from you, and mine was gone.

I saw the kids every day after work and paid all the bills for the one and a half months I was gone, and when I returned home, it was because Andy had been sent to another reform school for breaking his probation. He was released at the end of May, and since he was still a juvenile and on probation, he had to come home. Just as bad, I was held financially responsible for any trouble he got into. I couldn't wait until he turned eighteen, when I would be off the hook. I'd already spent plenty of money paying for the trouble he'd gotten into. Even though the courts remove children like Andy from your home and put them through the required programs and give them a court-appointed psychiatrist, they bill you for this. Since most people do not have $50,000 just lying around, they ask you to pay ten percent of your bill, which in my opinion is still a lot of money when you have two other kids. The psychiatrist's bill alone was almost $5,000. What a scam! He didn't see him that much, and as far as I was concerned, any counselor who could be conned didn't deserve to be paid.

Shortly after his release, Andy told me he was moving out. Since he had fewer than three months to go to reach legal age and was still on probation, I called his probation officer. She said to let him go and informed me that by willfully moving out on his own, I was released from any responsibility for him.

I did just that. My hopes were that Andy would go out into the world and learn to be accountable for his own actions, but that didn't happen. Instead, the parents of his numerous friends let him live with them after he told them how badly he'd been abused by his mother. He ended up stealing from most of those people, and they all caught onto him in the end. At that point, I learned to let go of Andy. By letting go, I don't mean I stopped loving him. That would have been impossible. I just stopped feeling that I could do something to help him.

Not too long ago, Andy told me that when he was a child, he used to sit around and think about what he could do next to get into trouble. He says it wasn't because I was a bad parent, but I'm not sure. I can't help but think I missed something along the way with Andy. I tried everything I could think of, but it wasn't enough, and I have put him in God's hands. Only God knows Andy's true heart, and only God can help him sort himself out. I'm glad I believe in miracles, or I would be in great despair about my son.

At least he was gone again, and I could resume attending to my well-deserving daughters, who once again had suffered silently through all this. We'd all paid the price for Andy and his obstinateness. The girls still loved their big brother to death, and even though they were young and knew right from wrong, they wanted to believe in their hearts that he was the best big brother anybody could ask for. They were such good girls that all the teachers who'd had Andy always said to me at conferences, "Wow, it's like night and day; not that we didn't like Andy!"

I knew what they meant, and I felt the same way. The girls were simply a breath of fresh air. Danielle and Liz both excelled at everything they set out to do. The difference was one daughter was very soft and sweet to almost everybody, and the other was more outspoken and temperamental. I couldn't have been more proud of them. They both were determined young ladies.

I wasn't attending church at this point. I still had my faith, but I had too many disagreements with how my church conducted itself on issues of homosexuality and how it seemed to side with one partner in a marriage and turned away from the other. In the end, our pastor was even standing up and telling the congregation not to have any ties with this person or that because they didn't fall in line with what he felt was God's will. I simply wasn't willing to bring my kids up in an atmosphere with those kinds of prejudices.

However, with Andy gone, I found it increasingly harder to live with Pat. He was now driving a truck and was on the road for six to seven weeks at a time and home only four or five days between trips, but I was having a hard time seeing any positive influence from him anymore. Not only was he not a hands-on dad who was available to his kids, but also his actions were teaching the girls to disrespect me. He routinely rolled his eyes when I spoke to them, and here I had to draw the line. If this went on any longer, I was saying without words to my daughters, "This is how a man should treat a woman." I wanted my daughters to grow up and find wonderful men and do so much better for themselves than I had done. Soon, whenever Pat called to say he was on his way home and only ninety minutes away, I instantly became sick with diarrhea.

With Danielle in junior high and Liz nearly so, I hoped they were coming to an age where I could tell them I could no longer stay in this situation. I paid close attention to the girls when Pat was next home. They were busy with friends and activities, and it was as though he weren't even present. Soon after this, I took my girls out to dinner and discussed my feelings with them. I told them I wanted to move on from the situation I was in with their dad. I told them I wanted to ask him to leave permanently. They seemed indifferent and remained respectful to me, and we left dinner that night without incident. All I had to do now was wait for the right moment to let Pat know how I felt.

The next time he was home, I tried bringing it up but to no avail. He didn't seem to understand what I was trying to tell him, and I wanted to choose my words carefully. The one thing I didn't want was for him to leave in anger, because if he did, he wouldn't see the girls at all. After I tried my best to convey my message to him, he acted strangely. It was Liz's birthday, and after the celebration, I went to dinner with him in the hopes of talking to him more. Out of the blue, he leaned over the table and told me, "I don't like Liz."

I was shocked. I looked at him and said, "How can you not like Liz; she's your daughter!" He had no undertone of meanness when he said this, and I was worried because it wasn't something he said angrily. He just explained in his Pat way that he loved her, but he didn't like her at all right now. He was so matter of fact it scared me to death, for he said this as though it were okay to feel this way about a child. I've been angry at each and every one of my kids, but never once did I not like them or love them.

When I left dinner that night, I had a pit in my stomach. I knew I needed to expedite asking him to leave and not come back, and I was angry, mostly because he'd verbalized something I'd begun to suspect. Now I had to face the fact that he *didn't* have a healthy love for his kids. Needless to say, I suffered those few days he was home, and I hated him worse than before. We'd now been divorced for nine years, and if you included the legal separation, it was eleven years. We'd been on good terms the past four or five years while he'd come and gone, driving his truck and so on, but it was time to end this once and for all.

Shortly after my revelation that he didn't truly love the children, I received in the mail the paperwork from the juvenile camp Andy had attended. It was part of their program to look into the family background, and they were so thorough in their investigation that included in these papers was Pat's police record. When I started to read, I nearly went into shock. This was the first time I'd ever seen his record, and it was not only huge, but it also included numerous assault charges "to do great bodily harm less than murder." This was a frightening revelation. I knew he'd had a few assaults, but the way he'd talked, they were nothing.

This paperwork also included a summary of Pat and me. They concluded that I was a mother who wanted to help her son and participated fully in their projects. On the other hand, they felt Pat was the root of a lot of the problems with Andy, and they believed they had less than his full attention in their family participation projects. In short, in more ways than one, they blamed Pat for Andy's problems. I wouldn't personally go so far as to agree with that, as my son was a smart kid, but these were the experts, and these were their observances. In any event, all this time I'd thought Pat had fooled everybody with his charm game, but I guess that wasn't so. Now I felt an even greater urgency to make him leave. I needed him to go, and I needed to feel safe from him.

He was on the road when I heard through the grapevine that my friend Delbert had moved back to Michigan from Arizona. We made plans to meet at a restaurant, and I was excited. It had been fourteen years since I'd seen him, and to my tremendous surprise, I didn't even recognize him. If he hadn't stood up and showed himself to me, I wouldn't even have looked at him. My first words were, "God, what happened to you?" He looked old, his hair was long and straggly, and his skin was wrinkled beyond the fourteen years of his absence. Frankly, he looked like a broken man, and when I looked into his eyes, I saw all the pain he had in his soul. I knew he had kept up a tough persona over the years, but he couldn't hide the pain from me. As we caught up, he told me he never wanted to be involved with a woman again. I could clearly see what had happened to him, but I knew this wasn't the time to say, "I told you so!" Even as he spoke, I could hear his heart crying out for the companionship of a good woman.

I wasn't thinking of a potential romance while Delbert and I talked. I was just happy to see him and sad at the same time. It was cold, rainy, and drizzling out when we got up to leave. I had to work the next morning, and so did he, and in the parking lot, I leaned over to give him a quick kiss goodbye. He kissed me back, and all of a sudden I remembered the feeling I'd had for him before, the one I'd prayed I wouldn't remember. This was the feeling I'd asked God to take away from me that one other night so many years before so that I could move on as Pat's wife, and until now I truly had forgotten how soft and sweet and wonderful Delbert's kiss was. As cold as it was, neither of us moved away from each other. Once again, this was the man I knew I loved and had always loved.

We talked in the freezing rain for a long time, with neither of us letting go of each other's hands. I realized the pain I'd seen in Delbert's soul might be a reflection of the pain I had in my soul. I'd been married twice, and what I felt with Delbert was something I hadn't experienced with either husband. I'd never known exactly what was missing before, but something sure was. I was now thirty-nine years old, and I felt like a schoolgirl. In spite of our troubled pasts, Delbert and I were determined not to let go of each other again, and as time went on, the girls saw the difference in me. They teased me about Delbert, and said things like, "Yeah, Mom, just a friend. How come you put makeup on and did your hair?"

They were right. This was different. It felt comfortable. It felt like I was home. Though I was afraid of these feelings, Delbert and I kept seeing each other, but our relationship remained platonic. He didn't want what was happening with us to be tarnished by sex. For now, he just wanted to be great friends, and that was fine with me. Though I knew he drank, and I didn't exactly like that, I didn't think it was a big problem. He never drank around me and certainly never in my home.

When Pat finally called to check in, I told him I'd run into Delbert and that we were seeing each other. He gave me no reaction, but he started calling home every night at all hours to see whether I was there. I knew it was time for Pat to be completely removed from the picture, but I was afraid of how I might achieve this and what his reaction might be.

The next time he was home was Thanksgiving. I was prepared to tell him this was the last time he was welcome, but because this was such a cherished holiday for the girls, I just couldn't do it. He soon noticed the bathroom sink that hadn't worked for eight years had been repaired. I told him Delbert had fixed it. I'd asked Pat to fix that sink on numerous occasions, and I told him that since the kitchen sink was also leaking, Delbert was going to fix that, too!

Funny, Pat finally fixed the sink that weekend, but there was nothing about Pat that was funny to me right now. A change in his personality wasn't necessarily a good thing. Even so, the holiday went by with some semblance of grace. The kids enjoyed themselves, and I was determined not to tarnish their memories. Then, like a flash, Pat was off on his next tour of duty on the road. While he was gone, Delbert and I had many talks about Pat, and I told him things weren't as simple as they seemed. I couldn't believe I was back in the position of being afraid of a man. I didn't want to admit this to myself, but I had to.

Delbert told me not to be afraid, that he would take care of me, but all I could think about was Pat's police record. Had I not seen his record, I wouldn't have hesitated a bit, but I knew Pat had gotten away with a lot due to technicalities and a very smart attorney. I was dreading the next call letting me know he was on his way home again. It came just before Christmas, and I told Pat on the phone that Delbert was going to stop by to play cards that night. My mom and brother Rod, who was in town to see Mom, stopped by, and they played, too. It wasn't a terrific evening. Delbert, to my dismay, had drunk too much by the time he'd arrived, and I didn't find it very pleasant to be around Rod, who had always made trouble for me. Pat refused to participate at all and went to bed. After we'd played, my brother and I drove Delbert back to his house, and when I got home, Pat's truck was running, and he was no longer in the house sleeping. I went outside to look for him and found him in the cab of his truck. He flew up from his bed looking like a half-crazed lunatic. His body was shaking like he was freezing cold, and I was afraid of him.

He screamed at me, saying, "When your man comes home from being on the road seven weeks, and I want to go to bed at 9:00, your ass should be in there with me. Ask your friends what they would do! They would have their ass in that bed!"

For a moment, I was frozen in fear as I watched Pat scream at me. Maybe it was my foolish nature, but in spite of my fear, I couldn't let him get away with that. I replied, "I guess you've forgotten who my friends are. You will find that none of them act on a man's demands." I then opened the door of the truck and started to make the long climb down to the ground. I reminded him this was

Christmas and that I was not going to ruin it for the kids. With that, I closed the door to his truck and went in the house.

As I lay in my bed, I was afraid he would come in the house and hurt me, but the sun came up bright Christmas morning, and soon the kids came in to wake me up. They were just as excited that it was Christmas morning as they'd been when they were small. They asked where their dad was, and I told them he was in the truck. They woke him up and then opened their presents. Of course, Pat didn't have a gift for me, even though he'd bought Barb one. This year, I knew I would have at least one gift under the tree. It was from Delbert, who also had gifts for the kids. This didn't please the already enraged Pat. I could tell from his expression that watching us open Delbert's gifts was like having hot coals poured on his head.

When his four days were up, Pat didn't leave. He didn't leave on the fifth day, either. He wasn't going to leave on the sixth day, but I told him to get going. Although he was reluctant, he left. He called a few days later, and I worked up my nerve to tell him I didn't want him to come back again. This didn't seem to bother him, which worried me. Within an hour, he'd called back. He asked whether this had anything to do with Delbert, and I answered him as honestly as I could, saying, "Yes!"

He was so angry he yelled, "How could you do this to me? How could you? I will never forgive you for this!" This in turn made me angry. I told him, "You of all people are not going to forgive *me*? How dare you after everything you've done!"

I hung up, and he called back a third time a little while later and asked whether this was our divorce. I knew then he'd snapped, and I was glad he wasn't anywhere near me. I reminded him that our divorce had been final nine years ago, when he'd wanted to marry Terry. He then had the nerve to try to make financial demands on me, but I would have none of it, and finally I told him to learn to live with my decision and to leave me alone.

It was done, and he never again used my home as a place to stay. To my relief, he eventually remarried, though not to Terry, and he was truly out of my life for once and for all. He was essentially out of the kids' lives, too, but they were older now and didn't any longer expect much from him. I was greatly relieved that this chapter of my life was finally over, and I looked forward to the peace and joy I knew a relationship with Delbert would bring.

Chapter 11

The Third Time's the Charm: Marriage to Delbert, and Ups and Downs with Our Kids

With Pat finally out of my life, I could at last breathe. I could now go to work, come home, and not feel overpowered by his presence or his impending return. The girls were handling it well, even though he tried to make them feel guilty on the rare occasions he called. He purposely made Danielle cry, saying, "Danielle, always love your music and Jesus because they will never leave you or let you down." He picked his easiest target using her, but he knew better than to play Liz this way. What a line! I knew a whole lot more than he did about being let down and left. As far as that goes, so did the kids!

Delbert was getting ready to go out to Arizona for a few months at this time to tie up some loose ends, and he wanted the girls and me to go with him. I thought long and hard about this. I knew I loved him, but before I made a commitment, I wanted to know for sure this was the man I could live with the rest of my life. Though we had a long history, Delbert had changed over the years. I was greatly concerned at how embittered he was about his failed marriages. Plus, I was a mom first. I had to make sure my next move would edify my family.

Though I'd always felt Delbert was a man of great integrity, he'd fallen short after his divorce with Sherrill and had begun to do drugs as well as drink. To me, this was a major personal weakness. I'd tried drugs when I was young, but dabbling in drugs on purpose at his age was unconscionable and hard to comprehend. I needed to at least understand what had happened to him, why it had happened, and how it had happened. I didn't need another man with a dependency.

Quite simply, I was not willing to leap into a full-blown relationship with a man who was an addict, and as far as I was concerned, drinking and doing drugs on any level met that definition. I wanted Delbert to walk away from it. Several times, I walked away from him. By the same token, there were periods when he stopped seeing or calling me. I knew he was fighting his own inward battles.

Interestingly, our lives paralleled each other in numerous ways. We both came from horrible family conditions. His father was an alcoholic who was mentally abusive and physically threatening to his family when drunk. He would be gone for days or weeks on end and would come home only after he'd spent all his money on other women and alcohol. Delbert's mother, God bless her, was a saintly woman who'd loved and cared for her children the best she could. She'd met her future husband when she was pregnant at age sixteen. He'd married her, "saving" her from her shame. He was sixteen years her senior and by today's standards would be considered a predator, but she didn't know any better; she just married the man who said he would love her and take care of her.

She had twelve children in all, five daughters first, with one infant daughter dying in her arms, and then seven boys in a row with barely a year between them. The family lived in a basement with dirt floors and no running water. Delbert's father was absent most of the time. He made plenty of money to support his family, but like mine spent it on his own interests instead. There was barely enough food to feed that many kids, so they went hungry often. His mother did her best, but when you have eleven children and you're worrying about how to feed them all, you're bound to overlook the personal needs of one or two of them. Delbert was one of them.

The difference between us was that Delbert had at least one parent who loved and nurtured him. The kids could always go to their mom, and she would soothe their hurts as best she could, sitting by the stove while they took turns on her lap as she sang to them. There was never a doubt in Delbert's mind that his mother loved him, and this made all the difference in the world.

The one thing I wasn't going to do was beat Delbert up for choosing his former wives unwisely. I myself had chosen unwisely. Our behavior patterns develop early on, and Delbert's father's behavior was bound to rub off on the little boys who looked up to him. Consequently, Delbert had always chosen the kind of woman his father had run around with, women with no moral values whatsoever who lied to and cheated on him. I'd also picked that type of man over and over again and had repeated this pattern all my life.

Delbert and I talked a lot about this, and what he didn't understand he was willing to explore. That meant the world to me, as I knew it would take more than love to hold us together. At least we had one of the most important factors going for us, and that was that we were friends first.

However, complicating our relationship were Delbert's ex-wives and his three children. All three daughters were older with lives and children of their own when we met again, but they all had significant problems. His oldest daughter, Ann, was one of his two daughters by his first wife, Charlayne. Ann had never married the father of her two kids, one little girl who seemed to be her major focus and one little boy whom she seemed to ignore and dislike. They lived in Michigan, too, several hours downstate. She occasionally called and invited us to visit, but as soon as we arrived, she'd take off with her friends, inevitably returning drunk or high or both. It seemed we were free babysitters more than anything. Her house was always in disarray, and her kids were perpetually dirty, though she herself was always clean. The only time she was interested in visiting with us was when we were ready to leave.

She didn't like me. I'd learned to read body language real well throughout my lifetime, and she did not appreciate seeing me with her dad. She came across more like a jealous girlfriend than a daughter. It was uncomfortable being treated as if I were the other woman, but Delbert said her rude behavior was a result of mannerisms she'd picked up from her mother. I knew better, since I'd seen her behave politely elsewhere, but I tried and mostly succeeded in keeping my mouth shut.

Charlayne had never gotten over Delbert and had always nurtured feelings of both love and hate for him. Ann and her mother didn't usually get along, but with Ann and her dad now spending time together, Charlayne became hopeful that Ann would be her vehicle to get Delbert back. In turn, Ann looked at her dad as the key to get close to her mother, who hadn't liked her all that well before but who now did.

Having me in the picture removed any reason for Charlayne to like Ann. It also removed any reason for Ann to like me. Soon, all Charlayne did was tell Ann how much she hated Delbert again. Both of Delbert's daughters with Charlayne lived their entire lives being told nothing but lies about their dad, and to this day, all they hear from their obsessed mother is how awful he is.

Right after their divorce, Charlayne had tried a different approach. She'd told Delbert the reason she had so many problems was that her father had molested her as a child. This was supposed to help Delbert understand why she was so frigidly cold, not only to him but also to the kids. Although Delbert believed her, he had no interest in resuming a relationship with her. She had so much anger inside that she was simply a miserable, hateful person to be around.

I wasn't quite as charitable as Delbert. While nobody has more sympathy toward women who have been molested in their early years than I do, from what I could see, Charlayne used this horrible circumstance as an opportunity. Even worse, she allowed her father to remain active in her life and her children's, even to the point that he regularly babysat them. She might as well have wrapped the girls in gift paper and put a bow on them for her father to molest. This just wasn't a woman who cared about her kids, and yet something about this situation has never felt right to me. Simply put, I've met too many women who've been molested, and the one thing they all have in common is their discomfort with their molesters as they get older. Invariably, they tend to stay away from them, not involve them in their lives. I couldn't help but suspect Charlayne's honesty.

Although Charlayne never withheld Delbert's daughters from him, she made his life hell. After every visit with their dad, his daughters were verbally accosted for loving him. This was a lose-lose situation all the way around. The girls truly were damned if they loved him and damned if they didn't. Accordingly, Delbert explained, his daughter Stormy, Ann's younger sister, was an extremely complicated young woman who thrived on drama and who made intrigue and lying an integral part of her life. At the time Delbert and I got back together, she was estranged from her father for reasons dating back to her teen years and hadn't spoken to him in a year and a half.

Meggie was Delbert's second wife and the mother of Marie. She was the extreme opposite of Charlayne, to the point of being an out-of-control, unpredictable nymphomaniac. After Delbert had been shot at and stabbed by Meggie, he left her and started a custody battle for his daughter. He lost, and though he had occasional visitations, Meggie used Marie as a pawn, and he seldom got to see her. I hadn't yet been reintroduced to Marie now that she was grown up, though I remembered her as a little girl from when I'd done Delbert's visitations with him. I was worried, because I knew her upbringing with Meggie had been horrific and that she, like her half-sisters, had been fed a stableful of lies by her hateful mother.

Delbert's third wife didn't do him any favors, either. In fact, thanks to Sherrill's actions, Delbert had returned to Michigan in handcuffs, having been arrested for failure to pay child support. Sherrill had controlled the money and paid the bills while they were married, and she'd deliberately failed to pay Delbert's child support. However, Sherrill didn't handle the finances *all* of the time, but, her selfishness, greed, jealousy, and constant bickering, always seemed to prevent Delbert from paying for and getting to see his kids.

Delbert admits that it was *his* choice to give in to Sherrill about the money he needed to have for his kids. He knows he should have been less understanding with her about her constant excuses as to why they never had enough money to support his children.

As a Christian woman, who had married a man with three children, she should have made sure his children were taken care of, as well as, if not better than her own children because Delbert's children had to live without him. Tragically, she was only concerned with herself and her children. Delbert takes full responsibility for his part in this wrong-doing and has paid dearly for it.

As soon as Sherrill heard that Delbert was seeing me, she told him she had lupus and was dying and she needed him to stay with her sons while she went off by herself to find some peace and tranquility. He'd been divorced from Sherrill for eight years at this point, but the boys were her shoe-in with Delbert like my kids were with me. He was easy to manipulate when it came to children, and he took people at face value. He just never understood how crafty women could be, especially women who wanted him back. Since he needed to return to Arizona anyway for a short time, seeing those boys became one more reason to go.

When he arrived at Sherrill's, to his surprise, nothing was out of the ordinary. Sherrill's health seemed fine, and though the boys were happy to see him, they were so busy being teens they hardly noticed him during his visit. Delbert then realized this was just another of Sherrill's ploys to try to get him back.

Regardless of what was going on with Sherrill, I felt this separation was going to do Delbert and me good. It would allow both of us time to explore our unanswered questions. In addition, I wanted him to miss me. I would have been a fool to think that incorporating such a man in my life was going to be easy, but at least he'd stopped drinking and doing drugs shortly before returning to Arizona and had decided I meant a whole lot more to him than they did. I knew there would be the usual problems combining kids, but I figured we could solve anything together. I never would have guessed the majority of our problems would come from outside interferences, nor did I realize how large the outreach of anger would span across the country.

I flew to Arizona in April to visit Delbert. This was the first vacation I'd ever taken, and I left the girls at home with my friend Barb. I was nervous about flying, but it was worth it: when I walked into the airport, there he was, smiling at me. My heart skipped a beat, and I got butterflies in my stomach. I was consumed with how wonderful it was to see this man I loved who was waiting with his arms wide open.

We had a wonderful two weeks, though I discovered I didn't care much for the Arizona landscape. I didn't appreciate the desert in the least or the lack of lush color. I was also concerned at the size of the city. It was not only huge, but it also boasted a great deal of crime. Delbert wanted to live there permanently, and I wasn't sure the girls or I would be happy in such an environment. Nonetheless, I had a wonderful time with Delbert. It was very hard leaving him when my two weeks were up, and I was glad he was returning to Michigan in another month. Being apart like this made it very clear to both of us how much we wanted to be together, and shortly after his return to Michigan and a surprise party he helped throw for my fortieth birthday, he asked me to marry him. This time I said yes for the right reasons. I truly loved him, and I knew he loved me.

Delbert wanted to get married outside at my home on a day close to when we had first met again, and we planned our whole summer around this day. We worked very hard on the inside of the house, and Delbert landscaped the yard and made flower beds. I was amazed at what a little paint, imagination, and elbow grease could accomplish. This house I'd once hated metamorphosed into some-thing beautiful! The yard was gorgeous, the house was gorgeous, and it didn't take a lot of money to do it. It really was just a matter of rolling up our sleeves and pitching in. I'd never been with anyone who'd worked side by side with me before, and I don't know about Delbert, but after what we did to that house and yard, I felt almost invincible.

This was the first time in my life I was proud of my home. I could tell the girls were proud, too, and between working days and coming home and working at the house at night, time flew by quickly. Though everything was right on schedule, the week of the wedding was nerve wracking. A few nights before the wedding, Delbert's daughter Ann called and reminded him that the night before the ceremony was his granddaughter's birthday. That was the night we had to put up the tent and decorate, and there was no way we could cram one more thing in. I told Delbert we should wait and celebrate the day after our wedding, but he and

Ann were both insistent that her birthday should be celebrated on her actual birthday. I put my foot down, and though Ann agreed to wait until the next day, she wasn't happy about it. I was pleased when the night before our wedding, she brought us each a rose. I knew she was struggling with her dad getting married, and I planned to give her a gift after the wedding. I hoped it would show her a friendship between us was possible.

It was past midnight the night before the wedding, and we were about to retire when my daughters came to me out of the blue and said, "You never once asked us how we feel about you guys getting married!" They were so upset I didn't know what to do. I asked, "Why did you wait so long to talk to me about this? Why now, when it's hours away?" I cried and told them I was sorry, but I'd taken it for granted they were fine with it as they'd never said otherwise. I went to bed very sad, but the next morning everybody arose with a much better outlook.

Delbert took his paintbrush and touched up the porch with his freshly manicured hands, and the girls woke up wishing us well. We couldn't have asked for a nicer day, and Danielle played her cello in a beautiful quartet as the guests arrived and sat down. Our wedding was simple and beautiful, and this time I had no doubts about the man I was marrying. Delbert was my one true love, and the way he looked at me, I could tell he felt the same. Somehow, I just knew my daughters would grow to love him the same.

The next day, we had nothing to do but have the birthday party. As soon as we got up, I called Ann and made arrangements for them to come over at one o'clock. Finally, when it was close to five and no one had come, I called her at Delbert's mother's house and asked what was going on. She informed me they were just getting ready to sit down and have the birthday party there. I asked, "Why didn't you call us?" She gave me no explanation, so we packed up the cake, decorations, ice cream, and presents and went to his mother's.

After we sang happy birthday, I presented Ann with a friendship card and a gift. It was a long, gold diamond-cut chain, with a beautiful embossed locket. She threw her arms around her dad and thanked him for it. He told her, "Rhonnie got you that," and she barely looked at me. I could tell she wasn't happy, and though I felt she'd tried to sabotage the birthday party on purpose, I was determined to win her over and wasn't going to give up yet.

In spite of Delbert's and my happiness, I soon began having a little trouble with Liz. She was thirteen now, and her grades started to fall, and she developed a bad attitude at home with both Delbert and me. I finally went to the school and asked what I could do with her or what they could do for her. We started going to counseling together, and she saw a counselor at school several times a week as well. It took a lot of effort from both of us, but it all paid off. By the time she was in the ninth grade, she was soaring. She not only made the honor roll, but she also earned a 3.95 grade point average. I couldn't have been prouder.

Danielle was much easier to deal with. She loved school and excelled in everything she tried. In spite of our challenges, things were coming along, and to my gratification, the kids both seemed to like Delbert more and more as time passed.

Andy at this time was in jail. Though he caused me continued pain and sorrow, I was glad he was suffering the consequences of his actions. He had found himself at a party where a fight was going on, and after his friends had knocked the other guy down to the floor, my son had taken a full bottle of Jack Daniels and cracked the young man in the head with it. For this, he was arrested on a high misdemeanor charge that carried one year in jail, so he wasn't present at Delbert's and my wedding. This was another of his bad decisions, but this time he stood alone as an adult. I didn't go to court with him, nor did he call and ask me for money. He knew better, as he'd been so hateful when he'd left here that I'd told him that if he got into trouble again, I wouldn't come to his rescue. And so, I hoped, he was learning.

Delbert and I had been married a year before I met Delbert's volatile daughter Stormy. Ann was scheduled for surgery, and we'd driven downstate to be with her. As it turned out, she was running a fever, so they couldn't operate, but Stormy showed up to support her older sister, and we all decided to have lunch together. I took one look and knew that Stormy was indeed a wild girl, a whirlwind of anger, anxiety, and confusion. Still angry at her father when we married, she had refused to come to our wedding, and I was leery of her. At lunch, she told her father that her stepmother Sherrill was her friend now, though she'd grown up hating her. As soon as I heard this, I knew it meant nothing but trouble. Two angry women putting their conniving heads together meant just that.

Stormy then presented her dad with pictures of the child she'd had at age sixteen and had given to its father in Arizona to raise. She said she'd done this because she couldn't stand to hear the baby crying and she was afraid she would have hurt her. I surely had to respect this very adult decision she'd made as a child herself, but now Stormy was re-entering her daughter's life, thanks to Sherrill. Somehow, Sherrill had managed to manipulate the little girl's father so that she controlled who could see the child and under what circumstances. This meant that if Delbert wanted to see her, his own granddaughter, the visit would have to be supervised by Sherrill. Bingo! That was the control she wanted over Delbert, and she went to great lengths to get it.

Upon learning this, I felt sorry for Delbert. Most ex-wives don't become stalkers, and though his ex-wives didn't stalk him outwardly, they stalked him by using his daughters and, now, his grandchild. I was also amazed by this turn of events since Stormy had hated Sherrill in the past, but Stormy had an angry heart, and Sherrill was another wolf in sheep's clothing when she approached Stormy with her new-found Christian love and ultimate goal of inciting her to hate her father even more.

By the same token, considering how troubled Stormy's past was, I guess nothing should have surprised me. When she was fourteen, Stormy had attempted suicide, and her mother had sent her to live with Delbert and Sherrill in Arizona. Delbert had done the best he could, but he simply wasn't able to withstand the hurricane force of trouble that the women in his life created. Sherrill hadn't cared whether the fourteen-year-old girl went to school and in fact had obtained a false ID for Stormy so she could work and pay her own way while she lived with them. Her intentions never were to help Delbert's biological children; she wanted him only for her own. After Delbert and Stormy got into a fight, her mother sent her the money to return home. When she got back home, she told everyone her dad had tried to molest her. This was a tactic a good friend of her mother's had used, and the two girls were both well aware of it. Thank goodness Stormy was sent to a mental institution, where her doctors saw through her lies. When she got out, she learned that her own sister had become pregnant by her boyfriend. This of course sent her over the edge, and she immediately returned to Arizona to stay with her dad again.

Delbert felt he couldn't say no to her, though he was reluctant to have someone so unpredictable around who would make such horrific accusations, but this was his daughter, and he loved her. Right away, she began an affair with a neighbor and soon got into another dispute with her father. Ultimately, she ran away with Steve, and they returned to Michigan. Charlayne didn't want to deal with Stormy, so she signed papers allowing her underage and now pregnant daughter to marry Steve. After their divorce, shortly after the baby was born, Stormy fled to Michigan to get away from her husband. This was when she'd discovered she couldn't take care of her baby properly, so she'd returned to Arizona where she'd signed over custody to Steve.

Stormy is thirty years old now, but she's still angry about all the nonsense that happened when she was a teenager, nonsense she brought on herself, and I soon found out that her nonsense could be lethal. She visited us in Traverse City shortly after I met her and immediately took the opportunity to sit up with my daughters and try to get them to hate Delbert. She also visited me at work and for three days spewed hateful stories about her dad to me, including a story she'd embellished years before about her dad slapping her mouth and putting her in her room, only now the story went that Delbert had bloodied her lips to the point that she saturated a bath towel full of blood and hid it under her pillow so she could show it to the authorities and press charges against him. This story became larger than life, and Sherrill "helped" her remember how it all went. Indeed, according to Sherrill, Sherrill herself had rescued Delbert from that horrible fate by sneaking into Stormy's bedroom and stealing the "blood saturated" towel out from underneath the pillow.

Basically, Stormy tried to perpetuate the same old lies over and over again. I told her to grow up and move on, and she didn't like that or me after that. She left town in a fury and again refused to speak to her dad until one day she called out of the blue and told him off, again! This was commonplace for her; she always had a crisis going and continuous drama. She thrived on it, and when there wasn't any, she created it.

I met Delbert's third daughter, Marie, and her husband, Collin, and their two children the following spring. They lived in Texas, and we stopped there on a trip to Arizona to get the rest of Delbert's things. At the time, Marie seemed like a breath of fresh air compared to her two half-sisters. That following summer, when her husband got out of the military, Marie and her family moved back to Michigan and into our home, where they stayed for almost seven months to save money. Though they essentially took over our house, I was determined to make the situation work. My girls were not happy about this, and there were lots of reasons why, not the least of which were Collin and Marie's potty training methods. They would take their son's and daughter's diapers off and let them run around naked. This wasn't so bad, except that they routinely climbed up on my couch and chair and peed in them, not to mention how they monopolized my daughters' chairs at the dinner table for their own kids.

Their discipline was also quite lacking, particularly with their son, who wasn't disciplined for bad behavior. On the contrary, he was almost humored for being naughty. He was a little boy with too much control. The very first day they arrived, this child was misbehaving at Delbert's mother's house, and I finally took his little shoulders, looked into his face, and told him "No." He spit at me, pulled his arm back, and punched me square in the face. Then he walked over to Marie, who coddled him.

There were other issues, too. It was apparent that Collin had no desire to live in Michigan. He was an uncooperative man, and I had a hard time liking him, though I loved their daughter, our granddaughter, tremendously. She was my girl right from the beginning. We had an instant, solid bond that surpassed all understanding. It was as if we'd known each other in another life. I could calm this little girl with just my touch when her parents lost control of her.

Things ultimately got so bad with our grandson that one night Delbert finally told Collin and Marie, "If you can't control your son in the evening when we are trying to relax, you must take him back downstairs." Well, how they handled being reprimanded seemed to be the common denominator with all three daughters. As long as they were on the receiving end and getting what they wanted, we didn't have any problems. However, if you crossed them in any way, you felt their wrath, and from then on, the perimeters were clearly drawn. Delbert and I didn't dare step outside the line they drew, or the grandchildren were withheld. Ann was already using her two children this way, and after Delbert's comment, Marie and her family soon moved out in a huff.

Two months later, Delbert suffered a heart attack. He was hospitalized and underwent a quintuple bypass, and it was simply terrifying. I sat with him all day in the hospital for nine days, and the day of his surgery, only his mom, Marie, my daughters, and my sister Jackie and I were present, though one of his sisters stopped in briefly and another called. Four of his brothers lived in the area, but they didn't bother to come by, though a few nieces and nephews did drop in. With all the brothers he has, not one of them asked whether there was anything they could to help, either while he was in the hospital or upon his release and during his recovery. All of his relatives seemed so caught up in their own worlds they forgot to be considerate. The only one who offered to help was Robert, whom Delbert had bailed out of trouble so many times in the past, and he expected to be paid for his contributions, though a sister did make food one time and brought it over.

Delbert's family talked a lot about love, but it was the same as with the church I'd previously attended. It was just lip service, and people weren't there when you really needed them. Delbert had always made himself available to those in need in his family, and this hurt him deeply. On top of that, quite frankly, we could have used some help. For three months following his surgery, Delbert wasn't allowed to pick up anything heavier than a gallon of milk. I finally asked Marie whether Collin would mow the lawn for me, as I didn't know how to use the riding mower, and she said he would, but he never came.

I learned a lot about Delbert's family thanks to this incident. This was after we had done so much for Collin and Marie and had let them stay with us for seven months and after I had taught Marie how to groom dogs, something that costs most people thousands of dollars. I now understood why Delbert had always said he could love his family just fine from thousands of miles away and that it wasn't easy coming back to Michigan.

Then Charlayne decided this was a good time to go after Delbert in court. It was only six weeks after Delbert's surgery, but we had no choice but to hire an attorney. The timing was bad, but it was now time to pay for his negligence. Thanks to two falls he'd had while living in Arizona, he'd fallen behind in his bills. He'd had two industrial falls, one from a two-story roof where he'd sustained a severe back injury and one from a palm tree where he'd fractured his neck. Even though Sherrill hadn't worked the first five years of their marriage, when she did, she figured her money was her money, and she refused to apply it to the bills coming in. However, she didn't tell Delbert this, so he had no idea his child support was going unpaid. She also made Delbert work even while his neck was broken, and he finally saw the light when she filed for a divorce from him after deciding he wasn't financially useful to her any longer.

When he'd learned he owed child support, he'd had a lean put on the house he owned free and clear so that he could come up with the money he needed for Charlayne, but in the meantime Charlayne had seen a potential gold mine for herself. Accordingly, she'd decided to falsely exaggerate the amount of monies owed her, and she refused to settle for one penny less than her inflated figures.

Now, many years after this mess first began, Delbert's attorney presented Delbert's offer, but Charlayne flatly refused. She even went so far as to ask each of her girls to go to court and lie for her, but they both told her to leave them out of it. Even they knew this was wrong. To our gratification, after a year and a half of fighting, Charlayne's lies were finally exposed, and she was forced to settle for what Delbert truly owed her, a sum only a third of the figure she'd been insisting on. To this day, Charlayne tells her daughters she won't be happy until Delbert's dead and buried. For his part, Delbert feels he should have found another way to catch himself up and also should have paid more attention to his own case files, because if he had, he could have disputed her claims a whole lot earlier.

We had one more child support bill to tackle, and that was Delbert's outstanding bill with Meggie, Marie's mom. She was pulling exactly the same trick as Charlayne and had inflated her numbers and lied about when her minor daughter had lived with her so she could keep her welfare checks rolling in. What Meggie was doing should have been considered welfare fraud, but the courts turned a deaf ear. We finally managed to straighten this out as well, but we couldn't believe the dishonesty of Delbert's ex-wives.

Soon after this was resolved, Collin and Marie moved to Phoenix and began living near Sherrill. They were still so angry at us they barely kept in touch, which broke our hearts. Then Sherrill convinced Marie to tell Delbert she was bringing Stormy's daughter to Michigan and would like to set up a visit with him. She convinced Marie she was not bringing the child just so she, Sherrill, could see Delbert. She explained that she wanted to introduce the little girl to the rest of her biological family in Michigan. Of course, she told Marie she had to supervise this visit, since Steve, the child's father, would trust only Sherrill with his little girl.

Delbert declined the supervised visitation, so Sherrill never made the trip, but we knew what her initial motivation was to see Delbert by using the little girl as her tool. What's more was that we knew Stormy had been involved in this as well. She was still angry with her dad and was an easy target for Sherrill's manipulation, since they had Delbert and their anger toward him in common.

Delbert and I had been married two years now, and I was getting burned out on the constant drama. For some reason, I'd thought that since I was with the man I loved, life would be easier than it was. I just never knew there were so many people in the world who would hate somebody simply because he'd finally achieved happiness and joy. A storm had been brewing in the evil hearts of his ex-wives ever since our marriage, and I finally began joking that I must have an invisible neon sign over my head that invited this type of garbage into my life. Foolishly, I'd expected Delbert's ex-wives to be like me. I was a great ex-wife. I never bothered Pat, nor did I care what he was doing, and I didn't have one jealous bone in my body when he remarried. Quite the contrary, I was glad he now had something to do with his time besides torment the girls. Likewise, I didn't care about Jack or what he was doing.

For his part, Delbert was becoming increasingly grumpy. He was unaware of his changing, but I was very aware of it, and I got the brunt of nearly every bad day he had. As those of us who are married know, it just works out that way. Delbert became more and more irritable and then began having what seemed to me to be flat-out tantrums. He finally went to the doctor and began counseling. He was also put on anti-depressants, even though he was convinced there wasn't anything wrong with him. In spite of what at times was an uncooperative attitude, I have to hand it to my husband as he continued to seek help and answers throughout this period, and his behavior exhibited strong character and determination.

Collin and Marie soon ran into a lot of trouble financially and ended up filing bankruptcy. At the time, they lived in a dangerous part of Phoenix that experienced regular drive-by shootings. After a little girl in their neighborhood was shot and killed, they decided they needed to get out. They'd been gone a year and a half by then and were too proud to ask us for money for some time, but Marie finally called her dad and explained their situation. Our resources were limited, but I told Delbert that if these were my kids, I would get them out of that dangerous situation and bring them home no matter what.

It just so happened that a friend's trailer was available to rent. It wasn't much, but it was something they could go to right away, and it was a whole lot better than the first few homes I'd lived in when I was young and struggling. I knew it would not be possible for them to live with us again. They'd taught me that lesson the first time.

Delbert called Marie and told her we would get them back to Michigan and had a place for them to move into right away. It was short notice, but somehow God knew there was urgency, and we were able to put our plan together in a matter of hours. We paid for the moving truck, sent them traveling money, and paid their rent several months in advance so they could find jobs and adjust.

They seemed relieved and moved back right away. Delbert was out of town when they arrived, and since my daughter Danielle had grown fond of them when they lived with us and couldn't wait to see them, she drove out to the trailer as they were unpacking. She came back in tears soon after she'd left. I asked what was the matter, and she finally told me that Marie was verbally thrashing Delbert right and left for finding her a place like that to live in.

Danielle loved Delbert. Marie never considered that, nor did Marie consider that Danielle loved me and also loved Marie! Danielle appreciated the fact that we had jumped to Collin and Marie's aid once again, using money we were going to take a vacation with. This would have been my third vacation in close to thirty years, but we simply put our plans on hold since their small children were in danger.

When Delbert got home, he went out to see them and invited them to dinner. They accepted, and I got home from work shortly after they arrived. When I walked in, they were all lying on the living room floor watching television. I said "Hi" and got absolutely no response from Marie or Collin.

This hurt my feelings terribly, and I walked to the bathroom and then went outside. Delbert followed me outside and hugged me, as I was crying. He apologized for his daughter's behavior, which of course wasn't his fault, and said he never would have believed this had he not seen it for himself.

Finally, the kids came outside, and Delbert said to them, "Aren't you guys going to say hello to Gramma?" With that, they ran over and hugged me up one side and down the other. I had missed them so much, but I could tell they weren't quite sure about me. I was sad their parents hadn't kept my memory alive as they'd done for Delbert. Plus, I knew they'd fallen under the spell of Sherrill and, of course, their parents' antipathy toward me.

As far as the money went, we never asked Collin and Marie to pay us back, even though getting them here and situated cost us thousands of dollars. Maybe that was a mistake, as it seemed they didn't appreciate how hard we'd worked for that money, but I wanted to stay on the best possible terms for the sake of the grandkids, whom I loved. Though the little boy especially had often behaved badly, he was just doing what he'd been taught was okay, and I certainly didn't hold his behavior against him.

I was also trying to think positively for the sake of my husband. I knew what it felt like to love your kids regardless of how badly they acted. For some reason, I still held out hope for Marie. She was the one I knew was capable of learning not to repeat the parenting mistakes she'd grown up with. Delbert and I consequently worked hard at our relationship with Collin and Marie, and soon it seemed they were also working on it. I bought them a new car seat for their brand new baby and a new bed for them, and we had the kids over often and enjoyed them greatly. Danielle loved them, Liz liked them, and I can honestly say we became a family. Andy was out of jail now, and we were getting along much better, and before long, Collin and Marie were even letting their kids call Andy "Uncle Andy."

To Delbert's and my great joy, it soon seemed we had stabilized a seemingly impossible situation. I found it fairly easy to let go of all the garbage that had happened previously by chalking it up to a bad upbringing. I loved Marie as if she were my own daughter, and I knew I would go to the ends of the earth for her and her family if that was what was needed. But now, we were a family. She assured me of this many times, and as far as I was concerned, that made everything worthwhile.

With Collin and Marie back in our lives, life settled down for us. Delbert and I had been together five years now, and catching up on old bills was a thing of the past. Soon, I was able to buy the first brand new furniture of my life. Delbert and I were just getting ready to take a vacation once again when Marie came upon a house she wanted to buy. It was a lot of money for them, and they were struggling as it was. I didn't want to see them get into debt over their heads again, and as the only parents around who could help, what were we to do? We knew owning their own house would finally stabilize their wanderlust and plant their feet firmly on the ground. For their children's sake, I felt this was imperative. Thus, for six weeks I worked ten-hour days grooming dogs and in the evenings and weekends worked at their new house, as did Delbert. I painted in every room of that house and hand-sanded the wood floors alongside Marie, and Delbert stained while Marie and I varnished the floors upstairs and down.

When they ran out of money, we applied what we could to help. Delbert paid to have the septic system pumped, dug and laid pipe, repaired the broken plumbing, patched the drywall, repaired the windows, patched the roof, and did numerous other things mostly out of his own pocket. This of course didn't touch all the miscellaneous items he purchased along the way. I bought paint, wallpaper, their counter top, and various other items that were needed as well. Even though we were all tired, we seemed to bond tighter than ever before. We worked fast and hard, and, by God, we finished in time for the closing inspection.

Collin and Marie were now homeowners! It was wonderful, and the grand-kids were elated to have their own bedrooms in their own house. However, right away, Marie rented the small apartment in the back to her brother. I was concerned about this, as she'd told me some very disturbing facts about both her brothers several years earlier. These were things she'd never revealed to her husband and had forbidden me to tell him or her father, though I'd told Delbert right away.

She'd confided to me the sordid details of her life as a child and how she'd suffered at the hands of her mother, who'd allowed her to be sexually molested by her uncles. These men were never prosecuted and in fact were protected by Meggie and her family from the law and went on to marry and have children of their own. Delbert had told me this part many years earlier; that's why he'd fought so hard for custody when Marie was a child. Unfortunately for Marie, the courts nearly always gave custody to the mother back then, and Marie had ended up in a life of hell with her mother. In addition to withholding his daughter from him, Meggie had gone on to say that Delbert had sexually molested Marie, which was why I'd done his visitations with him when Marie was small. In fact, Meggie was the one who'd befriended Charlayne after her divorce from Delbert, and it was from Meggie that Stormy had gotten the idea of lying about her dad molesting her. Meggie was proud of the fact that she was so cunning and had talked openly about this lie in front of Charlayne and her kids.

What was bothering me now was that I knew how frequently abused children, especially boys, tended to grow up and repeat the same patterns of abuse they endured as children. In Marie's family, the abuse was rampant, and none of the now-grown children, including Marie, had ever sought counseling. I told her I was concerned about this brother and how he might behave around her children, but she denied they were in any danger. What was relevant to her was the fact that if her husband ever found out the truth, he would forbid her brothers from being in her life. That seemed to be her concern, not the welfare of her children.

Delbert and I became somewhat frantic over this situation, but we knew we had to handle ourselves carefully. If we did the wrong thing, we were afraid the kids would be taken out of our lives. We decided the best thing to do was get closer to the brother so we could see how he behaved around the kids, but he'd just found out he had an eleven-year-old daughter and was busy trying to get to know her, and we didn't see much of him.

We didn't end up spending a lot of time at Collin and Marie's new home, but the grandkids came here often. They spent the night at least once a month, and they loved their grandpa and their grandma. With all our kids basically grown, this became our simple joy in life. Danielle was away at college now, and though Liz was still living at home, she, too, had graduated with honors and was working. There was just so much pleasure in having little children here. They were growing fast, and I wanted to be there every step of the way. I took them shopping for new clothes each fall before school began, and holidays were extra special now that Santa Claus and the Easter Bunny stopped at our house for them.

The year 2001 started out great for all of us, but then in March of that year,

Stormy re-entered the picture under the pretense of a new and changed person. She hadn't spoken to her dad for a couple of years at this point, but when she phoned, she was very apologetic about her past behavior with both Delbert and me. She explained that she had been going to therapy and was on anti-depressants, which seemed to be helping a lot. She was very sincere, and though I remained cautious, I wanted to give her a fair chance for Delbert's sake. He was head over heals happy that she was back in his life, but I couldn't help but feel she was on some sort of a mission. Still, she seemed very genuine in wanting to make amends, and seeing the despair on Delbert's face, I knew it was important that I accept his daughter.

As it turned out, she said she'd come to ask for our help. Ann, her sister, was in trouble. She'd been smoking crack cocaine for some time now, and her son no longer lived with her; he was living with his dad, a heroin addict. Ann's daughter was still living with her, but Ann's live-in was a crack addict, and they lived at what essentially was a crack party house. Stormy's description of what went on in that house made my skin crawl.

Stormy told us that Ann had just been beaten up by some girls pretty badly and that this was the second time it had happened. Stormy felt that not only was Ann jeopardizing her life but also she was putting her daughter at risk living in that house, and she said she needed her dad's help to get Ann on the right track. Because Stormy had told us so many lies in the past, I wanted to verify this was true, but Delbert's concern overrode any doubts at this point. Stormy soon brought Ann's son for a visit, and he told his grandfather this was not only true but also he and his sister had found needles in their dad's car and had almost sat on them. This nearly thirteen-year-old child also told Delbert his father had made him go to the doctor and say he was out of his prescription for Ritalin so he could get another one. His dad planned to sell this prescription's worth on the streets to buy heroin.

The concern for Ann and her kids was so great that Delbert, Stormy, and the girls' mother met in the city Ann lived in and went to the grandson's school and reported all this to his principal. After this, Stormy and Delbert went to Ann's home for an intervention. Delbert laid out to Ann what he needed her to do to keep him from reporting her to Protective Services, but ultimately he picked up the phone and did in fact report her. At the time, she was on government assistance for her depression, but her checks were based on how big her family was. Since she was lying and collecting for the son who had lived with his dad all these years, I called the fraud hotline and reported this as well.

Delbert's mission was not only to make a better life for his grandkids but also hopefully to make Ann realize she could have a better life, too. His poor little eleven-year-old granddaughter had pulled her own hair out of her head, not even realizing what she was doing. This sorrowful child felt so responsible for her mother's well being that she was afraid to leave her mom at any time for fear something would happen to her.

Once this crisis was on its way to being resolved, Stormy and I had several long talks about what it was that had made her so hateful in the past. She said she knew she used to be mean, but she didn't want to be that way anymore. She told me that as long as she was on her medication, she didn't feel like being mean at all. She seemed to be on the right track, but she'd been having marital problems with her second husband, a man my age, and was contemplating a divorce. Her dad encouraged her, but I warned him that Stormy wasn't serious. She had left this man many times before and had always gone back to him. Besides, I had to be the devil's advocate in this. Stormy was a hard person to deal with, and her husband stayed with her despite her disposition. Sometimes older men who marry younger women don't realize the package they're buying, and I'm quite sure this man got more than he bargained for. On the other hand, it served him right.

Stormy's husband was soon transferred to Kansas City, and Stormy thought the move would do them good. Even better, Steve had finally agreed to allow his twelve-year-old daughter a visit with her mom, and Stormy ended up making several trips to Kansas City and back again while her daughter was visiting her in Michigan. She even brought her daughter to stay with us while she got her things moved with the understanding that we would drive her to Kansas at the end of the week, and we had a very enjoyable time with this young lady. She was a real breath of fresh air, untainted by the wiles of not only her maternal grandmother but also of her mother. She was polite and considerate, something I hadn't seen much of in Delbert's children or in quite a few of his family members. We did all her school shopping in Michigan, and we let her go wild, picking anything she wanted. It was another of Delbert's big dreams come true to be able to reunite with this little girl after so many years of not seeing her, and the bonus was that Sherrill had lost her grip on the situation so that Steve, the father, didn't insist that Sherrill supervise her visit to Michigan.

When we arrived in Kansas, we noticed that Stormy's new house needed wallpapering, so we decided to wallpaper the kitchen, hallway, and laundry room for her. Thank goodness they had air conditioning, as it was over a hundred degrees every day we worked on the house. We bought a porch swing for their housewarming gift and of course all the wallpaper. We hadn't had a chance to do anything nice for Stormy in a long time, and she seemed to appreciate it.

We left there exhausted and came home to rest. She continued to call several times a week to stay in touch with her dad, and it was nice to see him smile when he heard from her. He felt as though his various relationships with his daughters were straightening out. He had a peace I'd never seen in him before. Instead of sadness and pain in his eyes, I saw love and compassion. On top of that, we were delighted with our relationship and with each other. To our relief, the worst thing we had to do that year was turn in Delbert's eighteen-year-old nephew for touching our granddaughter inappropriately during their play wrestling. He did this in the fall while he was staying with us with five grownups sitting nearby, and we promptly threw him out after we took the kids home to their parents.

With the most wonderful Christmas of our lives and a terrific New Year's over, in which the three grandkids and Collin and Marie spent the night in sleeping bags on our living room floor, we were looking forward to an even better year than the past one. Who could have known it would all fall apart with just a few cruel lies? I never would have dreamed it could happen.

Chapter 12

Where We Are Today

Though she had a brief spell of pretending to be changed, Stormy ultimately wreaked havoc in our lives. When she returned to Michigan in January of 2002 with her daughter and pets in tow after once again leaving her husband, she destroyed in a few short months relationships that took years to build. It started when she climbed into my son's bed. She was again toying with the idea of a reconciliation with her husband, of course, and she wanted to make him jealous. Andy ultimately realized a relationship with her was not a good idea and turned her away, and though at first she was angry, she soon moved on to her other stepbrother, Marie's brother. He initially embraced her advances, but when he, too, made attempts to tone down their relationship, she once again became irate.

In the meantime, her husband had finally had enough and had decided to sue her for divorce, so her dad put up the $2,500.00 retainer fee for her attorney in Kansas City as well as additional money to fix her car and pay for her trips to Kansas to go to court. As usual, she promised to pay him back, but she paid him only enough to make him think she was going to keep this promise. In the end, she ripped him off nearly $2,000!

She also tried to convince her dad she was suicidal during this period. Like her mother, she had perfected the role of victim and master manipulator, and thinking she was suicidal kept Delbert feeling responsible for her. He was afraid to say or do anything that would push her over the edge. I didn't buy it, and seeing her response when Andy broke it off with her convinced me she was no longer the new, changed Stormy she'd pretended to be. This was the old Stormy, the mean, destructive one, and I warned her father to pay closer attention to what her mission really was.

Then, during a fight with her lover/stepbrother, she raged into our home and was fuming with anger. This wasn't the first time she'd stormed into our house and was ranting and raving about this man, but this time, the things she said sent shivers up my spine. In response, I replied that with this man's mother having sex with her own brothers, I wasn't sure what lines she'd drawn when it came to her own children but that it wasn't normal for brothers to come on to their sisters or for brothers and sisters to have sexual relations! After I said that, Stormy stormed out. I was glad her dad witnessed everything I said, as it soon became apparent that Stormy lied to Marie about our conversation.

Our life as we knew it fell apart two days after. Easter morning, I thought it was strange that Marie hadn't yet called to see what time we wanted to have the egg hunt with the kids. Though it was only nine in the morning, I decided to give her a call. She said they'd already had their Easter egg hunt. I asked why she hadn't called, and she was snotty, unbelievably so. She replied that the kids had gotten up and wanted to do the hunt, so they had. I told her we would be right over and hung up.

When I told Delbert about this conversation, he jumped out of bed and dressed quickly. He, too, knew something was wrong. We hadn't been excluded from the kids' Easter egg hunt since the family had moved back to Michigan three years before. When we walked in, my fears were confirmed. As Collin walked by, I said, "Hi, Collin!" He kept walking and didn't say a word.

The atmosphere was thick, and then from the living room walked Stormy with a grin on her face. It was a grin of conquest, and Delbert and I both recognized it. She cheerfully said, "Hi, Dad!" and both daughters sat down with Delbert and ignored me. I passed the time by watching the kids go through the baskets we'd made for them, but Delbert soon told his daughters we had to leave.

We both cried all the way home, knowing everything we'd worked so hard to gain was lost. It wasn't long before we knew exactly what had happened, for Marie called and informed her dad I'd told Stormy the secret she'd confided to me long ago.

I didn't do that. I never would have disclosed Marie's secret to a volatile big mouth such as Stormy, but Stormy has a way of finding out what's none of her business as well as what is. Though I didn't tell her, I could hear Marie clear across the room when she called, and I couldn't believe my ears. She was convinced

Stormy was her friend and was looking out for her best interests, and I knew one thing was for sure: I would no longer be included in Marie's life. Sure enough, Marie then told her father I was not allowed to see her children again unless we were in a restaurant, another public place, or her home. I wasn't to be trusted, and they were no longer going to be allowed to come to our house.

Delbert replied, "You must be drinking too much. This is what your mother did to you; you're reminding me of your mother." Marie became even more irate and told her dad, "Make your choice between me or your wife."

I didn't want Delbert to have to make a choice between his children or me. I wanted him to continue his relationship with all of them. However, I made up my mind that this relationship would never again include me when it came to Stormy. I couldn't take another minute of her lies and cruelty, nor would I. My heart ached for those little kids, and I knew I would miss them forever, but I had exhausted my resources and patience with all three daughters. I had never tried so hard in all my life to help anybody, and this was more than a slap in my face. I knew I could no longer be their enabler, nor did I want to be used by them anymore. They were hellbent on manipulating people for their own gain, and I needed to completely distance myself from them.

Stormy called me at work two days before that fateful Easter morning and told me she was going back to Kansas City with her husband after all. In my opinion, she was returning to Kansas both in the hopes of making her lover/stepbrother jealous and because she realized she was losing her husband—she decided she couldn't afford that, so she pulled out all the stops in order to keep him! I've spoken to Marie only once since then, and that was later on that Easter day, and she was aloof at best. I've spoken to Stormy only once as well, on that same day.

Stormy was also leaving Danielle in the lurch. Once our nephew's funeral was over, I'd secured an apartment for Stormy and Danielle and had paid the first and last month's rent, as well as the deposit for Stormy's animals, with the understanding that she and Danielle would pay me back. At the time, it was a relief to have a few people out of our tiny house, and it also allowed the possibility of Stormy's temporary custody of her daughter to continue. I had also helped Stormy get access to legal help through the local women's resource center to fight for shared custody of her daughter, but once she started sleeping with her lover/stepbrother, she lost all sight of her daughter and began missing her appointments or canceling them.

Worst of all, in the end, Stormy didn't even try to get her daughter back, though I heard her promise she would. I also heard her tell her daughter she'd send her the clothes she left behind when her dad came to Michigan to get her, but instead of doing that, I saw Stormy wear them. In retrospect, not living with her mother is probably best for this little girl. She may not understand it at her tender age, but she has a gentle spirit, and I believe she will remain a sweet girl, untainted by her angry mom.

Stormy met with her dad one last time before moving back to Kansas City almost a year ago, and Delbert was shocked to hear the conclusion she and Marie had reached: I was a jealous woman, just like his last wife, who wanted to keep him from having a relationship with his daughters. In their view, I was pulling his strings as if he were some kind of puppet, and was making him do only what I wanted.

I have to admit it would sometimes be nice if this were true, but it's not. If it had been the way I wanted, Delbert would have continued to see his daughters very regularly. I prompted, urged, pleaded, and begged him to stay in their lives for everybody's sake, especially the grandkids, but Delbert decided this would not be wise. The children would have asked questions about me, and he could never lie to them, even for Marie. They would want to come over to our house and spend the night, and he didn't want to be the one to tell them they couldn't. Delbert's feelings were simple: "My daughters are not too old to learn how to be nice."

To my disgust, Stormy hasn't once called her dad since her return to Kansas City, and it makes me sad to think that not one of Delbert's daughters has ever taken the time to know who their father really is. They've accepted only their bitter mothers' opinions that he's a big loser, in spite of the fact that ever since I've known him, anytime his adult daughters have needed or wanted anything, he's been there to provide it.

Today, both of Charlayne's daughters hate their father. The investigation into Ann's drug-related problems forced her to straighten up, and to thank her dad, she called and told him she hates him for what he did to her, and now she refuses to talk to him. I know Ann and Stormy get kudos from Charlayne when they go after him, but they are currently thirty-one and thirty-three years old, and they need to quit wallowing in self-pity!

As for Marie, I cried for months about losing her family, and ultimately I sank into a deep depression. I finally went to the doctor and was put on medication, and I also started seeing a counselor to talk specifically about what had happened with Delbert's children, even though I knew there was nothing I was ever going to be able to say or do that would make a difference to Marie. Though Stormy was expendable as far as I was concerned, I'd treasured Marie and her kids, and what those two women had done was just too sad for me to comprehend. Those precious children were being used as an angry mother's tool, and I knew in the long run they would be the real losers.

Once we had our feet under us again, I decided to go ahead and end the torment I've felt all these years with my mother. I didn't see her very much, but when I did, she always managed a dig at me. It was obvious she still had an embittered heart towards me, and I didn't want to feel this way any longer. Though my sisters tried to make me feel guilty, the sad truth was I felt guilty anyway. I knew Mom was older now and all the damage had been done, but forgiveness is about repentance, about repairing those things that are wrong. They aren't repaired if you're still holding hostility and blame in your heart, and she clearly was with me.

I couldn't torment myself with this any longer. I didn't want to spend another year with my stomach churning as I tried to pick out a Mother's Day card for her, trying to find one I could honestly give her. They don't make cards that describe the kind of mother she was. I've read them all, and they don't exist. What's more is I'm a terrible fake, and I felt I would be betraying myself if I faked it with Mom, so I always ended up getting her a pretty card that was blank inside and writing "Happy Mother's Day, Mom" in it. In turn, for my last birthday, she sent me a generic birthday card with a "Touché, how does it feel?" written inside. I didn't want to live like that any longer, so I finally wrote her the following letter.

Dear Mom,

I thought I would write you this letter to try to explain what is going on in my life at the moment. Unfortunately, it involves my life as a whole and not just the here and now. I am suffering from depression and am on anti-depressants. I'm at a point where I need to be alone with those I know love me dearly.

To explain further, I need to tell you that this involves my life from birth until now. In explaining all this, some of this letter may be uncomfortable for you to read, but I hope that you do read it.

I started out in this world as a little baby, like all babies. But between infancy and adulthood, life has been tough. Many mistakes were made, and I don't think it's fair to grow up this way. Instead, I believe every child born is a child of God, and this would include me. I look back daily, even when I don't want to. I try to not look at all the bad things, and many times I've almost convinced myself that I wouldn't be the person I am today if all this stuff hadn't happened to me. I'm close to forty-seven years old, and I'm now at a point where I don't want to lie to myself any longer.

The facts are that I will never know what I would have been had I had the proper nourishment from loving parents who helped me through all the bad times, did homework with me, looked at my strong points, and said to me, "You go out there and do whatever you want, because whatever you do in life will turn out great," or maybe said, "Gosh, you're so good at that. I know you will be a success."

Guess what, Mom? I never knew any of that because none of it ever happened. I have struggled endlessly, and still I don't know where I belong. I have to tell you about a little girl in a family of six kids who grew up terrified and was treated like damaged goods. I have lived a life of horror. My beginnings were some of the worst I've ever heard of, short of being killed by abusive parents. I don't have childhood memories of school to speak of, of happy moments in the family, of good times where we all laughed. I have big huge gaps of nothingness, with only the horrible, sad thoughts of being ridiculed and abused sexually, physically, and mentally.

You know the punishment of being a "Joe Smith." Well, guess what, Mom? I'm still a "Joe Smith," still struggling for somebody to know I'm here. How about eating on the floor with the dog? Well, I guess I've eaten on the floor with the dog most of my life, not feeling any better now than I did back then. How about Dad making me have oral sex with him? I told you when I was small, and today you deny I even told you. How do you think that makes me feel? You didn't save me, and though I did the right thing by telling, you got mad at me and shook me and screamed at me.

It was from that point on that my life of hell became worse. How about trying to commit me to the state hospital? That was really fun. When that didn't work, what did you do? You sent me to Dad's to live. Now how about that? Those are the memories I live with daily and a whole lot more just like that.

I'm too old to have to climb uphill all the time. I'm working on these things that are part of me so I can deal with my terror dreams, but I need to move on from this, and I don't know how to without leaving that part of me and the causes behind. I wish you no harm in life; I just need to move on. Thank you for hearing me out.

Rhonnie

I don't wish my mother any harm; writing this letter was pure self-preservation. If the time comes when I'm needed for finances to help support her, I will be there with my checkbook wide open. I just don't want to deal with her in the meantime.

Many months have now gone by since the Stormy/Marie fiasco, and in retrospect, I've never felt more used than by Marie and Stormy. Somehow I thought I mattered to Marie, and I can't believe the lies of a vindictive woman could destroy our relationship so. As far as I'm concerned, it didn't take much to turn her away. Marie is repeating the patterns she grew up with, taking our pictures off the walls, out of photo albums, and avoiding places we might be, not realizing this will never destroy the love her kids have for us. What's more is, they are going to grow up feeling the same way about their mother that Marie does about her own mother. It is the nature of that beast.

Quite simply, I can clearly see many members of three generations of Delbert's family repeating the same patterns over and over, and though it is terribly sad, I can do nothing about it. It goes without saying that Stormy will never again be allowed in our home. Delbert and I both feel we can welcome only those who truly love us, and there are many who do, in spite of our shortcomings. These are the people we consider family, the ones who hold a true love for us, whether we are related or not. The saying "blood is thicker than water" simply doesn't apply to us. In addition, neither Delbert nor I would feel safe seeing the grandkids now without a third party present for fear Marie would fabricate lies about us as her mother did about Delbert when she was a child. With the pattern this clear, we have no choice but to protect ourselves.

Though I've bumped into many walls in my lifetime, I know I did one thing right: I kept my children from ever knowing my father while they were growing up. When they were old enough to understand, I told them why. My father is what he is, a predator, and he always will be. Though he's never spent a day in jail for the atrocities he committed, we all know he is the monster that lurks in the darkness who wants to rob another child of his or her spirit and innocence.

My dad's father, the grandfather no one ever spoke of, was also a predator. When I was in my twenties, I discovered that my grandfather molested his own children and actually impregnated one of his own daughters. When she found out, my grandmother went to her priest and asked his advice. In essence, he told her the deed was done and she needed to live with it.

Not satisfied with that, my grandmother went to the police and had my grandfather arrested. This was more than fifty years ago, and it resulted in a big trial in a small town. After that, my grandmother moved her family to the small town she'd grown up in, trying to put this embarrassment behind her. No wonder it was kept secret. My grandfather was found guilty of his crimes, and on the train en route to prison, he hung himself in the bathroom. The baby was given away and never spoken of again within the family.

As for Pat, my kids live with the knowledge that their father doesn't care enough about them to call or come see them. It's now been several years since they've heard from him at all. The murder that I suspect him of being involved in has never been solved, though thirty years have gone by. I pray for the wife and now-grown daughter of the store manager all the time and hope they will someday find peace in this matter. I know in my heart that someday Pat will have to answer for his misdeeds, and I will leave it up to God to deal with Pat and my father.

I'm sorry to say that after finding much success in business adventures, my sister Jackie began to sink into a deep depression a number of years ago. I wish she'd addressed her childhood trauma earlier, because that sleeping giant did emerge and take her down. The only way she's going to get any better is to get some help, but it seems the mere thought of that scares her. She also needs to come to grips with our mother, which she has yet to do. She has stayed in bed most of the past four years, unable to get up and face the world. Knowing this, I am profoundly grateful she came to be with me during Delbert's heart surgery and for both of my daughters' high school graduation parties.

My brother Bob remained in the Army until he retired and is still employed by the military as a civilian. He is just barely making ends meet. I have worried about Bob forever, always hoping he will find peace in his heart. He is a man who will forever be rescuing damsels in distress, drug addicts, and alcoholics. He is relentless in his efforts, though it sounds like the rewards are minimal. He realizes that most of the people he "rescues" go right back to drugs, alcohol, abusive relationships, and neglecting their kids.

Bob has been through therapy, as well. Of all us kids, he had the most to overcome, as Dad's abuse of him went further than it did with the rest of us. True to form, Bob has gone through life not quite fitting in anywhere, though he is a nice man with a big heart who has worked on self-esteem relentlessly. Inner peace and happiness seem to elude him, and I think he is the loneliest man in the world. Thank God he has his adopted daughter, her husband, and his little grandkids to make him smile. He was never romantic with the mother of his adopted daughter, and they didn't marry. Instead, he took on her family and helped her raise her kids by filling in for the absent father in their lives. Bob was married for a time, but he never had children, nor was he sure he wanted them, since he was afraid he would not be good to them. He knew what he was up against in terms of possibly repeating patterns of abuse, and he wasn't willing to take a chance and destroy another child in this world. I give him a lot of credit for this, but in the end he found out he had nothing but love to give to children. I feel this is his biggest victory in life. He is in my thoughts often.

I don't know much about my brother Rod. I haven't talked to him since 1995. At that time, he was very volatile and angry at the world, as usual. I've always felt there was something wrong with Rod. He was always a mean little boy, and he grew up to be a mean man. He moves around from state to state, which makes me wonder what he's really up to. I heard from my sister that he has a problem with young boys. He used to have an ice cream truck that he drove through neighborhoods, and one time he tried to coerce a young boy to go with him. The police were called, but to my knowledge Rod fled and wasn't caught. One of my nephews also told me that Uncle Rod came on-to him when he was small. Brother or not, if he's doing these horrible things, I want him locked up. My prayers to God are always to stop him, no matter what it takes, before he scars some young person for the rest of his or her life.

Tay is another sad story. She is now on the third and probably final episode in her life where she no longer will talk to me. I haven't heard from her in more than three years. I don't know what goes on in her head, even though I've tried for years to understand her. I can feel only that she may still be unstable and could snap at any given moment, as she has in the past. She's instructed my mother, who of course plays the game with her, to never allow me to have her phone number or address. This familiar antic was also used by Mom. She kept her telephone number from me for several years and shared it only with the kids whom she "trusted," just so her sister, my aunt, whom she despised, could never have it. How childish! The same goes for my sister Jackie, who Tay is convinced is a villain. She also claims Jackie poisoned her when she was a teenager living at Jackie's house. I hope she gets help someday so she won't end up just like Mom. Those two are the most alike.

Roger is the youngest of us six kids. Three and a half years ago, he was shot while being robbed in New Orleans. He was in intensive care for almost six weeks and almost died. I paid for a room for him at a nearby motel when he was finally released from the hospital, but I also called Dad and told him he needed to purchase a plane ticket for Roger to bring him home to be cared for. With a lot of prompting, Dad did that. Jackie took care of him for several months, and then he came to us.

He broke my golden rule and drank in this house after he'd been here a few months, and I immediately moved him to a local hotel full of drunks and addicts. He continued to drink, got a second drunk driving arrest, and now is sober. He is a brilliant writer and could do much with his life. He also has a little girl who's physically challenged whom he hasn't seen in a long time. He's just starting to come around again, and I like him much better as a sober man. I think he's beginning to realize just how fast time gets away from you when you drink. He's made a few comments to me about how big his daughter is getting, but he hasn't seen her in years other than in pictures. He does have a girlfriend I like a great deal. In most ways, she's good for Roger, but she drinks, which concerns me. I'd seen my little brother only once in the fifteen years before he was shot, and I guess you could say I never really knew him.

It is so sad that in a family like ours we don't have close relationships with each other. Our lives were so horrific that we've all automatically kept our distance from one another. When I see pictures of when we were small, my heart just aches. I see six beautiful children who just wanted to have normal childhoods, who never asked for the circumstances given to them. We were just kids trying to survive. The sadness in my heart will never leave me for those children. It bothers me so much I've had to quit looking at the pictures, and my heart grieves to this day.

All three of my children are now in their twenties. Danielle and Liz are currently living together and seem to be managing their lives quite well. They may be wobbly at times, but they are standing on their own. Since we live in the same town just minutes away from each other, I can keep my forever watchful eye on them, albeit from a slight distance. Despite the differences between Danielle and Liz, they love each other. I know both my daughters are going to be just fine, and I'm proud of them. They can be aggressive in achieving their goals, which I feel is an excellent quality, and they both miss their brother terribly.

Danielle continues to be very softhearted. She was incredibly hurt by Marie's betrayal, but hopefully, as time passes, the hurt will go away. She is currently working two jobs and attending college classes and seems to feel good about herself, though she's affected by the absence of her father and holds anger inside. We talk about this sometimes, and she doesn't know exactly what she should say to him or do about the situation. She wants to write him a letter, but she's afraid that when he gets to the parts he doesn't like, he'll simply throw it away and quit reading. I don't know what advice to give her. I just tell her she doesn't need her father to validate who she is; she is wonderful, and all who know her love her.

Liz is doing well, too. She is the more outspoken of my two daughters. Her summary of the Marie situation is, "Mom, you're just their bank. She doesn't care about you; she's just using you." I used to get angry when Liz said this, but now I think her view is more correct than mine. Liz doesn't seem to be having the chronic mood swings she used to have and is now very pleasant to be around. They are both hard workers, and though Danielle is still trying to decide what direction she wants to go in career-wise, Liz plans to open her own salon some day and in the meantime is busy learning all the ins and outs such a career will entail.

Though Andy had begun to show signs of maturity and responsibility in the last few years, he was convicted of conspiracy to distribute the drug ecstasy in 2002 and was sentenced to four to eight years in a federal correctional institute. I have no doubt whatsoever that he is reliving and rethinking every one of the bad decisions he's ever made. Amazingly enough, he sounds good when I talk to him on the phone. He's now on medication for anxiety and depression and to control the psychotic episodes he has as a result of his drug use. He has developed a heart arrhythmia as well. I'm worried for his life, but I know in my heart that he might well have killed himself had he not been put in jail and scared into stopping his drug use. He's just one of those people for whom something had to give or he would have completely self-destructed.

I talk to him often and miss him dearly. He has become closer to me than ever, as well as to his sisters. He worries about us all and misses us terribly and is homesick. He has poured himself into studying the Bible and wants to go to missionary school someday. He is worried not only about his own salvation but his sisters' as well. In short, he's finding his way through the muddled mess he's made of his life.

Before our most recent Thanksgiving dinner, I said a prayer, and everybody cried. That has never before happened in all these years. Thanksgiving has always been a joyful holiday for us, full of laughter and fun, but this year was very sad. Our hearts missed Andy so much, and the absence of the grandkids added sorrow to an already dismal mood. Needless to say, our appetites were not the same as in prior years.

As for the rest of the family, Delbert's nephew Aaron ended up being convicted for the sexual offense he perpetrated on our granddaughter and went to jail. His mother, Laurie, who'd moved back to Phoenix after Jon's burial, returned to Michigan to get her pickup truck when Aaron's time was up. After she collected him, they immediately began doing drugs together. The day after his release, he failed a mandatory urine test and was put back in jail. Thanks to breaking the terms of his probation yet again, he's now back in jail for the third time.

His father, Delbert's brother, is also still in jail thanks to his child molestation conviction. He apparently perpetrated his sex crimes on one little girl several times over a four-year period.

Nothing ever came of Jon's death. His all but forgotten body lay in an unmarked grave. There has never been a criminal investigation into it, and Sherrill's son will never be punished for the alleged role he played. Worse yet, this son will probably never get off heroin and may possibly suffer the same fate as his cousin. This situation is tragic all the way around.

Sherrill, of course, is still alive—her lupus must have miraculously gone into remission. How wonderful to go from a near-death experience to being the picture of health. She is a walking miracle!

Jo quietly passed away. She is such a wonderful memory. It was Jo's strength, determination and compassion that carried me through my difficult years. I am grateful that I had the opportunity to go to her and thank her and tell her that it was she who gave me the courage to stand up and keep looking forward. I feel so privileged to have known her. I love her.

As for me, I feel wonderful. Through every event and struggle in my life, I've learned a little more. I have faith that keeps me strong, and Delbert shares the same faith in Jesus that I do. Although I've met those along the way whom I would call the worst examples of Christians, they didn't cause my faith to waiver even slightly. I've always known God and Jesus were in my life. I can't explain how it all works; I can tell you only that I rely on my faith. I know Christ has been my mother, my father, my husband, my kids' father, and my companion. I have a very personal relationship with him and he with me. I know he is the sole reason Delbert and I can see light through the darkened clouds we've encountered along the way. We share this common bond between us; it's the glue that holds us together. Love helps, but love alone would certainly not be enough. There are spiritual reasons Delbert and I are together. Some of these reasons we can clearly see, but some are for only God to know. All I know is that what we have together is worth saving and that somehow, through all the pain and suffering we've endured, our marriage has matured. Now that we stand united, our lives are so much easier and more fulfilling. Neither of us misses the constant drama, and although saddened by some of life's facts, in his heart Delbert knows the truth of the matter. He knows my heart is a loving, compassionate one. He knows I've gone above and beyond the call of duty not only as his wife but also as a woman who has commiseration for his children. Now he feels he has to protect me from those who would like to hurt me, even if this includes his own children.

He will always live with a broken heart because of his daughters, but he understands that their behavior is not his fault. He also understands what denial is, and this has helped him understand that grown women make their own choices in life. It goes without saying that he will forever feel horrible about the dismal choices his children have made, as well as his own past poor choices, but he knows it's out of his control to change them. He can offer advice if his daughters come to him, but he knows he cannot make them do the right thing.

Essentially, we both know that in doing all we could for them, we enabled them to continue their bad behavior. If we were to continue this, we would be guilty of averting their growth. Simply, Delbert and I have made the conscious decision that we are not going to enable them any longer.

With all the excess turmoil gone from our lives, the energy now flows freely in our marriage. We very seldom have disagreements or arguments anymore, and wonderful things have been happening not only for me but also for Delbert. Not long ago, a company approached him about manufacturing and marketing one of his outdoor products. Finally, after all these years, somebody appreciates my husband's wonderful talents!

I'm still grooming dogs with my boss, Susie, who is my best friend and like a sister to me. She is one of my unsung heroes, and I don't know where I'd be without her. My job is physically demanding, and though I hate to even think about it, soon I will have no choice but to leave my position. I will be very sad when this day comes. Since I grew up without a family, other than my children, anything that resembles family is important to me. I have been at my job for eighteen years now and am attached to all the people who work in the small businesses around our shop. We all look out for one another, and it feels like a giant family, but I fell out of the bathtub at work 1 1/2 years ago and pulled my hip socket. Since then, I haven't been able to control my constant back pain and muscle spasms.

All in all, I feel very fortunate. I like who I am, and I like the fact that I'm not afraid to stand up for what I believe, even if I'm the only one who feels that way. I've seen much dysfunctional behavior throughout my life, but I've always believed that what I do with my life is my responsibility. Growing up abused is not justification to be mean or hateful to people. It's not an excuse, and we all can move on from it. Through women's groups and other organizations, there is help available today that simply didn't exist when I was a child.

For these reasons, I find it tragic that abuse and neglect remain rampant in some families. I fought hard to distance myself from those in my own family who leaned toward repeating patterns of neglect and abuse, yet I married men whose families were in some ways even harsher to be around than mine. Since Delbert's family, too, is challenging this way, I will forever be grateful that Delbert is as willing as I am to overcome his past and to change destructive patterns.

I have no shame about my past. My brothers and sisters and I were innocent children who were tortured, abused, neglected, and at times abandoned. I didn't grow up to repeat this pattern with my own children. After all, what kind of parents would wish a life with so many struggles onto a child of theirs? I broke this pattern consciously because I wanted my children to have the rightful joy and happiness they deserved, but I know too many others who continue to struggle with these patterns. It is my hope and prayer that reading my story can somehow aid these individuals.

Epilogue

New Beginnings

T hroughout my lifetime, I've met literally hundreds of men and women who've shared with me the living hell they endured as abused children. Even when they've achieved success in life, they've privately kept undeniable pain deep within them. The one thing they all have in common is quiet shame that blemishes their lives and keeps them from contentment and peace. It hasn't helped that some have never shared their pasts with their spouses, as they've felt too much shame to do so.

On the other hand, it hasn't helped that many women who did share felt sorry for doing so because of how their husbands reacted. Most were told this was something they needed to keep to themselves, as though it were embarrassing.

I don't know why I've been the one they've chosen to share their stories with, but I have a feeling it's because they know I'm a safe person who understands their pain. I, too, live with this pain. I, too, struggle with this unwanted and uninvited part of me. The difference is I'm not ashamed. What happened to me was no fault of my own. Formerly abused children, now women and men, need to know the abuse they suffered was not their fault and to rid themselves of their own guilt in this matter. The human body is designed so that when we are touched in those areas that are intended for enjoyment, a pleasant physical sensation is naturally stimulated. This is true even when we are little. As we grow older, the memory of this causes tremendous guilt.

This is why adult "child" victims are often ashamed and sometimes think that what happened may have been their fault. I don't think many know how to liberate themselves from this. We can see the damage everywhere we look if we choose to take our blinders off, but it's much easier to be told that "Children are resilient" and can "bounce back" into a normal life. What's normal? I can tell you from my experience and that of others I know that there is no such thing.

For me, what was abnormal was normal, and I'm not alone in this. On the contrary, I'm but one of millions who endured a savage childhood and who grew up with the total absence of love. I have strived to do the right thing, but it's been a struggle. Little by little, mistake after mistake, I've made headway. My life has been like riding the wildest roller coaster that exists, with many twists, turns, sharp rights, sharp lefts, slow climbs, and rapid descents. A portion of this ride has been enjoyable, but mostly I've wanted it to end so I could put my feet on solid ground.

Unfortunately, we tend to treat abused animals more humanely in our society than we do abused children. There are not only heavy fines for those who abuse animals, but also there is imprisonment. In addition, animals are rescued from those who neglect and abuse them and are never returned to them. Why is it that we don't have the same standards for our children? I find this horrifying, but our system feels it's better–and possible–to "fix the problem" and return children to their natural parents. Strangely enough, the first child abuse case argued before the court was represented by the American Society for the Prevention of Cruelty to Animals. At the time, there were no laws on the books to protect children from abusive parents, though in 1874 the New York Society for Prevention of Cruelty to Children began. In this first child abuse case, the little girl in question had been so badly abused by a stepmother that when she walked into the courtroom, the all-male jury wept. How sad that so many years later, it still remains the American Society for the Prevention of Cruelty to Animals that fully acknowledges the danger of abuse that lurks in abusive homes. Can we be that far from facing the truth about how evil human beings can be?

To my dismay, instead of protecting abused children from abusive parents forever, there is a movement nowadays to reintroduce such parents back into the family once they have been rehabilitated. I find this completely insane. I agree that intact families are best except in cases of sexual, physical, or emotional abuse from a parent. Such individuals are dangerous and will be dangerous forever. To be blunt, I don't think it's possible to rehabilitate pedophiles, though I would bet my bottom dollar that if their backgrounds were checked, the vast majority of sex offenders were child victims of abuse or neglect who didn't receive the help they desperately needed. After all, consider how many men are repeat offenders of violent sex crimes and pedophilia. "Repeat offenders" is the key phrase. You can't send pedophiles or sex offenders to prison and think they will come out rehabilitated. It's absurd to think rehabilitation is even possible in such an atmosphere. The only thing we can do is keep them away from children.

Unfortunately, you can bet there will always be women who will put a man ahead of the safety of their own children. A mother generally does know the truth; nobody will ever convince me she doesn't. When sexual abuse is present, a child behaves differently. There is always a sign, and I don't care if the abuser is the family meal ticket; that's not a justifiable tradeoff. If a perpetrator is caught and the mother remains in denial and fails to protect her children, she should be treated as if she committed the crime herself, or at least as an accomplice. Hiding a "child molester" in the family doesn't work. Denial in the family is the biggest perpetrator of this crime, and the "child molester" continues to molest.

Not long ago, I had the pleasure of explaining my book to our good friend Martin. This man is insightful and compassionate and knows how imperative it is for parents to take their mission seriously. We talked at length about these issues, and Martin's feelings, along with mine, are that when parents decide to have children, they need to make both the physical and emotional safety of their children their top priority. However, since there are so many divorces these days, this priority is sometimes shifted and all but forgotten. Martin went on to explain his belief that there should be a law on the books to ensure this safety.

I am ashamed to say that many women and men who would otherwise protect their children from harm don't seem to care about the emotional safety of their children. They tend to think that because they are angry with their estranged spouses, they have the right to take their hatred and pass it into their innocent children's minds. Thus, I agree that there should be strict laws about this. I know many states now recognize that mental cruelty is abuse, but it is hard to prove, and most of the time, children who are caught in the crossfire of hatred tend not to admit it even to themselves and fail to speak up out of fear.

Consequently, Martin and I both believe this theoretical law should demand and provide professional help through counseling not only to adults but also to children during the course of a divorce, counseling that lasts as long as is deemed necessary. Children often blame themselves for mommy or daddy being gone, and this is precisely why such a law is necessary. Though it may seem harsh to many, the safety of children should be of the utmost concern and in my view should surpass the rights of adults in many situations, as children simply are not capable of defending themselves.

Martin is a man who backs up his beliefs and words with actions. Not long ago, his daughter befriended a young girl at school, and one day she saw this child sitting in the hallway crying. She asked what was wrong, and the child painfully told Martin's daughter her story of being sexually abused at home. In turn, Martin's daughter related this to her father, and he went into action. He went to the school, told them what was going on, and refused to leave until something was done right then. Even the knowledge that there could be possible danger to him if things didn't work out legally didn't cause his commitment to help waver. He is the greatest example I can think of to illustrate the kind of compassion we all should possess.

For these reasons, I have begun a nonprofit foundation called Leaps and Bounds to help those who are struggling with such life issues as alcoholic parents, addictions, gay issues, and coming to grips in adulthood with childhood abuse. My greatest wish is that this foundation can help the victims of sexual, physical, and emotional abuse, whether they are children or adults who were abused as children. Too many people don't get the counseling services they need because of finances, and this will enable those who need help to get it. Likewise, this foundation will help fund safe houses for abused parents and children where they can learn alternate ways of living that result in healthy families. It is my goal and prayer that soon there never again will be one person on this earth who cannot get the help they he or she needs because of a lack of resources. By the same token, because this foundation acknowledges that abuse is an emergency with a patterned nature, it seeks to educate communities about abuse as well as to forge alliances with other nonprofit agencies so that it can help to systemically eliminate abuse.

I've known for a long time that helping victims is my calling, and I'm now at a point where I have time to devote to this cause. I not only *can* make a difference, but I *will* make a difference. Ultimately, I want to help victims of abuse see that drugs and alcohol and promiscuous sex will never give them peace. Peace must come from within, but I know that most don't know how to get there and that their children will suffer until they can find their way. There is a clear urgency to help. Granted, some of these moms and dads won't change, but for the sake of their children, they must be shown an alternative way to live, or the pattern will repeat in yet another generation.

Thus, I feel I have a destiny in life. I feel driven to communicate to these individuals and to all the millions of others globally who are still silently suffering that it is possible to overcome such abuse and to make a life that is good and solid not only for themselves but for the children they love, too.

Afterword

Victims of Abuse

By Denise Schmuckal, Victim's Assistance Coordinator

C hild victims are heartbreaking. Having worked in the court system as a victim right's advocate for more than sixteen years, three years as a volunteer and more than thirteen years in the prosecuting attorney's office, I can honestly say that physical, sexual, and emotional abuse lasts a lifetime. What's more is that victims of such abuse come from all walks of life, all backgrounds, and all socioeconomic situations. Sexual abuse frequently starts at an early age, but victims can range from infants to young adults to any age in between. Frequently, though not always, the abuser was also a victim during his or her childhood. Abusers are often male, but not always.

As a victim's rights advocate, I respond to the needs, cares, and rights of victims under the Michigan Crime Victim Rights Act. This means I refer them to specific agencies that can address their needs for counseling, shelter, and medical attention. If a child is removed from his or her home due to abuse, I contact the local Family Independence Agency that, working in tandem with the court system, finds emergency placement for them until the courts decide the fate of the child.

In most cases I've worked with, children generally have no idea the abuse they've endured is wrong. They may feel uncomfortable with their abuser, but they may not. They may even be uncomfortable with what is going on, but still they may not know it is actually wrong. Even when victims disclose what is going on, they still may not know it is wrong. Indeed, their disclosure may be accidental. They may be talking to someone and tell them, "So and so does this to me," or they may develop a medical problem that takes them to the doctor, and the abuse is discovered there.

In some cases, disclosure is more frequent when the perpetrator is not a relative. A child may disclose by saying, "Daddy never did to me what so and so does to me. How come?" In such situations, children have an undeveloped understanding that what has happened might not be right because it has not happened before.

Tragically, if and when they disclose what is happening, possibly to the other parent, there is often a tendency not to believe them, and they are told, "No, that didn't happen" or "You're making this up." Often the parent does not want to believe them. Such parents will not report the incident, often because they fear having their meal ticket taken away. The poor victims then wonder whether they did something wrong. Unfortunately, professionals frequently hear, "Was it my fault?"

I will never forget the case of the four-year-old child who was sexually abused by her mother's boyfriend. The mother did not believe the child and stuck by her boyfriend, but he was found guilty and is now in prison. The victim was unable to understand why her mommy did not believe this had happened, and eventually it became apparent that the child was beginning to second-guess herself. This victim will not only have to live with being abused as a young child, but she also has to live with having her mother turn her back on her when she needed her most. Unfortunately, this is something numerous victims have to live with.

The pain and suffering victims endure is indescribable. Even if they don't realize as children that their abuse was wrong, they are very aware of it as they grow older. Ultimately, they live with it their entire lives, and even when they receive the help they need, most find their abuse unbearable. In the years I've worked with victims, I've seen numerous suicides, attempted suicides, overwhelming depression, individuals who are unable to communicate or to trust, and individuals who struggle with basic relationships. In some cases, the abused in turn become abusers. Sometimes they don't even realize this is wrong! If they have never disclosed what happened to them, they may feel this is what every child goes through and that it is okay.

On the other hand, some abusers were not child victims themselves. They may simply have seen something happen in their own home between two adults and think this is the way it's supposed to be. Unfortunately, there are parents who do not sit down with their children and tell them what is right and wrong when it comes to abuse, both sexual and physical.

Those who recover from childhood sexual abuse are those individuals who have the support of parents, teachers, and others who repeatedly tell them this was wrong and it was not their fault. With in-depth counseling and such support, these victims can go on to live fulfilling lives, though their abuse will forever remain a part of them.

Thanks to the Michigan Crime Victim Rights Act, victims now have all the rights that defendants have had for years. For so many years, defendants alone had the right to an attorney, the right to a trial, the right to defend themselves, and the right to have their issues and concerns brought up before the presiding judge in hearing. One of the most important rights victims now have is to make an impact statement, written or oral, to the sentencing judge. This allows them to express their feelings and what they would like to see happen to their perpetrator. In addition, convicted abusers must undergo extensive counseling during their imprisonment and upon their release.

Many factors must be addressed in this counseling: their childhood were they abused physically or sexually? Disclosure had they disclosed and not been helped as a child? Morality did they know that what they were doing was wrong? Usually abusers are incarcerated, but a lot depends on the severity of the abuse and whether the defendant has a prior record, and not necessarily for sexual abuse. In some cases, the abuser can be put in prison for more than fifteen years. If it's a first-time offence, county jail with extended counseling may be the answer.

It is my belief that some abusers may re-enter the community, after extensive counseling and with simultaneous monitoring, but every case has its own circumstances and must be looked at independently. For example, was this the one and only instance of abuse perpetrated by the abuser? Was the abuser sexually deviant as a child? What is the family background? These are only three of the many issues that need to be addressed.

In the past two years, I have seen an increase in the number of sexually abused children coming into the court system. I think part of the reason is that more children are disclosing their abuse. In 2000, while the U.S. Department of Health and Human Services (HHS) reported that maltreatment dropped to 12.2 per 1,000 children, the second lowest level in the past decade, the HHS agency estimated that child protective service agencies received about three million referrals of possible maltreatment. Of these, approximately 879,000 cases were substantiated after investigation. Sixty-two percent of these children suffered neglect, 19 percent were physically abused, 10 percent were sexually abused, and 8 percent were psychologically maltreated.

Consistent with previous years, 84 percent of the victims were abused by a parent or parents. Mothers acting alone were responsible for 47 percent of the neglect and 32 percent of the physical abuse. Nonrelatives, fathers acting alone, and other relatives were responsible for 29 percent, 22 percent, and 19 percent, respectively, of the sexual abuse. Approximately 1,200 children died of abuse or neglect in 2000, a rate of 1.71 children per 100,000 children in the population. The increase, up from 1,100 in 1999, is thought to be attributable to improved reporting.

Many schools now teach the difference between good and bad touching, among other things, and there are also groups to help nonoffending parents in cases where they might legitimately be afraid of losing the financial support of an abusing partner. Laws also exist today that require individuals to report any sexual or physical abuse they are aware of. These laws were not in effect several years ago, so for this reason, as well more, victims are being helped.

I am thankful that more and more victims are disclosing their abuse, and I am equally thankful that the law is now on their side. The fight to end child abuse is far from over, but at least now many of the perpetrators are being brought to justice.

Thank You

In purchasing this book, you have taken the first step in becoming part of the solution. Ten percent of the cost will go directly to Leaps & Bounds, a nonprofit foundation dedicated to aiding the victims of abuse. You have joined the fight and are a "ray of hope" in the dark face of abuse. If this book touched you in any way, please pass on what you have learned to others. Knowledge is the key, and it only takes one person to break the cycle of abuse. One person can make a difference.

For more information about Leaps & Bounds please visit us at:
www.livingafterafterabuse.com
or write to:
Leaps & Bounds
3535 3 Mile Rd. N.
Traverse City, Michigan 49686
231.929.3223